Finn Dammann, Dominik Kremer (eds.)
Geographical Research in the Digital Humanities

Editorial

Digital Humanities is an evolving, cross cutting field within the humanities employing computer based methods. Research in this field, therefore, is an interdisciplinary endeavor that often involves researchers from the humanities as well as from computer science. This collaboration influences the methods applied as well as the theories underlying and informing research within those different fields. These implications need to be addressed according to the traditions of different humanities' disciplines. Therefore, the edition addresses all humanities disciplines in which digital methods are employed. **Digital Humanities Research** furthers publications from all those disciplines addressing the methodological and theoretical implications of the application of digital research in the humanities.
The series is edited by Silke Schwandt, Anne Baillot, Andreas Fickers, Tobias Hodel and Peter Stadler.

Finn Dammann is a research assistant at the Institute of Geography at Friedrich-Alexander-Universität Erlangen-Nürnberg. His research interests lie in digital geography, GIScience and interdisciplinary infrastructure research. He works on questions of contested spatialities of digital sovereignty in Germany, on new methods at the intersection of GIScience and Critical Cartography as well as on Political Geographies of digital infrastructures.
Dominik Kremer works at the Department of Digital Humanities and Social Studies at Friedrich-Alexander-Universität Erlangen-Nürnberg. After a doctorate in Applied Computer Science at Otto-Friedrich-Universität Bamberg and experiences as an IT consultant in the industry, he joined the working group for Digital Health Geographies at FAU in 2020. His research addresses climate change and climate resilience, place-based GIScience and geo-content management in education.

Finn Dammann, Dominik Kremer (eds.)

Geographical Research
in the Digital Humanities

Spatial Concepts, Approaches and Methods

[transcript]

We acknowledge support for the publication costs by the Open Access Publication Fund of Bielefeld University and the Deutsche Forschungsgemeinschaft (DFG).

Bibliographic information published by the Deutsche Nationalbibliothek
The Deutsche Nationalbibliothek lists this publication in the Deutsche Nationalbibliografie; detailed bibliographic data are available in the Internet at https://dnb.dnb.de/

First published in 2024 by Bielefeld University Press, Bielefeld
© Finn Dammann, Dominik Kremer (eds.)
An Imprint of transcript Verlag https://www.transcript-verlag.de/bielefeld-up

Cover layout: Maria Arndt, Bielefeld

https://doi.org/10.14361/9783839469187
Print-ISBN: 978-3-8376-6918-3
PDF-ISBN: 978-3-8394-6918-7
ISSN of series: 2747-5476
eISSN of series: 2749-1986

Contents

Spatial Concepts, Approaches and Methods for Digital Humanities – An Introduction to the Book

Finn Dammann & Dominik Kremer

With the arrival of large data sets in Digital Humanities, demand has risen to analyse theses data sets also with regard to their spatio-temporal contributions and patterns. Surprisingly, the development of tools and methods within the field has evolved largely detached from the both conceptually and methodologically rich traditions of Human Geography and Geographic Information Science. This may be partially rooted in the fact that research in Human Geography has been focussing on the development of theories, concepts and perspectives on spatial relationships, processes and transformations in the last decades more than on the development of ready to use toolings. Nevertheless, the Digital Humanities could take immense profit embracing those conceptual perspectives both to spatial ways of investigating and to the methodological operationalisation of related empirical research.

At the same time, with Geographic Information Science, an independent scientific discipline has developed alongside Geography, which specialises both in the modelling and formalisation of spatial patterns and processes as well as in the analysis, visual representation and generally the processing and provision of spatial information. Interestingly, since the 1990s, Geographic Information Science as a technical discipline has been increasingly opening up to concepts and theories of cultural and social science in spatial research. Since then, new research procedures and methodological approaches for modelling, analysis and visualisation of society/space or people/space relationships have been developed under the terms of "Critical GIS" (Schuurman, 1999; Wilson, 2017), "Feminist GIS" (Kwan, 2002a, 2002b), "Qualitative GIS" (Elwood, 2006; Cope, 2009) or "Place-based GIS" (Goodchild, 2011; Goodchild, 2015) – sometimes also referred to as "Platial GIS" (Westerholt et. al. 2018). Geographic Information Science thus offers transgressions (Burns, 2021) of the classic methods of cartography, Digital Humanities can take profit of for the purpose of conceptual clarification and methodological operationalisation.

Despite these promising overlaps, interdisciplinary spatial research has not yet been visible in this context – apart from a few studies that point to the relevance and diverse possibilities of such research within the Digital Humanities (Gregory et al.

2015, Porter 2018). Thus, spatial studies in the Digital Humanities have often been oriented towards the more basic methods and artefacts of Geographic Information Science – which are provided in the form of ready to use digital toolings. As a result, space in the Digital Humanities often appears only as a description of the shape and position of objects or as a Cartesian dimension for locating, analysing and visualising (data) objects in maps and map-like artefacts. However, the social meaning, construction and transformation of spaces – to which human geography repeatedly points – can not be addressed appropriately by these approaches. In parallel, this is the purpose, alternative Geographic Information Systems – such as Platial Information Systems (Mocnik, 2022) or Geographical Imagination Systems (Bergmann & Lally, 2021) – are explicitly designed and developed for in Geoinformation Sciences. However, these concepts and toolings had little impact on spatial research within the Digital Humanities so far.

At the same time, both human geography and geographic information science have offered surprisingly few direct and explicit conceptual or methodological interfaces and interdisciplinary exchange platforms for the Digital Humanities so far – which also points to the reproduction of disciplinary boundaries on this end. With this volume, we would like to contribute to overcoming these disciplinary boundaries and to stimulate an interdisciplinary exchange as well as to present impulses for the development of new research procedures and methods at the interface between human geography, geographic information sciences and the Digital Humanities. From this vantage point, compiling this collection as a result of an interdisciplinary workshop on the topic "Geography meets Digital Humanities. New Approaches to Spatial Modelling" held in March 2021, we want to inform and encourage further exploration research utilising of out of the box models and approaches to space and place, as it is exactly the richness of social and cultural theory in humanities that allows for building study designs that mirror theory-informed concepts in data-based analysis workflows. In general, we believe conceptual theory on space to provide a strong framework for operationalisation and modelling in spatial data analysis:

- **operationalisation**: identify spatial concepts of interest to be investigated by data analysis
- **conceptual modelling**: inform feature recognition or indicator sets by those target concepts
- **evaluation of results**: compare patterns in the data to expectations from theory
- **ontological evaluation**: evaluate the applicability of theory on specific research questions

Results will depend heavily on the underlying conceptualisation of space. What do e.g., places of wellbeing look like in human society? In a naïve determinist approach, one could try to identify the amount of urban green space in a specific part of a city as a first rough indicator in a spatial data analysis. In a phenomenological, place-related approach, methods of self-reported health could be applied to look for variances in perception between different participants using mixed-method-approaches. Finally, in the vantage point of cultural geography, additional automated language processing techniques well known from the Digital Humanities could be used to investigate how healthy places, but also situated wellbeing itself are discursively produced and negotiated in a specific society.

About this Book

Compiling the collection, we followed three complementary goals: (1) Provide a conceptual framing covering promising conceptualisations ranging from cultural geography to geo-information science for a broad audience from Digital Humanities. (2) Present current work in the Digital Humanities dealing with data pointing to different conceptualisations of space. (3) Present current work in the Digital Humanities offering innovative methods for the analysis of space and place.

In a first conceptual section Günter Görz shows how a perspective from the geo-information sciences helped to develop projects from historical geography. Boris Michel's contribution deals with the challenge of translating certain concepts and social science theories of space and society into digital techniques and methods – and at the same time emphasises the importance of the technical design and constitution of geoinformation systems for geographic knowledge production. The contribution suggests a productive cooperation between cultural geography and Digital Humanities in the search for new and alternative forms of (digital) representation of space. Georg Glasze provides a short introduction into spaces as settings produced under specific socio-cultural conditions. In the concluding part, Blake Walker provides a vision on how conceptual knowledge from cultural geography can help to shape a more detailed understanding of investigating health and wellbeing in times of a pandemic.

In a second section we compiled approaches from different disciplines for novel or innovative approaches to space in the Digital Humanities. Maike Flüh, Mareike Schumacher and Julia Nantke show how Named Entity Recognition (NER) can be used in Computational Literary Studies to extract spatial categories as 'stages of the scene' from narrative texts and historical letters. Ramona Roller discusses in her historical study requirements for a discursive complete analysis of power dependencies between medieval states and evaluates the feasibility given the sparse and fragmentary data at hand. Florian Windhager, Saminu Salisu, Johannes Liem and Eva Mayr present an assistance system capable of visualising spatio-temporal lifelines of objects from arts and humanities with maps, graphs and sets. Finally, Dominik Kremer and Blake Walker introduce a novel approach using association rule mining to assist analysis of wellbeing in health geography with the text analysis of interview data and news media.

References

Bergmann, Luke/Lally, Nick (2021): For geographical imagination systems. Annals of the American Association of Geographers 111 (1), 26–35.

Burns, R. (2021). Transgressions: Reflecting on critical GIS and digital geographies. Digital Geography and Society, 2, 100011. https://doi.org/10.1016/j.diggeo.2021.100011

Cope, M., & Elwood, S. (Eds.). (2009). Qualitative GIS: A mixed methods approach. Sage.

Elwood, S. (2006). Critical Issues in Participatory GIS: Deconstructions, Reconstructions, and New Research Directions. Transactions in GIS, 10(5), 693–708. https://doi.org/10.1111/j.1467-9671.2006.01023.x.

Goodchild, M. F. (2011). Formalizing Place in Geographic Information Systems. In L. M. Burton, S. A. Matthews, M. Leung, S. P. Kemp, & D. T. Takeuchi (Eds.), Communities, Neighborhoods, and Health (pp. 21–33). Springer New York.

Goodchild, M. F. (2015). Space, place and health. Annals of GIS, 21(2), 97–100. https://doi.org/10.1080/19475683.2015.1007895.

Gregory, I., Donaldson, C., Murrieta-Flores, P., & Rayson, P. (2015). Geoparsing, GIS, and textual analysis: current developments in spatial humanities research. International Journal of Humanities and Arts Computing, 9 (1), p. 1–14.

Kwan, M.-P. (2002a) Is GIS for women? Reflections on the critical discourse in the 1990s. Gender, Place, and Culture, 9, 271–279.

Kwan, M.-P. (2002b) Feminist Visualization: Re-envisioning GIS as a Method in Feminist Geographic Research. Annals of the Association of American Geographers, 92, 645–661.

Mocnik, F.-B. (2022). Putting Geographical Information Science in Place – Towards Theories of Platial Information and Platial Information Systems. Progress in Human Geography, 46(3), 798–828. https://doi.org/10.1177/03091325221074023.

Pavlovskaya, M. (2017). Qualitative GIS. The International Encyclopedia of Geography: People, the earth, environment, and technology.

Porter, C. (2018). Introduction: The Importance of Place and Openness in Spatial Humanities Research. International Journal of Humanities and Arts Computing, 12 (2), p. 91–101.

Schuurman, Nadine (1999): Critical GIS: Theorizing an Emerging Science. Cartographica Monograph, 53. Toronto: University of Toronto Press.

Westerholt, Rene/Mocnik, Franz-Benjamin/Zipf, Alexander (Hg.) (2018): On the Way to Platial Analysis: Can Geosocial Media Provide the Necessary Impetus? Proceedings of the First Workshop on Platial Analysis (PLATIAL'18). https://doi.org /10.5281/ zenodo.1475269.

Wilson, Matthew W. (2017): New Lines. Critical GIS and the Trouble of the Map, Minneapolis: University of Minnesota Press.

SPATIAL CONCEPTS, APPROACHES AND PERSPECTIVES

Digital Spatial Humanities – Some Methodological Remarks and Two Historical Examples

Günther Görz

Abstract *The introduction briefly discusses the so-called Spatial Turn as an impulse for the Computational/Digital Humanities. This is followed by a discussion of methodological questions on digitisation, (Big) Data and Computational/Digital Humanities. Digital Humanities is associated with a transformation into data-centred sciences, but semantics is still the central issue. Our thesis is that Digital Humanities including semantic techniques stand in a relationship to the Humanities like "Computational Science" to the natural sciences or "Computational Engineering" to the engineering sciences. With "Spatial Humanities" we want to point out the special relation to the geosciences, whereby we follow a cognitive-epistemic perspective in the direction from geography to cultural studies. Following the discussion of some methodological questions such as operationalisability and the problem of conceptual change, the approach of the Semantic Web is proposed on the technical side for knowledge modelling, processing and publication (Knowledge Graph, Linked Open Data). Finally, two examples are presented in which historical maps (and texts) are thematised as cognitive maps and which are processed with the help of the Virtual Research Environment WissKI.*

Keywords: Computational/Digital Humanities, Spatial Turn, Spatial Cognition, Semantic Web/Linked Open Data

Introduction: Spatial Turn as an Impetus for Computational/Digital Humanities

For more than a decade, there has been word of a Spatial Turn in the cultural and social sciences. This refers to a movement that pays special attention to space, especially in critical social theory, and an overarching new discipline of "Spatial Humanities" has been proposed many a time. The anthology on the Spatial Turn edited by Doering and Thielmann (2008) is a plea for this perspective by pointing out commonalities of the many individual scholarly justifications for the repeated attention of space, although the editors are well aware of the different claims to validity and scope: "From large-scale paradigm to heuristic platform". Cartography plays a central role here, and Dünne argues in his contribution (pp. 49–69) that the Spatial Turn is even a reaction of the "turn to space" in the early modern period. Günzel (pp. 219–237) refers to quite justified criticism of the concept of Spatial Turn and instead disambiguatingly proposes a more precise definition of a "Topological Turn" – in the mathematical sense. In this way, he aims at a relational understanding of space as opposed to that of space as a substance or container; see also comprehensively Günzel (2010).

Digitisation, (Big) Data and Computational/Digital Humanities

In order for a new discipline such as the Digital Humanities to form, a number of prerequisites had to be met: A comprehensive digitisation of cultural assets, i.e., primarily of texts and images, had to be set in motion along with comprehensive networking. For data collections, standards for storage, description (metadata) and access had to be developed and implemented, as well as suitable algorithms. With the end of the second decade of the 21st century, comprehensive text corpora and image archives are now available, digital libraries and virtual research environments are part of everyday scientific life. European and national networks such as CLARIAH (Common Lab Research Infrastructure for the Arts and Humanities), a distributed research infrastructure for the humanities and social sciences, have made important preliminary contributions with public start-up funding.

Foster (2011) has already impressively pointed out the changes that the transformation into data-centred science(s) entails under the title *How Computation Changes Research*: How are data obtained and processed, how are hypotheses generated – including through the use of simulation methods – and how are the results communicated? Through various approaches to spatial and temporal data exploration using visual metaphors, there is a direct connection with Geographic Information Systems (GIS). In *Data-Centric Biology*, Sabina Leonelli (2016) has also presented a noteworthy detailed study in the philosophy of science on such changes, which is also relevant for many general aspects beyond biology. In the geosciences, the availability of topographical, geological and geophysical, but also geo-referenced social science Big Data (see e.g., Cheatham (2018)) not only raises new questions about the characteristics of the data, their acquisition and management. There are also parallels in terms of the influence on knowledge production and theory formation and the development of the discipline as a whole.

Without doubt, there are discipline-specific research questions which, for quantitative or methodological reasons can – in whole or in part – only be operationalised and processed by means of computer science, and the results obtained will cause follow-up questions. At the same time, methodological questions of modelling arise, whereby we give preference to a fundamentally cognitive-scientific – as opposed to a purely technical – approach. Here, *semantics* is the central issue: it is about assigning meaning and about inference – just think of the processing of ambiguities and inconsistencies in the data. From a hermeneutical perspective, this must be supplemented by a well-founded source critique so as not to fall prey to a data positivism that is unfortunately still widespread.

This gives the Digital Humanities – or, as I would prefer to say, "Computational Humanities" – an important role in their contribution to the "sciences of understanding". At its simplest, it is only a now common catch-all term for computer science applications in the humanities and cultural studies, but there are many claims that go far beyond this, see e.g., Berry, Fagerjord (2017). Thus, a characterisation of the Digital Humanities as a transformational science is obvious,[1] because they introduce a digital transformation of the research methodology as an extension. There seems to be a widespread consensus that digitisation and informatisation generally act as accelerators as well as trend amplifiers of social developments. The discussion is now about what is new, if anything. First of all, we have an addition to the inventory of methods. One thing is certain: new scales of magnitude in the data require new methods of analysis. But to stick with the analogy: What has been added decisively are modelling and simulation. Whether something new will also emerge on an epistemological level remains to be seen; perhaps it will be an expansion of epistemology to include an algorithmic and experimental dimension (see Wedekind et al. (1998), Görz (2018)).

The study of symbolic structures, as we encounter them in antiquity, the Middle Ages, the early modern period and in non-European cultures, is largely new territory. Conceptual systems have their own historical dynamics: it is about the development and use of standards for names, designations, technical terms and their systematisation in thesauri and formal ontologies, which at the same time take into account their historical change – influenced by diverse transfer relationships. In general, computer science is asked what contributions its research approaches and methods can make, for example to conceptual modelling, knowledge representation and inference, informed search, text analysis and semantic indexing, image analysis and object recognition, visualisation of complex data structures, planning and problem solving as well as cognitive aspects.

In view of relevant cognitive performances in the interaction of the disciplines, such as perception, memory, analysis and synthesis, it is not easy for the cognitive sciences – as long as they do not only understand themselves in a natural-scientific-reductionist way, i.e., address the understanding of action in the sense of

1   Cf. Jannidis et al. (2017).

hermeneutics – to come up with approaches of operationalisation: if you reduce action to behaviour, you are right back to the natural sciences. Naturalistic hermeneutics is a contradictio in adiecto. The problem becomes clear, for example, in the discussion about the role or the gain of knowledge in imaging procedures: They only show correlations, but no causality.

It is therefore suggested that a fruitful synthesis be sought in an epistemologisation of cognitive science approaches, i.e., in a reinterpretation at the level of knowledge: what types of knowledge are at play when certain cognitive science models are constructed, and of what type of knowledge are these models themselves – taking into account the historical dimension? Nelson Goodman once put it this way: historically, the structure of the mind – i.e., mentalism – has been replaced by the structure of concepts and these in turn by the various symbol systems of the sciences and philosophy. To avoid everything dissolving into postmodern arbitrariness, reference must be made to the unity of scientific rationality.

The question of whether something genuinely new emerges through the Computational/Digital Humanities thus depends on the degree to which they transcend the required interdisciplinary cooperation. This is what Mittelstraß (1989) calls "transdisciplinarity", a term that is unfortunately used inflationary today. Originally, it meant tackling problems that could not be solved additively within a given disciplinary framework; rather, by working on them, a new integrated form of science was meant to emerge. Natural and cultural sciences have in common that they occur in two forms: a propositional form (theory form) and a research form – methodological action, which is reflected in the distinction of context of discovery vs. context of justification. A fundamental problem orientation requires crossing disciplinary boundaries and leads to a reconstitution of the unity of science – i.e., scientific rationality, not systems. This is ultimately due to the unity of scientific language, which provides a framework for conceptual modelling and for procedures of justification (practical unity) and thus constitutes meaning.

Digital Humanities including semantic techniques would then be related to the humanities like "Computational Science" to the natural sciences or "Computational Engineering" to the engineering sciences. However, it would be misleading to see this as the advent of a new science – just consider what has become of the claims of the supposed super-science of cybernetics in the 1950s. On the other hand, it is far from clear that computer science must remain an auxiliary science. Particularly from a cognitive science perspective, computer science can contribute a variety of offers in modelling and simulation based on its decades of experience with descriptive and algorithmic-procedural description methods. Knowledge processing – representation and inference – has been taken up again in a special way in the context of the so-called Semantic Web and has certainly gained in attractiveness for numerous corpus projects, to name just these, through the standardisation based on XML. Suddenly, compatible connection and extension possibilities are opening up, which also promise considerable endurance tests for algorithmic procedures due to the newly acquired data volumes. Things will also change with regard to our understanding of inference: In addition to the explication of implicit knowledge, the processing of mass data, above all with statistical methods, will take place, which has only become possible since the mid-1990s with their availability through the internet and grid-like organised massive storage and processing capacity.

"What do you do with a million books?" asks Gregory Crane (2006), pointing out that "close reading" for in-depth exploration of individual works is now being joined by what Moretti calls "distant reading" for identifying patterns and trends in large digital text corpora. Finally, the issues of non-monotonicity and reasoning management, long explored in the context of inference systems, receive new attention. Procedures for revising inferences derived from statements that are retracted or changed are directly relevant to the processes of hypothesis formation and testing in research. It may be instructive here to look at the relationship between computational linguistics and AI-related language processing: Natural Language Processing, which has numerous applications in the Digital Humanities itself, has its own accentuation. It differs from computational linguistics primarily in its cognitive interest and in its application, even if both use the same algorithmic means: Speech processing has no primary interest in grammatical structures from a linguistic point of view, but sees them as an intermediate representation on the way to semantic-pragmatic content analysis – communicated meanings in social communication processes represented in symbolic form. This does not exclude the use of stochastic methods, but ultimately it is not about probability distributions, but about communicative content represented in formal linguistic form, i.e., explanatory models, not just functional models.

Thus, in the medium term, it can be expected that the use of digital techniques will probably also lead to a change in research methods and strategies in the respective disciplines of the humanities, so that a real interaction can be expected here (see also Foster (2001) above). Juan Barceló (2009) points out a possible direction in which this can steer in his book Computational Intelligence in Archaeology: static archaeological knowledge is to be logically reconstructed as dynamic, operationalisable knowledge, so that algorithmic methods of machine learning can be used for the perception, classification, interpretation of objects. Ultimately, he aims at an algorithmic representation of scientific methodology and speaks of "experimental epistemology". Interconnected science must focus on semantics, on systematics and methodology – this marks a development from simple, partly uninformed reference structures to argumentation contexts, and opens up the chance for an Epistemic Web worthy of the name. However, the pragmatic dimension must always be considered in the process; continuous consensus-building between the scientific communities and cultures is necessary; this, too, is taught by the critical engagement with the cultural tradition.

Spatial (Computational/Digital) Humanities and Spatial Cognition

The Spatial Turn in the Digital Humanities should be considered here primarily from a cognitive-epistemic perspective.[2] This assumes that we can draw on – at least qualitatively – georeferenced or georeferencable data from cultural studies. The following considerations focus on the historical dimension of cultural geography, exemplified in the last section by two projects in which historical maps play an important role. The general framework in which we reflect on spatial cognition and cognitive maps is accurately spanned by Schemmel (2016) with *Historical Epistemology of Space – From Primate Cognition to Spacetime Physics*: It is about natural conditions of spatial cognition, culturally developed mental models of space, but also their context-invariant aspects, social control of space, the expansion of experiential spaces and finally the disappearance of an autonomous concept of space in modern physics.

Concerning the Spatial Humanities, preference will be given here to a viewpoint directed from the geosciences to cultural studies, as Bodenhamer et al. (2010) also comprehensively suggest in the book edited with this title. The idea of Spatial Humanities was to revitalise and reorient the humanities by reintroducing geographical spatial concepts for the purpose of studying the influence of geographical spaces on human behaviour and cultural development. Nowadays, we are witnessing an ubiquity of Geographic Information Systems (GIS) – as applications of "Geographic Information Science" (equally "GIS") – through online maps, navigation systems, etc. Map-making has been an important part of the Digital Humanities from the beginning; interactive maps in particular enable the acquisition of new knowledge.[3] GIS face the task of combining two views of spatial knowledge, mathematical/scientific and cognitive mapping. While GIS were not developed for the cultural sciences, they have, as recent research shows, had a considerable impact on the Spatial Turn in the humanities and social sciences, especially in their web-available variants. This not only concerns visualisation through – also interactive, dynamic – thematic maps and the underlying representations, but also has methodological and epistemological consequences. For example, for the analysis of geographical texts and (historical) maps, the matching of place names with the help of gazetteers for georeferencing has now become a standard technique, as has the study of spatial relationships and their use for social communication through network analyses.[4]

---

2   See especially Kuhn (2013).

3   See also contributions in Kent and Vujakovic (2018).

4   On the methodological foundations of GIS, see also Tambassi (2019). A good practical introduction to digital cartography, GIS and the analysis of spatial data is provided by the *Spatial Humanities Workshop* by Lincoln Mullen (2015): https://lincolnmullen.com/projects/spatial-workshop/ [27.03.2023].

"In the last analysis all maps are cognitive maps" – this thesis attributed to Blakemore and Harley names an important topic of recent research in cartography and cartographic history. Structuring knowledge according to cognitive criteria, i.e., according to strategies of perception, learning, memory and associative reasoning, is not an invention of modern times. Georeferencing, i.e., referring to geographical locations, is the underlying principle for the organisation and presentation of all kinds of information in maps. People, buildings and other artefacts, historical and fictional events are perceived at specific locations, associated with them and remembered and recalled in this way; temporal sequences of events are mapped onto spatial relationships.[5]

A simple approach to cognitive mapping can be achieved by systematically examining the questions *where, what* and *when*. For the *where*, i.e., spatial information in the narrower sense, we take naming ("appellation") as the elementary means of determining identity. For a description of places, depending on the frame of reference, a specification of states or processes, as well as of distance and direction must be added. An example of a process specification would be a way description of how to reach a certain place. *What* – the goal – and *when* become important for solving spatial problems: a set of appropriate properties must be specified in order to find a solution using cognitive mapping. In other words, we must first identify the elements necessary for an epistemological organisation of spatial knowledge. The second step is then to develop a formal representation that is suitable for machine processing. Obviously, regions and their relative positions to each other play a key role, as do direction or orientation and distance. To perceive these elements, to identify them and to refer to them in discourse is a feat of abstraction that in any case also has a cognitive foundation. To counter objections to this approach that it is unhistorical, I am convinced that there are elementary epistemological expressions of spatial orientation that are largely invariant to cultural conditions. On culturally invariant "cognitive universals" see also Thiering (2018); Smith and Mark (2001) speak of "primary theory". In our case, this cognitive approach will also serve as a starting point for the construction of concept models, so-called "formal ontologies". A concept model consists of a hierarchy of concepts (classes) from the general to the particular, to which properties are assigned in such a way that the class definitions are abstractions over the explicitly named properties. Extensionally, a concept or class consists of the set of all individuals ("instances") given by filled-in schemata of at least the necessary properties. Formal ontologies thus serve as a conceptual basis for the formation of theories.[6]

---

5   Kitchin and Blades (2002) and MacEachren (1995) provide representative overviews from the perspective of psychology and cognitive science.

6   From the numerous publications on formal modelling and ontology, examples are: Jansen (2008) and Arp et al. (2015); Schulz et al. (2012) is systematic and very well suited for intro-

Today, it is largely common to group generic terms and properties for objects, time and space, events, agents, processes, etc., in a so-called reference ontology, so that domain-specific concepts can be derived from the generic ones. The event-based Conceptual Reference Model (CRM) of ICOM/CIDOC, defined in Bekiari et al. (2021), is such a generic reference ontology, which was originally specified for the field of cultural heritage and has been recognised as an ISO standard 21127 since 2006. The advantage of a standardised ontology such as CRM is that it guarantees interoperability between the models and metadata schemas formulated using it and opens up linkage to many web resources, which has proven very useful especially in the documentation of cultural heritage. The ontological representation with CRM as the top conceptual model, which is event-based in its basic design, provides, for example, a generic "assignment event" that has open slots to fill or is linked to the semantic roles of agents, constituents of a material and immaterial nature, a time span and a location.

A special conceptual model is usually also called a "formal domain ontology". It represents the conceptual core of a theory of an object domain and thus the semantics through the terminologically standardised linking of concepts, which is sometimes also referred to as "sense-relational semantics".

The particular conceptual challenge of formal ontologies for the field of geosciences is that they need to bridge conceptual systems from three domains: general spatial/topological/mathematical, concepts of physical geography and human geography, as e.g., Tambassi (2018) has pointed out.[7] A basic orientation for modelling is given by Kuhn (2012) with his proposal of ten core concepts for spatial information. When building ontologies, the depth of indexing must always be considered. For modelling depth, it is ultimately decisive which distinctions should be explicitly modelled in the concept hierarchy and included in conclusions and which technical terms merely serve to refine or specify descriptions and thus do not have to be modelled as concepts in their own right. Using the example of modelling places, it quickly becomes evident what methodological questions arise. Place, according to geographer Tim Cresswell (2009) in the introduction to an article on the subject in the *International Encylopedia of Human Geography*,

"lies at the heart of geography's interests. In common usage, geography is about places. But the everyday use of the word place belies its conceptual complexity. While the word place has been used for as long as geography has been written, it is only since the 1970s that it has been conceptualised as a particular place that

---

duction outside biology. Hitzler et al. (2010) and Allemang et al. (2020) give excellent introductions in the context of the Semantic Web (see below).

7   An implementation in this sense has been done by Lana et al. (2016) through a modular layered model in the "Semantic Web Ontology Language" OWL (originally Smith et al. (2004)).

has acquired a range of meanings and attachments. A place is a meaningful location that combines location, site and sense of place. Place refers to an absolute point in space with a specific set of coordinates and measurable distances to other places. Locale refers to the "where" of the place. Locale refers to the material framework for social relations – the way a place looks. Sense of place includes buildings, streets, parks and other visible and tangible aspects of a place. Sense of place refers to the more nebulous meanings associated with a place: the feelings and emotions that a place evokes."

Whenever we refer to places, "we encounter a combination of materiality, meaning and practice". Practice refers to the fact that actions are performed in places and that these actions and events constitute to a large extent the meanings associated with the place. For a *formal* representation of places, the latter dimensions also play a role in accordance with the Spatial Humanities and require appropriate means of expression[8], for which the reference ontology CIDOC CRM is particularly suitable.

However, one must pay attention to the important aspect of historical epistemology: Often historical concepts are understood in the light of modern concepts or even identified with them. In our particular case, this is the question of the applicability of modern geographical concepts ("geographical features" in the sense of the OGC standards) to ancient or early modern texts. Actually, a formal historical reconstruction is needed, but considering our current logical language means, there is still a considerable need for research. An interesting attempt using means of knowledge representation, so-called "dynamic frames", can be found in Andersen et al. (2006) in their application to Thomas Kuhn's *Copernican Revolution*. However, they remain in the realm of feature logic and leave the concepts themselves static, which is ultimately not very convincing. For concepts in the context of cognitive science, one could argue that the cognitive approach directly refers to perception. But here, too, there is still a need to clarify to what extent cognitive categories can be considered culturally invariant, considering the hermeneutic, culturally covariant level of so-called reading habits. From a formal point of view, the CIDOC CRM, through its event orientation, offers in principle expressive possibilities for modelling time-dependency of naming, especially in the case of place and personal names. There is no fundamental obstacle to using this also for terms, i.e., the conceptual words that denote the respective semantic content of the term.[9]

---

8   See also Ballatore (2016), Bosse (2019), Vasardani and Winter (2016).

9   For place names see Schneider et al. (2021), for the general problem see Masolo et al. (2019).

"Semantic Web" as a Technical Solution Framework for Semantic Representation and Publication of Linked Open Data

For the technical implementation of the task of knowledge modelling relating to geo-referenced data, which is undoubtedly central in the intersection of Digital Humanities and cultural geography, its collection, (partial) processing and publication as Linked Open Data, the use of techniques of the Semantic Web (Hitzler (2008), Allemang et al. (2020)) is obvious. The following goals should be supported:

• Reconstruction of the contexts of the creation and use of the sources (texts and maps): contexts of their production and social use, especially communication;
• Interdisciplinary merging of data from the fields of cultural and natural science;
• knowledge representation, i.e., purpose-oriented formal reconstruction of knowledge (creation of conceptual models) and its implementation in a formal (logical) language;
• A semantic level in the narrower sense only arises when there is a possibility of formal (logical) reasoning.

Additional technical challenges arise in the use of standard-compliant presentation formats, in the handling of different indexing depths, in providing heterogeneous forms of access as well as long-term availability, long-term stability and measures to ensure the quality of the data.

Knowledge representation languages from the family of Description Logics ("DL", Baader [2003]) have proven themselves for the representation of formal ontologies or concept models and associated object descriptions. Description Logics and among them in particular the Semantic "Web Ontology Language" OWL-DL (originally Smith et al. [2004]) are decidable sublanguages of standard first-order logic, for which efficient reasoning algorithms are available, which in turn guarantee complete and correct inferences from complex, logically composed queries. The publication of data identified and linked by "Uniform Resource Identifier" (URI) as "Linked Open Data" (LOD),[10] enables their integration into a worldwide knowledge network, the so-called "Linked Open Data Cloud".[11]

The set-up of complex knowledge networks is supported by so-called Virtual Research Environments with ontologies such as CRM as a semantic backbone; they enable interoperability and data exchange beyond mere linking. WissKI[12] is such a web-based virtual research environment, which at its core is based on Semantic

---

10   For linked geodata see in particular Hart and Dolbear (2013).
11   https://lod-cloud.net [27.03.2023].
12   Görz (2011); http://wiss-ki.eu [27.03.2023].

Web technologies for the representation of curated knowledge.[13] WissKI must first be configured with an ontology – usually CRM and extensions. Then the data model is defined in the form of so-called ontology paths: For each selected object type – e.g., "map" – the metadata, i.e., characteristics in the form of triple sequences of the ontology "concept – property – concept ..." are defined using WissKI's "pathbuilder" tool. For each object type, WissKI generates an input form – and also a corresponding search form – based on the paths. Whenever the value of a metadata component – e.g., "title" – is entered, the underlying ontology path is instantiated and decomposed into triples, which are stored in a triple database. These triple data form a large knowledge graph, ready for publication as standardised Linked (Open) Data.

Two Examples for the Indexing of Historical Geographical Maps and Texts

The two projects presented below with a cultural-geographical historical character may illustrate the procedure in the context of the Digital Humanities; their focus is on the content indexing of historical maps and geographical texts. In this context, special reference should be made to the pioneering knowledge modelling by Gkadolou and Stefanakis (2013, 2015); there, metadata schemas for the bibliographic recording of historical maps and, beyond that, for their in-depth indexing on the basis of CIDOC CRM are presented. Scheider et al. (2014) take a different Description Logics approach to *Encoding and Querying Historic Map Content*.

A central problem here lies in the operationalisability, which I would like to call the "operational gap". The starting point of many cultural studies projects are very general scientific questions for which it is anything but immediately clear which data are to be collected and how they can then be "broken down" into concrete questions about the data. A methodological proposal that goes back to the British philosopher Robin Collingwood – who, by the way, was also successful as an archaeologist – and which has become known as the "Complex of Questions and Responses", offers itself as a research heuristic at this point. For Collingwood, the meaning and thus also the truth of a proposition depends on a complex of questions, insofar as it gives an answer to them and thus the two must be seen in conjunction.[14] In his argument against analytical philosophy's propositional concept of truth, he focuses on temporal and spatial contextualisation, which cannot be dealt with by standard logic with its model-theoretical semantics, and emphasizes the indispensable role of presuppositions.

---

13   Cf. also the similar system "Research Space" of the British Museum, https://researchspace.org [27.03.2023].

14   See, among others, Collingwood (1955), ch. V.

The second project described below ("Biondo") is an apt example of this. It began with the formulation of a research interest in very general research questions such as the perception of geographical space in the Renaissance and its change on the basis of historical geographical texts and maps. This was based on the assumption that precise research questions can be derived from them, which lead to operationalised hypotheses that can in turn be tested on data. At this point, however, there is an epistemological gap – operationalisation does not arise automatically but requires hard differentiating work on the concept. In our case: What does "perception of geographical space" mean? On the basis of which – culturally covariant – parameters can this be specified, e.g., in linguistic expression on the basis of certain linguistic forms, cognitive-semantic categories, etc.? And analogously, this also applies to (map) images and their pictorial elements and graphic structures, the inscriptions, etc. – also following the modern semiotic slogan of maps as text. Which spatial relationships expressed in text and image allow conclusions to be drawn about perception and its change?

Visual indexing: The Behaim-Globe

Behaim's "Erdapfel" (literally "Earth Apple") from 1492 is the oldest preserved earth globe; today it is one of the most prominent exhibits in the Germanisches National Museum (GNM) in Nuremberg (Bott (1992)). Commissioned by the council of the imperial city of Nuremberg, it was made by local craftsmen under the direction of Martin Behaim during a stay in his hometown, a merchant and seafarer from a patrician family in Nuremberg who had also lived in Portugal. Nevertheless, the globe must be regarded as an achievement of the entire Nuremberg humanist community. Although the eventual reasons for its production are unknown, many of its inscriptions point primarily to economic motives.

With its diameter of 50 cm, the globe is relatively large and, with three continents, it shows a map image of the earth on the threshold of modern times, which is mainly influenced by Ptolemaic cartography; however, it also contains iconographic elements of medieval universal cartography and portolans (nautical charts) and follows their inscription conventions. Due to its extensive and ornate decoration, which includes over 110 miniatures, sixty flags and heraldic figures, more than 2000 place names and over 50 long-form inscriptions, it is an expression of pre-Columbian knowledge about the world. Its current state of conservation is precarious; many inscriptions have faded to the point of illegibility and numerous passages of text had been overwritten until the 19th century.

Since the only still relevant but partially outdated monograph by Ravenstein was published in 1908, we have begun research in cooperation with the GNM to prepare a new digital and printed edition of the globe. Basis for this is the digital indexing of the globe, which includes a database of all available images, a new critical reading of all globe inscriptions including all historical readings as well as a comprehensive catalogue of all visually relevant places on the globe surface.

Historical maps are first and foremost cognitive maps, which requires a formal qualitative representation of (abstract) regions and their relative positions to each other, but also of direction, orientation and distance. Points of orientation, buildings, persons, historical or fictional events are perceived at certain locations, are associated with them and memorised and recalled accordingly. With the aim of a semantic representation of the visual content of the globe, the first step was to create a catalogue of all visually relevant places on its surface and their connections, consisting of annotations of named places, miniatures and transcribed inscriptions. The data model for such a catalogue is based on a domain ontology extending the CRM with cognitive parameters, i.e., a systematic classification of all visual object types and object properties representing geographical and non-geographical elements and relations anchored in positions on the map image. The entries of the position catalogue consist of structured descriptions with given data fields, which are built in a systematic way along. paths given by a conceptual model. Around 1990, a new reading of the globe inscriptions was carried out by U. Knefelkamp (unpublished); on the basis of his research journal, approx. 3000 data sets were created in a joint project, in which all historical transcriptions of the longer inscriptions are also included.

The place catalogue was implemented with WissKI.[15] In the specific case, the modelled object types are geographical regions, toponyms, inscriptions, historical readings, miniatures and comments, for which WissKI automatically generates data entry and query forms. By embedding the ontology and the place catalogue database as well as the images in WissKI, the publication of Linked Open Data is immediately given. CRM as a basis enables interoperability: if there are similar place catalogues for other maps, a multitude of comparative procedures for texts and images comes within reach and a new quality of comparative working emerges.

The question of a formal-logical representation of cognitive categories, especially for the representation of qualitative spatial knowledge and spatial reasoning, only provides added value if there are complex queries to a cartographic database in a research context that can only be answered by other means with an unjustifiably high cost or not at all. There are various formal approaches to spatial reasoning for qualitative theories of geographical (Euclidean) space, e.g., Egenhofer (1995) and Vieu (1993). Their integration into a general Description Logics framework results in a system for hybrid reasoning[16] for processing complex spatial queries over the place

---

15   https://behaim.wisski.data.fau.de [27.03.2023].
16   Cf. also Pellet-Spatial: Stocker, Sirin (2009).

catalogue of the globe, which has been tested in a feasibility study (Jelinek [1997], Deang [2000]).

Historical Spaces: Flavio Biondo

Texts and maps do not simply depict spaces, they create them. The project *Historical Spaces in Texts and Maps*[17] of the Bibliotheca Hertziana, Max Planck Institute for the History of Art, Rome, aims at a cognitive-semantic analysis of Flavio Biondo's "Italia Illustrata" (1474/2005) in connection with contemporary maps. Using Biondo's example, this project investigates the spaces a literary account of Italy conceptualises by combining in a particular way topographical and historical information since antiquity. The cognitive-semantic analysis of the text is accompanied by the examination of historical map material, which visually prepares and stores historical spatial knowledge. By examining the relationships between historical maps and texts, the historical understanding of space and the knowledge associated with it will be explored. Cognitive-semantic parameters such as toponyms, landmarks, spatial frames of reference, geometric relations, Gestalt principles and different perspectives are combined with computer-assisted linguistic analysis. This results from the strong belief that all maps are cognitive maps that depict culturally specific spatial knowledge and practices.

In the first phase of the project (2016–2020), the analysis and interpretation of Biondo's text within the framework of cognitive semantics was about the identification and geographical verification of toponyms and definite descriptions that name places and geographical objects, as well as the spatial relations in their linguistic coding, in their use and in occurrence frequencies. The same was done in an analogous way for 15th century maps of Italy. In the text analysis, in addition to the linguistic information about single words provided by tools such as Collatinus,[18] information about grammatical structures was also used, especially dependency structures, which are particularly important for semantic representation.[19] Since no general tools for "Spatial Role Labelling" are available yet, a semi-automatic annotation procedure was used with the help of the annotation tool Recogito 2,[20] which contains a powerful component for recognising "named entities", among others. In addition, there is an integrated geographical verification mode utilising various gazetteers.

---

17   Tanja Michalsky in cooperation with Klaus Geus, FU Berlin, Günther Görz and Chiara Seidl, FAU Erlangen-Nürnberg, and Martin Thiering, TU Berlin, c.f., e.g., Görz et al. (2018, 2021). https://www.biblhertz.it/en/dept-michalsky/historical-spaces-texts-maps [27.03.2023].

18   https://outils.biblissima.fr/en/collatinus-web/ [27.03.2023].

19   Cf. Fischer and Ágel (2010), Straka and Straková (2017).

20   https://recogito.pelagios.org/ [27.03.2023].

This was applied in the same way to over 40 maps of the 15th century. The annotation results can be exported in various formats, including as Web Annotation/RDF data,[21] as tables and in GeoJSON.[22] Furthermore, Recogito also allows to annotate map images and to display (annotated) locations on different map types.

The most important step in text processing is the marking of spatial object descriptors and the relations between them. Therefore, annotations are complemented by cognitive-linguistic spatial role markers (Thiering [2018]; see also Taylor and Brunyé [2013]) by marking spatial relations, for which the "brat rapid annotation tool"[23] is used.

The annotations described so far are bound to the linguistic level, i.e., they refer directly to the text and map image "surface". In order to reach a deeper and more generic semantic level, a transition is made to the methodological level of general knowledge representation. In this way, the toponyms and other place descriptions in the cognitive-linguistic spatial role annotations, primarily constructions of the form "figure – spatial relation – background", can be identified, enriched with general geographical information and linked to a variety of (online) resources. For this purpose, we have defined a domain ontology based on the event-based CIDOC CRM and its spatio-temporal extension CRMgeo in OWL-DL, complemented by a domain ontology for the description of historical maps and their contents. Using formal ontologies, we provide an answer to the question: What is the meaning of annotations? At the same time, we can immediately publish the annotations transformed into semantic representations as Linked Open Data.

For the ontological enrichment and processing of the primary data, we also used the Virtual Research Environment WissKI.[24] In this case, the modelled object types are images, image series, maps and collections. With the help of special mappings, the annotations exported into the format CSV (or RDF or JSON) can be transferred. For this purpose, paths were defined for the annotated content, which enables a semantic interpretation of annotations, so that, for example, an instantiated CRM description in subject-predicate-object triple format is generated for each location. This applies in the same way to the results of the spatial role annotations, which encode cognitive parameters in triple form. All triple data form an extensive knowledge graph; they are the "raw material" for further research steps, i.e., the exploration of the historical understanding of space and the knowledge associated with it.

---

21   https://www.w3.org/TR/annotation-model/ [27.03.2023].
22   https://geojson.org [27.03.2023].
23   https://brat.nlplab.org [27.03.2023].
24   https://wisski.biblhertz.it [27.03.2023].

Conclusion

With the two examples, it has been shown in principle that a rational reconstruction of cognitive maps is possible on an epistemological level that includes the elements necessary for organising spatial knowledge and that can be compatibly integrated into a comprehensive knowledge network. Furthermore, qualitative conclusions can be automatically drawn with the semantic operationalisation presented. However, this only addresses one aspect of spatial research in the Digital Humanities.

Regarding theory-building, the final word is surely yet to be given on which components "spatial knowledge" encompasses. This has emerged clearly from the comments on "place": on the one hand topology, on the other communicative-social space. For integrated modelling, a hermeneutic approach to understanding action will be necessary.

In general, many questions are still open in the relationship between geographical information science or "data science" and a cultural studies approach. How is mutual beneficial interaction possible? And can, as has been claimed in this article, a cognitive science orientation offer bridges? In the future, hybrid strategies in which interpretative (theory-driven) and explorative (data-driven) methods work in tandem will probably become increasingly important.

The challenge of how to effectively operationalise research questions in the humanities has already been addressed. Spatial data entail special requirements for semantic analysis and processing, as Janowicz et al. (2022) currently explain in the context of "Knowledge Graphs". In my opinion, a successful example is the "Sphaera" project (Valleriani et al. [2019]), which also has spatial references. At the same time, it is also an excellent lesson for the currently very popular network analyses, which are concerned with the problems of combining topological and social science components. Especially in historical projects, spatial and temporal vagueness are a central problem; other aspects of historical epistemology such as conceptual change have already been pointed out.

Further challenges are posed by (cognitive) maps, where topological and social science aspects meet in equal measure. This is not only about the extremely important questions of visualisation and interaction, as far as active media are concerned (user interfaces, augmented and virtual reality). The latter are only mentioned; they are outside the scope of this article.

However, the most important desideratum in Spatial Digital Humanities is a fruitful cooperation between the various disciplines. This can only succeed if there is equal potential for relevant research questions in the cooperation of geoscientific, cultural science and information science disciplines for each of the participants. It is to be hoped that the disciplines will then change in a transdisciplinary sense and grow beyond themselves.

References

Allemang, D., J. Hendler, F. Gandon (2020). Semantic Web for the Working Ontologist: Effective Modeling for Linked Data, RDFS and OWL. 3rd ed. San Rafael: Morgan and Claypool Publishers.

Andersen, H., P. Barker, & X. Chen (2006). The Cognitive Structure of Scientific Revolutions. Cambridge University Press. Cambridge.

Arp, R., Smith, B., & Spear, A. W. (2015). Building Ontologies with Basic Formal Ontology. MIT Press.Cambridge, MA.

Baader, Franz et al., (Eds.) (2003). The Description Logic Handbook: Theory, Implementation, and Applications. Cambridge University Press.

Ballatore, A. (2016). Prolegomena for an Ontology of Place. In Onsrud, H., Kuhn, W. (Eds.), Advancing Geographic Information Science: The Past and Next Twenty Years (p. 91–103). GSDI Association Press. Needham, MA.

Barceló, Juan A. (2009). Computational Intelligence in Archaeology. Information Science Reference. Hershey PA and London.

Bekiari, C., Bruseker, G., Doerr, M., Ore, C. E., Stead, S. &Velios, A. (2021). Definition of the CIDOC Conceptual Reference Model, Version 7.2. CIDOC CRM Special Interest Group, September 2021. https://cidoc-crm.org/Version/version-7.2 [27.03.2023].

Berry, D., & A. Fagerjord (2017). Digital Humanities – Knowledge and Critique in a Digital Age. Cambridge. Biondo, F., White, J. A. (2005). Italy illuminated. Vol. 1. Harvard University Press. Cambridge.

Bodenhamer, D. J., Corrigan, J. & Harris, T. M. (2010). The Spatial Humanities. GIS and the Future of Humanities Scholarship. Indiana University Press. Bloomington and Indianapolis.

Bosse, A. (2019). Place. In Hoston, H. & Walnig, T. (Eds.), Reassembling the Republic of Letters in the Digital Age (p. 79–95). Göttingen University Press. Göttingen. https://doi.org/10.17875/gup2019-1146 [27.03.2023].

Bott, G., & J. Willers, (Eds.) (1992). Focus Behaim-Globus. Ausstellungskatalog 2 Bde. Germanisches Nationalmuseum Nürnberg.

Cheatham, M., Hitzler, P. & Janowicz, K. (2018). The GeoLink Knowledge Graph: Big Earth Data. P. 1–13. https://doi.org/10.1080/20964471.2018.1469291 [27.03.2023].

Collingwood, R. G. (1955). Denken – Eine Autobiographie. Köhler. Stuttgart.

Crane, G. (2006). What Do You Do with a Million Books? D-Lib Magazine 12 (3). https://doi.org/doi:10.1045/march2006-crane [27.03.2023].

Cresswell, T. (2009). Place. In Thrift, N. & Kitchen, R. (Eds.), International Encyclopedia of Human Geography (p. 169–77). Elsevier. Oxford.

Deang, D. M. (2000). Geometrical and Logical Modelling of Cartographic Objects. Master Thesis in Computational Engineering. University of Erlangen-Nuremberg. Erlangen.

Doering, J. & Thielmann, T. (Eds.) (2008). Spatial Turn – Das Raumparadigma in den Kultur- und Sozialwissenschaften. transcript Verlag. Bielefeld.

Egenhofer, M., & D. Mark. (1995). Naive Geography. In Frank, A. U. & Kuhn, W. (Eds.), Spatial Information Theory. Proceedings of Conference on Spatial Information Theory (COSIT'95): A Theoretical Basis for GIS. 988 (p. 1–15). Lecture Notes in Computer Science. Springer. Berlin.

Fischer, K., & V. Ágel (2010). Dependency Grammar and Valency Theory. In Heine, B., Narrog, H. (Eds.) The Oxford Handbook of Linguistic Analysis (p.223–55). Oxford University Press. Oxford.

Foster, I. (2009). How Computation Changes Research. In Bartscherer, Th., Coover, R. (Eds.) Switching Codes. Thinking Therough Digital Technology in the Humanities and the Arts (p. 15–37). University of Chicago Press. Chiacago.

Gkadolou, E., & Stefanakis, E. (2013). A Formal Ontology for Historical Maps. In Buchroithner, M. et al. (Eds.), Proceedings of the 26th International Cartographic Conference (p. 813–28). International Cartographic Conference. Dresden. https://icaci.org/files/documents/ICC_proceedings/ICC2013/_extendedA bstract/182_proceeding.pdf [27.03.2023].

Gkadolou, E. & Stefanakis, E. (2015). Historical Maps on the Semantic Web. In Sarris, A. (Ed.), Best Practices of GeoInformatic Technologies for the Mapping of Archaeolandscapes (p. 189–98). Archaeopress. Oxford.

Görz, G. (2011). WissKI: Semantische Annotation, Wissensverarbeitung Und Wissenschaftskommunikation in Einer Virtuellen Forschungsumgebung. Kunstgeschichte. Open Peer Reviewed Journal (urn:nbn:de:bvb:355-kuge-167-7, http://w ww.kunstgeschichte-ejournal.net/ [27.03.2023]), 17pp.

Görz, G. (2018). Some Remarks on Modelling from a Computer Science Perspective. Historical Social Research Supplement 31, p. 163–69.

Görz, G., Geus, K., Michalsky, T., Thiering, M. (2018). Spatial Cognition in Historical Geographical Texts and Maps: Towards a Cognitive-Semantic Analysis of Flavio Biondo's 'Italia Illustrata'. E-Perimetron 13 (4), p. 182–99.

Görz, G., Seidl, C. & Thiering, M. (2021). Linked Biondo: Modelling Geographical Features in Renaissance Texts and Maps. E-Perimetron 16 (2), p. 78–93.

Günzel, S. (2010). Raum – Ein Interdisziplinaeres Handbuch. Verlag J. B. Metzler. Stuttgart, Weimar. DOI 10.1007/978-3-476-05326-8.

Hart, G., & Dolbear, C. (2013). Linked Data: A Geographic Perspective. CRC Press. Boca Raton (Florida) etc.

Hitzler, P., Rudolph, S. & Krötzsch, M. (2010). Foundations of Semantic Web Technologies. Chapman & Hall/CRC Press. Boca Raton (Florida).

Jannidis, F., Kohle, H. & Rehbein, M. (2017). Digital Humanities – Eine Einführung. Stuttgart.

Janowicz, K. et al. (2022). Know, Know Where, KnowWhereGraph: A Densely Connected, Cross-Domain Knowledge Graph and Geo-Enrichment Service Stack for

Applications in Environmental Intelligence. AI Magazine 43, p.30–39. https://d oi.org/10.1002/aaai.12043 [27.03.2023].

Jansen, L. (2008). Categories: The Top-Level Ontology. In Munn, K., Smith, B. (Eds.), Applied Ontology: An Introduction 8/9 p.173–96. METAPHYSICAL RESEARCH. Ontos Verlag. Frankfurt am Main.

Jelinek, R. (1997). Räumliches Schließen in einer Kartographischen Datenbasis. Master Thesis in Computational Science. University of Erlangen-Nuremberg, IMMD 8. Erlangen.

Kent, Al, J., & Vujakovic, P. (Eds.) (2018). The Routledge Handbook of Mapping and Cartography. Routledge. Milton Park and New York.

Kitchin, R., & Blades, M. (2002). The Cognition of Geographic Space. I.B. Tauris Publishers. London and New York.

Kräutli, F., Chen, E. &Valleriani, M. (2022). Linked Data Strategies for Conserving Digital Research Outputs – The Shelf Life of Digital Humanities. In Golub, K., Liu, Y. (Eds.), Information and Knowledge Organisation in Digital Humanities – Global Perspectives (p. 206–24). Routledge. London, New York.

Kuhn, W. (2012). Core Concepts of Spatial Information for Transdisciplinary Research. International Journal of Geographical Information Science 26 (12), p. 2267–76.

Kuhn, W. (2013). Cognitive and Linguistic Ideas in Geographic Information Semantics. In Raubal, M., Mark. D. M. & Frank, A. U. (Eds.) Cognitive and Linguistic Aspects of Geographic Space: New Perspectives on Geographic Information Research (p. 159–74). Springer Berlin Heidelberg. https://doi.org/10.1007/978-3-64 2-34359-9_9 [27.03.2023].

Lana, M., Borgna, A., Ciotti, F. & Tambassi, T. (2016). Ontologies and the Cultural Heritage. The Case of GO! Proceedings of SWASH 2016, Semantic Web for Scientific Heritage, 1595, p. 7–18. CEUR Workshop Proceeedings. http://ceur-ws.o rg/Vol-1595/ [27.03.2023].

Leonelli, S. (2016). Data-Centric Biology: A Philosophical Study. The University of Chicago Press. Chicago and London.

Masolo, C., Sanfilippo, E., Lamé, M. & Pittet, P. (2019). Modeling Concept Drift for Historical Research in the Digital Humanities. 1st International Workshop on Ontologies for Digital Humanities and Their Social Analysis (WODHSA) 2518, 12 pp. CEUR Workshop Proceeedings. Graz. http://ceur-ws.org/Vol-2518/ [27.03.2 023].

MacEachren, A. M. (1995). How Maps Work: Representation, Visualization, and Design. The Guildford Press. New York and London.

Mittelstraß, J. (1989). Der Flug der Eule. Von der Vernunft der Wissenschaft und der Aufgabe der Philosophie. Suhrkamp Taschenbuch Wissenschaft 796. Suhrkamp. Frankfurt/M.

Onsrud, H., & Kuhn, W. (2016). Advancing Geographic Information Science: The Past and Next Twenty Years. GSDI Association Press. Needham, MA.

Ravenstein, E. G. (1908). Martin Behaim. His Life and His Globe. George Philip & Son. London. http://digilib.ub.uni-freiburg.de/document/318545497/ [27.03.20 23].

Scheider, S., Jones, J., Sánchez, A. & Keßler, K. (2014). Encoding and Querying Historic Map Content. In Huerta, J. et al. (Eds.), Connecting a Digital Europe Through Location and Place (p. 251–73). Lecture Notes in Geoinformation and Cartography. Springer International Publishing Switzerland. Cham. https://do i.org/10.1007/978-3-319-03611-3_15 [27.03.2023].

Schemmel, M. (2016). Historical Epistemology of Space. From Primate Cognition to Spacetime Physics. SpringerBriefs in History of Science and Technology. Springer. Cham etc. https://doi.org/10.1007/978-3-319-25241-4 [27.03.2023].

Schneider, P., Jones, J., Hiltmann, T. & Kauppinen, T. (2021). Challenge-Derived Design Practices for a Semantic Gazetteer for Medieval and Early Modern Places. *Semantic Web 12* (3). P. 493–515. https://doi.org/10.3233/SW-200394 [27.03.2023].

Schulz, S., Boeker, M. & Jansen, L. (2012). Guideline on Developing Good Ontologies in the Biomedical Domain with Description Logics. GoodOD Guideline, v.1. Universität Rostock, http://www.purl.org/goodod/guideline [27.03.2023].

Smith, B., & Mark, D. M. (2001). Geographical Categories: An Ontological Investigation. Int. J. Geographical Information Science 15 (7), p. 591–612. https://doi.or g/10.1080/13658810110061199 [27.03.2023].

Smith, M., Welty, C. & McGuinness, D. L. (2004). OWL Web Ontology Language Guide, W3C Recommendation. World Wide Web Consortium Geneva, February 10. https://www.w3.org/TR/owl-guide/ [27.03.2023].

Stocker, M. & Sirin, E. (2009). PelletSpatial: A Hybrid RCC-8 and RDF/OWL Reasoning and Query Engine. In Hoekstra, R., Patel-Schneider, P. (Eds.) Proceedings of OWL: Experiences and Directions 2009. http://www.webont.org/owled/2009 . [27.03.2023].

Straka, M., & Straková, J. (2017). Tokenizing, POS Tagging, Lemmatizing and Parsing UD 2.0 with UDPipe. Proceedings of the CoNLL 2017 Shared Task: Multilingual Parsing from Raw Text to Universal Dependencies, p. 88–99. Association for Computational Linguistics. Vancouver.

Tambassi, T. (2018). The Philosophy of Geo-Ontologies. Springer. Cham. Tambassi, T. (Ed.) (2019). The Philosophy of GIS. Springer. Cham.

Taylor, H., & T. Brunyé. (2013). I Go Right, North, and over: Processing Spatial Language. In Waller, D., Naderl, L. (Eds.), Handbook of Spatial Cognition (p.229–48). Washington DC.

Thiering, M. (2018). Kognitive Semantik und Kognitive Anthropologie. De Gruyter. Berlin.

Valleriani, M. et al. (2019). The Emergence of Epistemic Communities in the Sphaera Corpus: Mechanisms of Knowledge Evolution. Journal of Historical Network Research 3. P. 50–91. https://doi.org/10.25517/jhnr.v3i1.63 [27.03.2023].

Vasardani, M. & Winter, S. (2016). Place Properties. In Onsrud, H., Kuhn, W. (Eds.) Advancing Geographic Information Science: The Past and Next Twenty Years, p. 243–254.

Vieu, L. (1993). A Logical Framework for Reasoning about Space. Spatial Information Theory. A Theoretical Basis for GIS. European Conference, COSIT'93, 716. p. 25–33. Lecture Notes in Computer Science. Springer. Berlin.

Wedekind, H., Görz, G., Kötter, R., & Inhetveen, R. (1998). Modellierung, Simulation, Visualisierung: Zu aktuellen Aufgaben der Informatik. Informatik-Spektrum 21, p. 265–27.

The Digital Humanities and Geography's Spatial Thought

Boris Michel

Abstract *In recent years, a new interest in questions of space and spatial theory has emerged in the Digital Humanities. As a contribution to a discussion between geography and the Digital Humanities, this text discusses some key points of geographical engagement with space and highlights some of the risks and pitfalls of the transition.*

Keywords: Production of Space, Geography, Spatial Humanities

Introduction

Within the Digital Humanities, a new interest in space, spatial concepts and spatialisation has emerged in recent years. On the one hand, this can be understood as part of the broader *spatial turn* in the social sciences and humanities that for the last 30 or so years argued for a closer attention to space. Part of this argument is the assumption that the social sciences and humanities have a tradition of neglecting space over time (Massey 1992). At the same time, this engagement with space and spatial modes of questioning raises particular questions and challenges for Digital Humanities. These questions and challenges are related both to the respective disciplinary backgrounds and the way space can be integrated within their concepts and theories as well as to the ways in which digital technologies and rationalities influence thinking about space. Especially the spatial ontologies of software such as Geographic Information Systems (GIS) shape to a significant degree the way space can be understood and represented – it is extremely difficult and perhaps impossible to turn something like the concept of place into a data base or to digitise the phenomenology of space. Making concepts machine-readable affects these concepts. In turn, there is a lot social and cultural geography can learn from the humanities and the way Digital Humanities approach questions of space and the digital, especially when searching for modes of representation that go beyond the cartographic reason of maps and GIS (Pickles 2004). This is also evident in the wide range of concepts of space used in the contributions to this volume.

Engaging in a discussion between geography and the Digital Humanities it might be productive to take a closer look at geographical approaches to space and geographical spatial thought. This is not to say that the discipline of geography has or should have a privileged position on spatial thought and most concepts discussed here do not have clear disciplinary origins. Nonetheless, geography has a long history of thinking about space and using space as a perspective or method. Understanding itself throughout its history as either a discipline in whose centre is a spatial perspective at nature and culture, a spatial science or a form of spatial studies, geography has a long tradition of implicit and explicit engagement with space. Also, geography provides or influences many of the methods and methodologies used in the spatial humanities.

Space as a Social Product

One of the central assumptions of critical approaches in geography is that theories and concepts of space are historically and geographically specific. The respective social conditions shape the understanding, experience and the social reality of space. This is true for societies writ large as well as the sciences and arts. It has become conventional wisdom to agree that "(social) space is a (social) product" (Lefebvre 1991: 26) and that the *spatial turn* (Jameson 1991: 154; Soja 1989: 39) is deeply connected to both, a historical materialist and/or constructivist understanding of space and the historical experiences of what is frequently called *postmodernity* . Therefore, Harvey's point is important that "The question 'what is space?' [should be] replaced by the question 'how is it that different human practices create and make use of different conceptualisations of space?'" (Harvey 1973: 13–14).

This is not the place to go into the histories of theoretical discussions about spatial concepts in more detail nor is it the place to single out a specific understanding of space. Instead, this contribution is a mere call for a sensibility for the multidimensionality of space and spatial concepts – not in a relativist sense but in a context sensitive one (Harvey 2006). Such a perspective is present in a number approaches and concepts that are prominent in geography. Be it in the dialectical tensions between absolute, relative and relational understandings and productions of space Harvey illustrates in his "Space as Keyword" or his earlier "Social Justice and the City" (1973), a triad he links to the names of Newton, Einstein and Leibniz or in Lefebvre's *trialectic* of material space (the space of experience and perception), representations of space (conceived and represented space) and spaces of representation (the lived space) (Lefebvre 1991: 31–53) . These two triads – both coming from a Marxist and historical materialist background – insist that space is deeply linked to social practice and that these practices are the result of specific social relations – in the case of Lefebvre and Harvey the prime interest is directed towards capitalist social relations and their main frame of reference are European and North American societies since the 19th century. Such a perspective on the social production of space can also be found in the discussions around the social construction of scale – be it in a Marxist (Smith 1992) or post-modernist/assemblage perspective (Marston et al. 2005), in debates about space and place (Massey 1994, Cresswell 2004) or the genealogy of territory as a political technology of making space calculable and legible (Hannah 2009; Elden 2013).

Following Harvey, it is important not to read this as a progression, for example a historical progression where a concept of absolute space is replaced by a relative one and this in turn by a relational understanding. Instead, all these spaces are modes of productions of space. While private property or the nation state can be described in terms of absolute space – and the history of private property as one of producing absolute space – economic interactions, centrality of and mobilities are best understood in terms of relative space.

Episodes of Geographical Understandings of Space

While not a to be confused with a historical progression, it is frequently argued that absolute concepts of space dominated late 19th to early 20th century academic geography. Often describes as regionalist geography or landscape geography the focus of geographical inquiry was on the local inter-relations of geographical conditions from the abiotic to flora and fauna up to the build environment and human societies. This was an ideographic and inductive endeavor that was interested in the uniqueness of places and the unique way nature and culture came together in place. It was a geography that relied on extensive field work by individual geographers and a deep and embodied understanding of places, regions and landscapes (Livingstone 1992). The classical and modern map is a good example of such an understanding. Not only is it a central instrument of visualisation of geographic knowledge and geographic argumentation. Rather, it can be understood in this form as an epitome of an inventorying perspective, a realistic ontology of regional description. This form of geovisualisation is a cataloging of the where of things. It is easy to see how such a holistic approach runs counter to much or modern 20th century science in particular and modernity in general – insofar as both are driven by abstraction, specialisation, dynamisiation and the promise of keeping nature and culture in neatly separated.

This understanding of geography was challenged, especially after 1945 and in the context of cold war science and the growth of state-led spatial and regional planning. Under the impression of locational theories in economics, the emerging cybernetics and mid-20s century social physics, geography turned towards both application and planning as well as theory and abstraction (Bunge 1962). Instead of regional description the goals of geographical inquiry were seen to be the search for spatial laws and models – researching, for example, the spatial distribution of cities and settlements, urban hierarchies or the spatial patterns of rivers and highways. Many of those models and theories where derived from physics and mathematics such as gravitational or potential models (Stewart, Warntz 1958) and some geographers where starting to become interested in the use of digital computers (Hägerstrand 1967; Tobler 1959). Related to this new geography – often described as quantitative and theoretical and the whole turn as the quantitative revolution in geography – is a radically different understanding of space. Instead of space as the container this paradigm was heavily reliant on relative understandings and abstract models of space. Whereas the map of the older geography was a register of things in space cartographic representation now becomes much more diagrammatic, relational and dynamic. It becomes the visualisation of abstract spatial models of relations between elements such as population or functions of urban centres and their mutual influence. As it was argued that geometry was the language of space, these spatial models were often described and visualised in simple geometric shapes and patterns (Michel 2016). What is important within the discussions about spatial humanities is how this shaped early computational approaches and many of them are influential in current methods in geoinformatics and digital spatial analysis – most of all the influence of Tobler's infamous "first law of geography" on geostatistics (Tobler 1970).

From the early 1970s onward Marxist, postmodern or humanistic geographers challenged these assumptions and opened geography to a much more pluralistic and open understanding. Arguing against deterministic spatial models and their reductionist understanding of social and natural phenomenon as well as against the neglect of the role of human perception, experience, and agency human geography saw an intensive discussion about theoretical conceptions of space. For example around the social production of scale and its relation to the formation of the modern nation state or the changing relation between space and place under globalisation. Instead of physics and economics geographers increasingly turned towards the social sciences and humanities for inspiration.

Additionally and somewhat counter-intuitive an important discussion in geography highlighted the problems and pitfalls of a spatial way of thinking (Belina 2008). Especially since the 1980s geography has gained a sensitivity for the problems of spatial argumentation, on the theoretical as well as on the practical and methodical level. In a way, the theoretical debates of the 1990s in geography were partly characterised by a counter-movement to a spatial-turn in the social sciences and humanities, namely a growing caution against an understanding of social relation in term of spatial relation. This led to a critique of spatial explanations of the social and a renewed critique of geographical determinism – for example in geopolitics – as well as of problematic spatial abstractions. From a more methodological perspective, geographers warn against specific pitfalls of spatial research such as the implications of spatial segmentation and regionalisation (e.g., the *modifiable area unit problem*) or challenges of spatial autocorrelation for statistical analysis.

Conclusion

The previous sections of this short contribution were intended to point out the broad range of spatial concepts in geography and make the point that those concepts are historical and context specific – though the focus here remained western-centric and ignored the broad and diverse literature on indigenous concepts and relations to space and land (see Liboiron 2021). For the digital and spatial humanities, I would argue, a particular challenge lies in the interweaving of methods and ways of thinking in the humanities with digital technologies.

While the humanities have a rich history of thinking about space, technologies such as maps, diagrammatic representations or GIS bring about their own rationalities. This becomes particularly clear with GIS. Developed since the late 1960s, GIS is a child of geographies quantitative revolution and the emergence of digital computers, GIS has frequently been criticised for its inability to go beyond quantitative methodologies and *thin* modes of spatial description and analysis (Schuurman 1999, Pickles 1995; Wilson 2017). The banal fact, that GIS forces knowledge to be turned in to a database and its spatial properties into the spatial ontologies of this particular piece of software forces a specific understanding of space onto potentially very different social and historical settings. GIS, in general, requires exact coordinates and is not very good in dealing with fuzziness, contradiction and ambiguities. This partly the reason why GIS has had it much harder in social and cultural geography than in this field of physical geography.

A simple and classical example is the mapping of states before or beyond the territorial nation state. While states have always been spatial, the territorial understanding and this mode of mapping are decisively modern and European. As Wood argues, cartography – not to be confused with the practice of making maps – is a through and through modern technology that goes hand in and with the rise of the nation state and private property (Wood 2010). Using cartographic tools to visualise the spaces of pre-modern or non-western political entities is in constant danger of presentism.

At the same time there is a long discussion around the possibilities of opening GIS and cartography to other modes of spatialisation and spatiality. Be it in the (not to easy) search for a *qualitative GIS* and ways to use thick and rich qualitative data in GIS and cartography (Cope; Elwood 2009), in discussions around ways to bring place into GIS and develop something like *platial-GIS* (Westerhold et al. 2020), in attempts to fuse GIS with art and artistic research (Knowles et al. 2015) or the broad field of critical cartography and counter-mapping (Dammann; Michel 2022; Michel 2022). All of these are attempts to go beyond the modern understanding of the map and its translation into GIS. While it is very interesting to see what Digital Humanities do with the tools of geography and cartography and how questions of the humanities are translated into questions of spatial research, I think that in the exchange and discussion between geography and the spatial and Digital Humanities there is also a great potential for a critical advancement of geographical analysis and visualisation.

References

Belina, B. (2008). No Go Areas historisch-materialistischer Raumdebatten. Zur Kritik von Raumfetischismus und Raumidealismus. In: Alex Demirović (Ed.): Kritik und Materialität. Münster: Westfälisches Dampfboot, p. 89–109.

Bunge, W. (1962). Theoretical Geography. Lund: C.W.K. Gleerup.

Cope, M.; Elwood, S. (Ed.) (2009). Qualitative GIS. A mixed methods approach. Los Angeles, Calif.: SAGE.

Cresswell, T. (2004). Place. A Short Introduction. Oxford: Blackwell.

Dammann, F./Michel, B. (Eds.) (2022): Handbuch Kritisches Kartieren. Bielefeld: transcript Verlag.

Elden, S. (2013). The Birth of Territory. Chicago: University of Chicago Press.

Hägerstrand, T. (1967). The Computer and the Geographer. In: Transactions of the Institute of British Geographers 42, p. 1–19.

Hannah, M. (2009). Calculable territory and the West German census boycott movements of the 1980s. In: Political Geography 28 (1), p. 66–75.

Harvey, D. (2006). Space as a Keyword. In: Noel Castree (Ed.): David Harvey. A Critical Reader. Malden: Blackwell, p. 270–293.

Harvey, D. (1973): Social justice and the city. London: Edward Arnold.

Jameson, F. (1991). Postmodernism or, The Cultural Logic of Late Capitalism. Durham: Duke University Press.

Knowles, A. K.; Westerveld, L.; Strom, L. (2015): Inductive Visualization. A Humanistic Alternative to GIS. In: GeoHumanities 1 (2), S. 233–265. DOI: 10.1080/2373566X.2015.1108831.

Lefebvre, H. (1991): The Production of Space. Oxford/ Cambridge: Blackwell.

Liboiron, M. (2021): Pollution in Colonialism. Durham, London: Duke University Press.

Livingstone, D. N. (1992): The geographical tradition. Episodes in the history of a contested enterprise. Oxford: Blackwell.

Massey, D. (1992): Politics and Space/Time. In: New Left Review 196, p. 65–84.

Massey, D. (1994): Space, Place and Gender. Minneapolis: University of Minnesota Press.

Marston, S.; Jones, J. P., III; Woodward, K. (2005): Human geography without scale. In: Transactions of the Institute of British Geographers 30/4, p. 416–432.

Michel, B. (2016). Seeing Spatial Structures. On the Role of Visual Material in the Making of the Early Quantitative Revolution in Geography. In: Geografiska Annaler B 98 (3), p. 189–203. DOI: 10.5194/gh-69-301-2014.

Michel, B. (2022). Kritisches Kartieren als reflexive Praxis qualitativer Forschung. In: Geographica Helvetica 77, p. 153–163.

Pickles, J. (Hg.) (1995). Ground Truth. The Social Implications of Geographic Information Systems. New York: The Guilford Press.

Pickles, J. (2004). A History of Space. Cartographic Reason, Mapping and the Geocoded World. London: Routledge.

Schuurman, N. (1999): Critical GIS: Theorizing an Emerging Science. Cartographica Monograph, 53. Toronto: University of Toronto Press.

Smith, N. (1992). Contours of a Spatialized Politics: Homeless Vehicles and the Production of Geographical Scale. In: Social Text 33, p. 54–81.

Soja, E. W. (Hg.) (1989). Postmodern Geographies. The Reassertion of Space in Critical Social Theory. London/New York: verso.

Stewart, J. Q.; Warntz, W. (1958). Physics of Population Distribution. In: Journal of Regional Science 1 (1), p. 99–123.

Tobler, W. R. (1959): Automation and Cartography. In: Geographical Review 49 (4), p. 526–534.

Westerholt, R.; Mocnik, F.-B.; Comber, Alexis (2020). A place for place: Modelling and analysing platial representations. In: Transactions in GIS 24 (4), p. 811–818. DOI: 10.1111/tgis.12647.

Wilson, M. W. (2017). New Lines. Critical GIS and the Trouble of the Map. Minneapolis: University of Minnesota Press.

Wood, D. (2010). Rethinking the Power of Maps. New York: Guilford.

Language(s), Discourse(s), Space(s)
– and their Transformations in the Digital Age
Research Approaches from Cultural and Social Geography

Georg Glasze

Abstract *With the reception of social and cultural theories in the 20th century, studies in Cultural and Social Geography developed a new perspective on spaces: societal spaces were no longer conceived as given but as always (re-)produced. In particular, discourse-theoretically oriented research was (and still is) interested in how texts (and other sign systems such as maps and wider assemblages of practices) delimit, describe and thus produce specific spaces. The digital transformation is now leading to changes in socio-spatial relations: New networks of digital interaction are being established and, at the same time, new digital boundaries are being defined. Digital information helps shape the world we live in. Against this background, Cultural and Social Geography as well as the emerging field of Digital Geography are developing new conceptual approaches to understand these changes – such as "digitally augmented spaces". The approaches from Cultural and Social Geography therefore offer the Digital Humanities theoretical impulses for questions about the conceptualisation of spatiality. At the same time, with regard to empirical work, there are numerous points of convergence that may make a closer exchange fruitful.*

Keywords: Cultural Geography, Social Geography, Digital Geography, Discourse, Space; Digital Humanities

On the Prospects of a Conceptual and Methodological Exchange between Digital Humanities and Geography

This book section discusses how language(s), discourse(s), and space(s) have been conceived and rethought in Social and Cultural geography. Traditional Cultural Geography in the 19th and early 20th centuries assumed that spaces of different cultures were given and could be delimited. Mapping the distribution of different languages was supposed to contribute to describing such a mosaic of cultural spaces.

With the reception of social and cultural theories in the 20th century, studies in Cultural and Social Geography developed a radically new perspective: societal spaces are not just given but always (re-)produced. In particular, discourse-theoretically oriented research was (and still is) interested in how texts (and other sign systems such as maps and wider assemblages of practices) delimit, describe and thus produce specific spaces.

The digital transformation is now leading to changes in socio-spatial relations: New networks of digital interaction are being established and, at the same time, new digital boundaries are being defined. Digital information helps shape the world we live in. Against this background, Cultural and Social Geography as well as the emerging field of Digital Geography are developing new conceptual approaches to understand these changes – such as "digitally augmented spaces". Empirically, Cultural and Social Geography is increasingly concerned with the question of which specific spaces are (re-)produced in these socio-technical settings.

The approaches from Cultural and Social Geography therefore offer the Digital Humanities theoretical impulses for questions about the conceptualisation of spatiality. At the same time, with regard to empirical work, there are numerous points of convergence that may make a closer exchange fruitful.

The World as a Mosaic of (Cultural) Spaces: Language and Space in Traditional Cultural Geography in the 19th and early 20th Centuries

Traditional Cultural Geography assumed that the world could be described and understood as a mosaic of cultures. The mapping of "language areas" was one approach to delineate and describe such cultural areas (such as the 1917 mapping of the distribution of languages and religions in Europe in the elaborate cartography of Justus Perthes, fig. 1).

Predominantly, however, traditional Cultural Geography focused on material culture – not least the systematisation and mapping of traditional settlement and landforms (for an introduction to the perspectives of traditional Cultural Geography, see Glasze et. al. 2021a). This Cultural Geography, which focused on the description of regions, came under increasing criticism in the 1960s – described as theory-free-descriptive, backward-looking, and socially irrelevant (Fig. 2). With the turn to quantitative-theoretical approaches in Geography since the 1960s as well as to socio-critical positions since the 1970s, the concept of "culture" lost importance for the discipline as a whole. Questions of social differentiation and economic processes came to the fore.

Figure 1: "Languages and Religions in Europe and the Boundaries between western- and eastern European Culture"

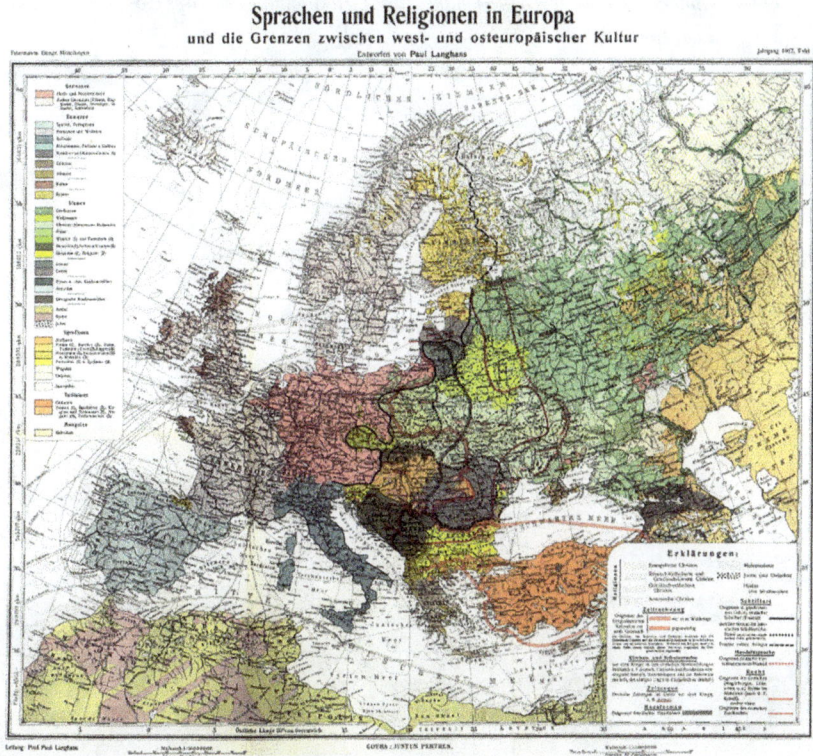

Source: Petermanns Geographische Mitteilungen 1907.

However, until today there are still works that tie in with the traditional perspective of Cultural Geography and, in this context, occasionally also linguistic geographic studies that understand language as an element of cultural-spatial differentiation (e.g., Kreutzmann 1995) or ask, with a stronger social and cultural theory orientation, to what extent linguistic differentiation is used as a symbol of spatially defined identities (e.g., Rowley 1985).

Figure. 2: *The title page of the special issue of the student journal "Geografiker" published on the occasion of the German Geographers' Day in Kiel in 1969 makes fun of traditional Landscape Geography*

Source: Textarchiv Kritische Geographie; http://kritische-geographie .de/textarchiv-kritische-geographie/ [15.09.2022].

Moreover, we should not fail to mention that there have been creative approaches in German-language Geography early on to analyse the production of geographical concepts in and through language. Gerhard Hard, especially, explored the conjuncture and connotations of the concept of landscape as early as the late 1960s in a critique of traditional Cultural Geography. Not least with his linguistic-analytical work, he was able to show what problems arise for Geography when it implicitly incorporates these connotations into its scientific argumentations: for example, a supposedly neutral analysis of "landscapes" as sections of the earth's surface mixed with certain normative-aesthetic notions of harmonious landscape images and corresponding social relations.

Figure 3: Hard (1969) visualises the increase of academic papers using "Landschaft" in their title in early 20th century (orig.: German-language essay titles in which the word "Landschaft" occurs ("1" absolute number (ordinate: titles per year); this real curve can be approximated by exponential ("a", "a'") and growth curve ("b"). ("a" starts in 1878 with the value 1 and shows doubling every 1,5 years). "2" a comparison curve, which shows the increase with reduced values (according to the increasing total production); the curve is exaggerated tenfold compared to "1").

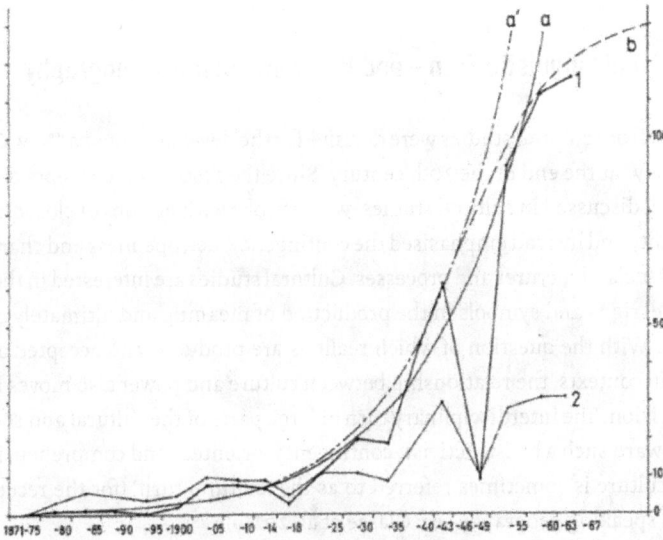

The Production of Spaces: Lines of Development of Social Geography in the 20th Century

In 1974, the French urban sociologist Lefebvre published the book: "The Production of Space". Even though the book itself was not received until years later in English- and German-language Geography, the title stands for a fundamental and comprehensive paradigm shift in Geography as well as in the broader social-scientific examination of social spatiality. In the late 1960s and early 1970s, it were mainly Marxist-oriented geographers who argued that the spatial structures of the world, be it the differentiation of cities into affluent neighbourhoods and poor districts (e.g., Harvey 1973) or global inequalities (e.g., Smith 1990), were not simply given, but were and are produced in specific social contexts.

This political-economic and Marxist-oriented Social Geography paved the way for a more theoretically-conceptually oriented Social and Cultural Geography. Even though the reception of Marxist approaches was marginalised for a long time in German-speaking Geography, these impulses nevertheless prepared the way for a Social and Cultural Geography being much more in exchange with social and cultural theories. For the German-language debate, the works of Benno Werlen were particularly influential here, who, starting in the 1980s and based on approaches of action theory and structuration theory, designed a Social Geography that aims at the geography-making of the individual agent (Werlen 1987, engl. 1993). This context also gave rise to some works that ask about the linguistic uses of spatial terms as part of everyday geography-making (e.g., Schlottmann 2005; Felgenhauer 2007).

Cultural and Linguistic Turn – and the "New" Cultural Geography

Impulses from cultural studies were decisive for the development of a "New Cultural Geography" at the end of the 20th century. Since the 1960s, new concepts of culture have been discussed in cultural studies, which broke with notions of closedness and essentiality and instead emphasised the contingency, i.e., openness and changeability, of all social structures and processes. Cultural studies are interested in the role of language, signs and symbols in the production of meaning and ultimately of social realities. With the question of which realities are produced and accepted as given in certain contexts, the relationship between culture and power also moves into the field of vision. The interdisciplinary turn of large parts of the cultural and social sciences toward such a constructivist, contingency-oriented, and comprehensive concept of culture is sometimes referred to as the "cultural turn" (for the reception in German speaking geography see: Glasze et al. 2021b).

Building on these impulses from the cultural turn, the New Cultural Geography radicalises the perspective of a production of space. Thus, the New Cultural Geography also questions the notion of supposedly given social structures or supposedly given actors. This New Cultural Geography wants to work out how meanings and thus ultimately all social realities are produced. As an approach to this production of meaning, it is not least interested in language: "[A] revitalised cultural geography must go beyond the mapping of languages and the geography of dialect towards the study of language itself as the medium through which intersubjective meaning is communicated" (Jackson 1989: 169).

For German-speaking Geography, the reception of post-structuralist and discourse-theoretical studies from English-speaking geography has been influential. Authors such as Derek Gregory have stimulatingly adopted perspectives work from cultural studies (1994) to raise awareness of how geographical ideas are produced not least in language and become a powerful element of social realities (see also the contributions in Philo 1991 or the development of a "critical geopolitics" on the basis of Foucauldian perspectives Ó Tuathail 1996).

Discourse Studies in Geography

A larger discussion context around geographical discourse studies emerged in German-speaking Geography at the beginning of the 2000s. The aim was to take up the conceptual but also the methodological challenges of the cultural and linguistic turn and to use them for a fruitful further development of Social and Cultural Geography.

Conceptually, for example, a spatially oriented development of poststructuralist oriented discourse theoretical work was discussed intensively: Thus, following the work of Foucault, Laclau and Mouffe, it can be argued, for example, that the discursive production of identities is reproduced and naturalised not least through spatial differentiation (for a German speaking introduction see: Glasze and Mattissek 2009, Engl. see: Mattissek and Glasze 2016). Methodically and methodologically, on the one hand, impulses from interpretatively oriented, "social science discourse research" (Keller 2004, engl. Keller, Hornidge and Schünemann 2018) were taken up. On the other hand, however, the focus was on the reception and translation of approaches that strive for a more consistent methodological translation of poststructuralist approaches – such as, for example, lexicometric-corpus linguistically oriented approaches from the French school of discourse analysis (see Mattissek and Glasze 2016).

This research context has given rise to numerous works that empirically investigate the discursive constitution of spaces. For example, an extensive German-French-Polish project has comparatively investigated how the settlement form of large housing estates is being specifically charged with meanings in public discourse in the media and politics (Glasze et al. 2012).

Interestingly, just at the beginning of the 2000s, when discourse studies gained momentum in German-speaking Geography, the first swansongs on the reception of the cultural and linguistic turn were already published in British Geography. Nigel Thrift, for example, problematised the cultural and linguistic turn already in 1991 for reducing the world to words and in the 2000s demands for a "materialist return" already dominated the debates in English-language Social and Cultural Geography (e.g., Whatmore 2006).

Thus, the German-language debate differs from the English-language debate by a later but then more intensive engagement with discourse-theoretical foundations and discourse-analytically oriented methodologies and methods (Korf et al. 2022). Thereby, the debate in German-language Cultural and Social Geography, especially in the 2010s, also turned to an engagement with materiality and technology (Bittner et al. 2013; Schurr & Verne 2017, Wiertz 2021), with bodily practices and affect (Strüver 2011, Schurr 2014, Baumann et al. 2015). However, discourse theoretical studies in Cultural and Social Geography largely work with a broad concept of discourse that asks how spaces and social realities are produced in discursive relations of different elements. Therefore, this turn was elaborated to a large extent less as a fundamental break than as a complementation and extension of post-structuralist approaches in the sense of a "more-than-representational geography".

Figure 4: Key words in the French large housing estate discourse, from Le Monde, 1995–2006 (Glasze et al. 2012)

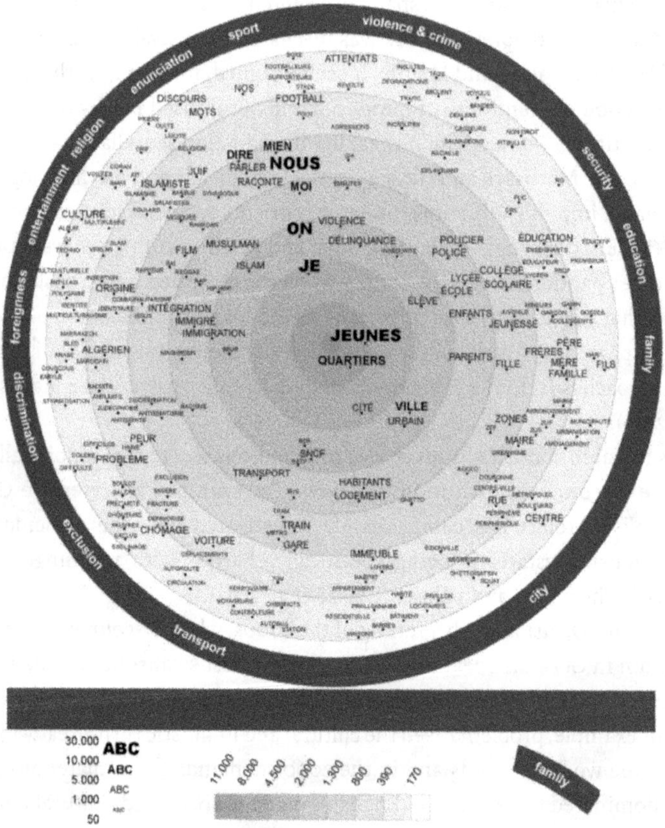

Potentials and Challenges of Discourse Studies in Geography in the Digital Age

The increasing datafication of the world, i.e., the digital "translation" of more and more processes into data, is both an opportunity and a challenge for research in Cultural and Social Geography. Various techniques are leading to more and more of these data being georeferencable, i.e., being (able to be) linked to a specific location on earth. The proliferation of the mobile Internet and mobile digital devices also means that the use of location-based digital information merges with the appropriation of specific places. In a sense, "imaginative geographies" thus coincide with the concrete appropriation of places.

Figure 5: Digitally augmented geographies – location-based digital information is used, for example, in tourism or increasingly also in education (Photo: Glasze 2022)

We increasingly live in "digitally augmented geographies" (see fig 5; for an overview on the conceptual debates see: Leszczynski 2019, Bauder 2021). At the same time, the digital transformation is fundamentally changing the media landscape – in increasing ways, digital media are shaping how we communicate and what we know about the world. In this outlook, I discuss what methodological challenges but also opportunities this poses for research in Cultural and Social Geography.

Georeferencing of Text Corpora

More and more text corpora are instantly stored in digital form and are thus available for computational linguistic, lexcometric studies. For Cultural and Social Geography, the question of how certain spaces are defined and linked to meanings within texts continues to be of interest. Named entity recognition (NER) techniques partially automate the identification of toponyms.

Figure 6: Results of a diachronic frequency analysis of the mentions of country toponyms in the German Bundestag in the 16th and 17th legislative term, visualised as anamorphic cartograms. (Dammann et al. 2021)

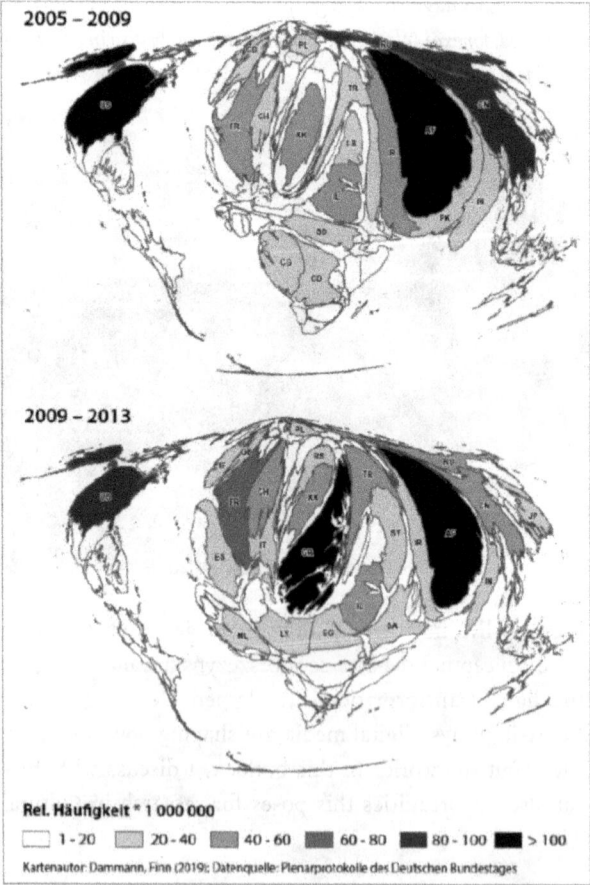

At the same time, digital location databases (gazetteers) link spatial terms (toponyms) with coordinates. They thus make it possible to relate textual information directly to places and territories on the earth's surface thus enable the use of GIS in computational linguistic studies (see fig 6).

Conceptually, however, it must be kept in mind that an exact locatability of toponyms in the coordinate system is rather the exception than the rule. In many cases, toponyms are rather fuzzy, ambiguous, controversial and dynamic – and therefore cannot be unambiguously related to a coordinate system. And it is precisely these cultural and social dynamics that are often the focus of research in Cultural and Social Geography (for example, place names such as "the Orient", "the problem districts", "old Europe", the "rogue states" or "Franconian Switzerland" etc. cannot be clearly located in the coordinate system).

A new form of geographical analysis of meaning production is opened up by the georeferenced semantic content on the Internet. In an early analysis, Mathew Zook and Mark Graham, for example, analysed in 2010 how frequently "church" is mentioned above or below average in place names in Google and were thus able to reconstruct the "bible belt" in the USA on the geoweb.

Figure 7: The virtual 'bible belt' (Zook & Graham 2010)

Monica Stephens works with Twitter data. She takes advantage of the fact that tweets in the USA are often posted with geo-referencing. In this way, she could work out a geography of hate tweets.

Figure 8: The "geography of hate" in georeferenced Twitter posts in the USA (Stephens 2013)

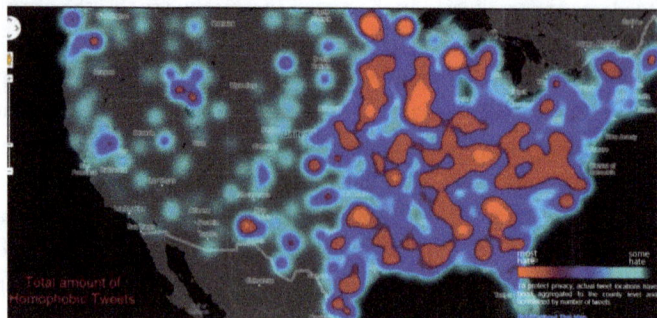

Communicative Interaction in Digital "Social" Media

The new digital, "social" media change how we communicate and contribute to shaping what we know about the world. It thus becomes the concern of cultural and social science discourse studies to address the production of meaning in social media. Compared to traditional print media, which have often been the focus of social science discourse studies, the media techniques and associated practices are changing fundamentally. Social media, for example, enable much more communicative interaction than traditional print media, radio and television with their privileged gatekeepers.

Figure 9: Clusters of Twitter account interaction among political elites in the Arabian Gulf (Schuhn 2020)

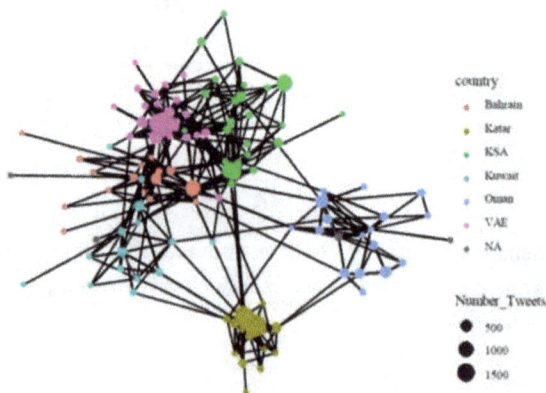

Against this background, works from Cultural and Social Geography try to reconstruct these interactions (see fig 9) or the thematically definable communicative condensations (see fig 10) that emerge in such specific interactions, for example, in Twitter. At the same time, the forms of communication are changing with social media – orientations to affect and attention generation are becoming more significant. This is where, for example, more ethnographically oriented research on social media comes in (Militz 2022).

Fig 10: Clusters in the network of accounts and retweets within the 1.5 millions Tweets related to the federal elections in Germany in 2017 (Wiertz & Schopper 2019)

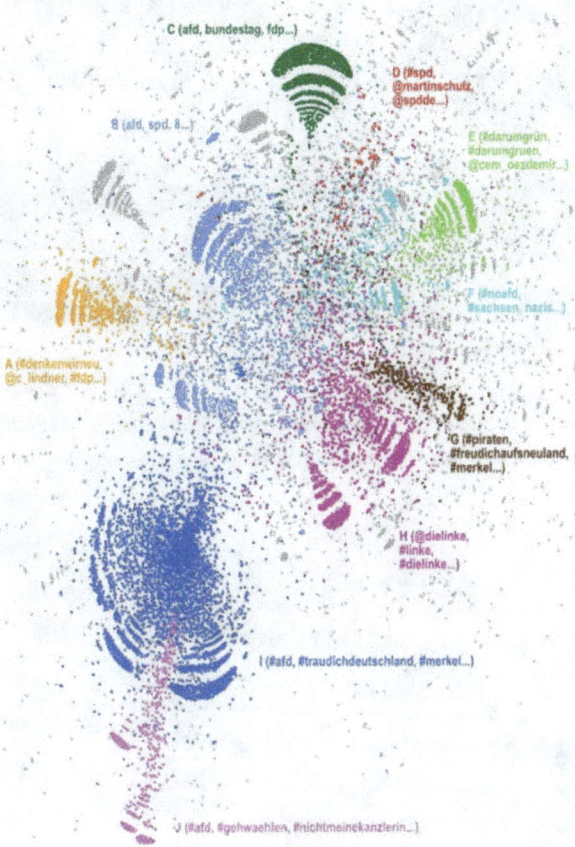

Socio-technical Production of Geographical Knowledge

Overall, the importance of socio-technical interactions in the production of meaning is coming more into research focus with digital media. For example, work on the production of geographic knowledge in Wikipedia (Graham et al. 2015, see fig 11) and OpenStreetMap (Bittner 2014, Schröder-Bergen et al. 2021) was quick to point out that data production is shaped by numerous inequalities that lead to biases in the nature and spatial distribution of the data collected.

Figure 11: Geotagged Articles in Wikipedia (Graham & Dittus 2021)

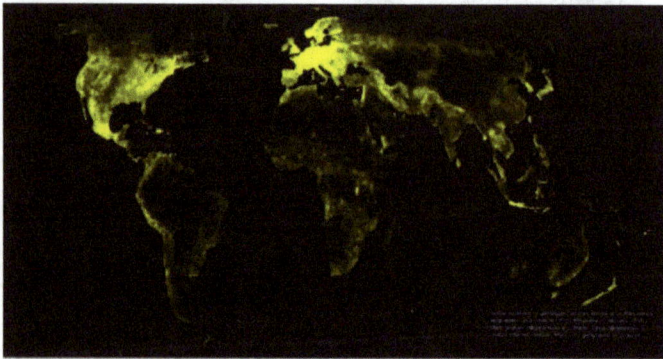

Figure 12: The Production and Use of Geographic Information as Socio-technical Assemblages (Bittner et al. 2013)

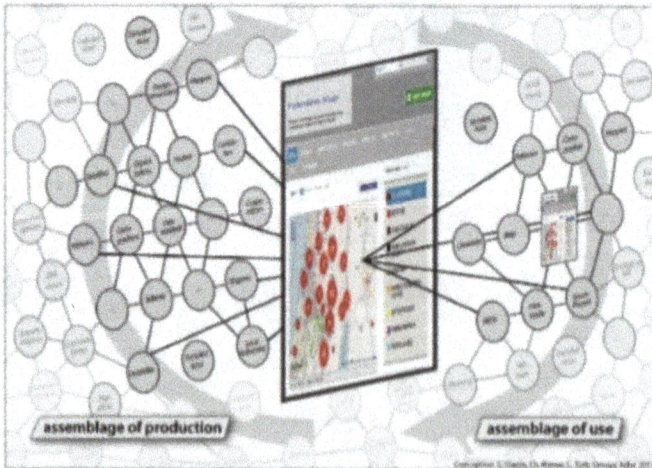

To conceptualise the production of geospatial data, Bittner et al. (2013) proposed to analyse complex socio-technical assemblages, specifically identifying exclusions (fig 12). Such a perspective ultimately also requires an examination of the design and functioning of technical infrastructures, not least software (see for example: Plennert et al. 2019).

References

Bauder, M. (2021). Raum. In Bork-Hüffer, T., Füller, H., Straube, T., (Eds.), Handbuch Digitale Geographien: Welt – Wissen – Werkzeuge (p. 77–91). UTB.

Baumann, C., Tijé-Dra, A., & Winkler, J. (2015). Geographien zwischen Diskurs und Praxis – Mit Wittgenstein Anknüpfungspunkte von Diskurs- und Praxistheorie denken. Geogr. Helv. 70, p. 225–237. https://doi.org/10.5194/gh-70-225-2015.

Bittner, C. (2014). Reproduktion sozialräumlicher Differenzierungen in OpenStreetMap: das Beispiel Jerusalems. Kartographische Nachrichten 64, p. 136–144.

Bittner, C., Glasze, G., and Turk, C. (2013). Tracing contingencies: analyzing the political in assemblages of web 2.0 cartographies. GeoJournal, 78, p. 935–948.

Felgenhauer, T. (2007). Geographie als Argument: Eine Untersuchung regionalisierender Begründungspraxis am Beispiel "Mitteldeutschland". Steiner, Stuttgart.

Glasze, G., Pütz, R., Germes, M., Schirmel, H., and Brailich, A.(2012). The Same But Not the Same: The Discursive Constitution of Large Housing Estates in Germany, France, and Poland. Urban Geography 33, p. 1192–1211. https://doi.org/10.2747/0272-3638.33.8.1192.

Glasze, G., Husseini de Araújo, S., Michel, B., & Miggelbrink, J. (2021a). Einleitung: Kulturgeographien. In Schneider-Sliwa, R., Braun, B., Helbrecht, I., and Wehrhahn, R., Westermann (Eds.), Humangeographie (p.296–302). Humangeographie Schulbuchverlag, Braunschweig. https://doi.org/10.5555/9783141603798.

Glasze, G., Husseini de Araújo, S., Michel, B., & Miggelbrink, J. (2021b). Kultur in den Ansätzen einer „neuen Kulturgeographie". In Schneider-Sliwa, R., Braun, B., Helbrecht, I., and Wehrhahn, R., Westermann (Eds.), Humangeographie (p. 303–309). Humangeographie Schulbuchverlag, Braunschweig. https://doi.org/10.5555/9783141603798.

Graham, M. & Dittus, M. (2021). Wikipedia's Global Geography. https://geography.oii.ox.ac.uk/wikipedias-global-geography/.

Graham, M., Straumann, R. K., & Hogan, B. (2015). Digital Divisions of Labor and Informational Magnetism: Mapping Participation in Wikipedia. Annals of the Association of American Geographers 105, p. 1158– 1178. https://doi.org/10.1080/00045608.2015.1072791.

Gregory, D. (1994). Geographical Imaginations. Blackwell, Oxford. Harvey, D. (1973). Social justice and the city. Edward Arnold. London.

Jackson, P. (1989). Maps of meaning: An introduction to cultural geography. Unwin Hyman, London, Boston.

Keller, R., Hornidge, A. K., & Schünemann, W. J. (2018). The Sociology of Knowledge Approach to Discourse: Investigating the Politics of Knowledge and Meaning-making.

Korf, B., Verne, J., Oßenbrügge, J., Hannah, M., Glasze, G., and Mattissek, A. (2022). Book review: Handbuch Diskurs und Raum. Geogr. Helv. 77, p. 433–442. https://doi.org/10.5194/gh-77-433-2022.

Kreutzmann, H. (1995). Sprachenvielfalt und regionale Differenzierung von Glaubensgemeinschaften im Hindukusch-Karakorum. Erdkunde 49, p. 106–134.

Lefebvre, H. (1986). La production de l'espace. Anthropos. Paris.

Leszczynski, A. (2019). Spatialities. In Ash, J., Kitchin, R., and Leszczynski, A. (Eds.), Digital geographies, (p. 13–23).

Militz, E. (2022). Affekte und Emotionen. In Steiner, C., Rainer, G., Schröder, V. Zirkl, F. (Eds.), Mehr-als- menschliche Geographien (p. 87–109) Franz Steiner Verlag. Stuttgart.

Ó Tuathail, G. (1996). Critical Geopolitics: The Politics of Writing Global Space. Borderlines, 6, Univ. of Minnesota Press, Minneapolis.

Philo, C. (1991): New Words, New Worlds: Reconceptualising Social and Cultural Geography. Cambrian Printers. Edinburgh.

Plennert, M., Glasze G., and Schlieder, C. (2019). The Socio-Technical Background of an Unconventional Software Architecture in OpenStreetMap: Understanding the Implementation of 'Folksonomy', Computational Culture 7.

Rowley, A. R. (1985). Dialekte und regionale Kultur – Sprache als Symbol des Ortsbewußtseins. In Maier, J. (Ed.), Regionales Bewußtsein und regionale Identität als Voraussetzung der Regionalpolitik, Arbeitsmaterialien zur Raumordnung und Raumplanung 43. Bayreuth, p. 15–32.

Schlottmann, A. (2005). RaumSprache. Ost-West Differenzen in der Berichterstattung zur deutschen Einheit. Eine sozialgeographische Theorie. Franz Steiner Verlag, München.

Schröder-Bergen, S., Glasze, G., Michel, B., and Dammann, F. (2021). De/colonizing Open-StreetMap? Local mappers, humanitarian and commercial actors and the changing modes of collaborative mapping, GJ 8, 232. https://doi.org/10.1007/s1 0708-021-10547-7.

Schuhn, Laura (2020). The Gurdians of the Gulf – Der Golfkooperationsrat auf Twitter im Spannungsfeld zwischen einer epistemischen Gemeinschaft und regionaler Konkurrenz. Masterarbeit an der FAU Erlangen-Nürnberg.

Schurr, C. (2014). Emotionen, Affekte und mehr-als-repräsentationale Geographien. Geographische Zeitschrift, 102, p. 148–161.

Schurr, C. and Verne, J. (2017). Wissenschaft und Technologie im Zentrum der Geographischen Entwicklungsforschung: Science and Technology Studies meets development geographies. Geographische Zeitschrift, 105, p. 125–144.

Smith, N. (1990). Uneven Development: Nature, Capital and the Production of Space. Blackwell. Oxford. Stephens, Monica (2013). The Geography of Hates. Floating Sheep-Blog. http://www.floatingsheep.org/2013/05/hatemap.html (3.10.2022).

Strüver, A. (2021). Der Konstruktivismus lernt laufen – "Doing more-than-representational geography". Social Geography, p. 1–13.

Thrift, N. (1991). Over-wordy worlds? Thoughts and worries. In Philo, C. (Ed.), New words, new worlds reconceptualising social and cultural geography (p.144–148). St Davids University College, Lampeter.

Werlen, B. (1987). Gesellschaft, Handlung und Raum: Grundlagen handlungstheoretischer Sozialgeo-graphie. F. Steiner Verlag Wiesbaden, Stuttgart.

Werlen, B. (1993). Society, Action and Space. Routledge. London, New York.

Whatmore, S. (2006). Materialist returns: practising cultural geography in and for a more-than-human world. cultural geographies, 13, p. 600–609, https://doi.org/10.1191/1474474006cgj377oa.

Wiertz, T. & Schopper, T. (2019). Theoretische und methodische Perspektiven für eine Diskursforschung im digitalen Raum, gz 107 (254), p. 254–281. https://doi.org/10.25162/gz-2019-0008.

Wiertz, T. (2021). Materialität. In Glasze G., Mattisek A. (Eds.), Handbuch Diskurs und Raum (p.291–308). transcript Verlag.

Zook, M. & M. Graham (2010). Featured graphic: The virtual 'bible belt'. Environment and Planning A, 42, p. 763–764.

Petrichor and Positionality: Occasion for a Situated Spatial Epidemiology in the Digital Humanities

Blake Byron Walker

Èisd ri gaoth nam beann gus an traoigh na huisgeachan.

[Listen to the mountain wind until the waters abate.]
Scottish Gaelic Proverb

Abstract *Within months of the first COVID-19 outbreak in 2020, map-based dynamic platforms for disseminating population-level incidence, mortality, and later hospitalisation and vaccination data quickly grew to near total ubiquity (Rosenkrantz et al. 2021). As digital artefacts reproducing a reductionist factualisation (Kitchin et al. 2015) and statist sociopolitical anchoring (Everts 2020) of the pandemic, dashboards and interactive maps have featured prominently in public discourses of anxiety and othering as non-expert citizens sought to understand the pandemic as a sociocultural, political, and public health phenomenon, somehow manifest in spatial administrative units and spreading in shades of red as 'hotspots' emerged and dissipated. Simultaneously, these technologies have come to serve as a hybrid figurisation (Wilson 2009) of society's confrontation with geospatial and epidemiological methodologies and epistemologies, as rationalisations of the situation are contested via argumentations based on largely deterministic constructs such as hotspots, spatial and temporal lag, raw versus standardised rates versus case counts, covariates and confounding, and 'the curve'.*

The Digital Humanities concern themselves in part with reading the human condition through the digital artefacts we create and produce. Maps and geodata are among the many digital art forms that we can analyse through a Digital Humanities lens. In this disquisition, I draw primarily on critical GIScience perspectives grounded in the ongoing COVID-19 pandemic, presenting navigable inroads towards a more context-aware applied geostatistics, particularly in the context of spatial epidemiology. I argue that the increasing prominence of geostatistical concepts and their instrumentalisations for producing Lefebvrian space (Pierce & Martin 2015) underscore the need for a humanities-adjacent geostatistics that embraces the social, cultural, and situational, and optimistically suggest that amidst long-standing epistemological incongruencies (Schuurman 2000; Wilson 2017) stands a middle-ground between hermeneutic phenomenology and deterministic reductionism.

Keywords: Digital Humanities, Spatial Epidemiology, Geographic Information Science, Health Geography, COVID-19

Fragrance of a Storm

In the initial months of the pandemic, state actors encouraged the individual to take shelter and wait for the tempest to pass. Gazing into open laptops and smartphone screens, we anxiously sought to make sense of the pandemic's digital traces of the struggle in hospitals, care facilities, and communities worldwide. In the various narratives and discourses concerning COVID-19, the storm metaphor rapidly devolved into cliché, albeit in many ways a fitting one. Even in the realm of digitalities and the psychosocial, the sheer quantity, pervasiveness, and impact of data regarding the pandemic was not unlike a squall, confronting experts and non-experts alike with irregular and often conflicting interpretations, narratives, and criticalities. I do not intend in this paper to ruminate on the storm, rather, I lead a meditation on its digital petrichor, considering the Digital Humanities as an inroad towards a hybrid, *situated* spatial epidemiology, in which the creator and the consumer of digital (geo)data are increasingly challenged to critically reflect on positionality and context beyond traditionally reductionist and factualising readings of (geo)statistics.

The Digital Humanities seek in part to read the human condition through the varied digital artefacts that we create and produce. Traditionally considered and practiced as a subdiscipline of the natural sciences and therefore subject to positivist epistemological and empiricist/reductionist methodological underpinnings, the use of maps, geodata, and geospatial/geostatistical analysis to understand human health and illness has played a central role in how society and the individual view and craft understandings of disease (Koch 2011; Lucas-Gabrielli & Eliot 2019). However, challenges to a purely deterministic spatial epidemiology practice continue to mount, as the inherent contestations of the social-political context and the latent subjectivities and positionalities of the data analyst/cartographer are drawn to the forefront of the discourse. Decades of scholarship in geographic information science and health geographies, and more recently in the Digital Humanities, continue to strive for a contextually-aware, reflective, and critically-informed digital health geography praxis. Guided by these efforts, I submit that the ubiquity of maps and geodata, multiplied by the sociopolitical complexities of the COVID-19 pandemic, present us with a ripe opportunity for spatial epidemiology to both embrace, and be embraced by, the aforementioned paradigm and join the ranks of other culturally-informed, contextually-rich methods of inquiry in the Digital Humanities.

A 'Dashboard Pandemic'

Following in the footsteps of its predecessors the 'swine flu' of 2009–10 (Nerlych & Koteyko 2012) and the more recent Ebola outbreak of 2013–16 (Koch 2016), the emergence of COVID-19 in early 2020 as the next global pandemic quickly drew the attention of cartographers, web developers, and (both armchair and professional) spatial epidemiologists. Their attention to the implicit spatiality of epidemics-becoming-pandemics, fueled by an anxious (and at times morbid) public fascination, gave rise to what Jonathan Everts coined "a dashboard pandemic" of its own (Everts 2020), as map-based dynamic platforms for disseminating population-level incidence, mortality, and later hospitalisation and vaccination data quickly grew to near total ubiquity across various news/social media (Rosenkrantz et al. 2021).

These digital traces of the pandemic were instrumental in the (re)production of narratives concerning, for example, public health services and facilities (Nyashanu et al. 2022), schools (Kim et al. 2021), religious institutions (Deeg 2021), and restaurants and hotels (Im et al. 2021), and in discourses within academic debate (Pase-Sousa et al. 2020), social media (Cinelli et al. 2020a,b), and state or corporate news media (Nekliudov et al. 2020). As digital artefacts, the circulation and translation of COVID-related data into short-format talking points served to reproduce a reductionist factualisation (Kitchin et al. 2015) of the virological and epidemiological realities, in that contextual and experiential aspects critical to an holistic understanding were left by the wayside in favour of simplistic forms tendentially viewed as hard fact, due largely to their quantitative nature. Their geographical incarnation as spatial data, dashboards, and maps therefore served to reinforce anxiety, provoke othering, and buttress a statist sociopolitical anchoring (Everts 2020), as publics sought to understand the pandemic as a sociocultural, political, and public health phenomenon. For example, early hotspots in European border regions were referenced in social media debate concerning border closure policies and (often rather xenophobic) allegations of migrant persons as carriers of the virus.

The complex psychosocial mechanisms underlying the public reaction were (and certainly will continue to be) influenced by the ways in which geospatial and spatially aggregated epidemiological data were packaged and disseminated. For example, spatial administrative units quickly became the common denominator in public discourses, given their centrality as the template by which visualisations of the pandemic's spread were curated for the public eye. In Germany, COVID-19 data were published daily at the *Landkreis* scale (roughly equivalent to county, municipality, or district), and these formed the basis for the designation of areas as "risk zones" such as Tirschenreuth and Gütersloh (Brandl et al. 2021; Fuchs & Daniell 2020).

Naturally, the use of municipalities, counties, regions, and other subnational political units as the basis for containerisation has administrative, technical-methodological, privacy/anonymity-related, and quite plainly pragmatic bases, and I do not intend herein to problematise, contest, nor offer alternative methods for mapping disease data. Decades of inquiry in critical geographic information science (GIScience) do however underscore the importance of recognising narratives' placial bindings as being driven by the means through which geographical data are produced and mapped (Koch 2011; Thatcher et al. 2016; Crampton 2010). This is also true for placial bindings at the neighbourhood scale. For example, state-imposed measures to contain the virus accentuate the differentiation between private and public spaces, the latter being labelled "unsafe", whilst categorisations of various sites' functions reproduce perceptions and experiences of anxiety bound to sites considered to be high-risk, e.g., grocery stores, schools, and restaurants (Stadlmeier et al. 2022). Associations between health risk and the built environment are certainly rooted in the literature (Vialard et al. 2019; Walker et al. 2020a; Walker et al. 2022) and provide important space for critical analysis and methodological development (Walker & Schuurman 2015). It is therefore becoming increasingly important for the research agenda to consider how digital geographical information plays a role in society's confrontation with the epidemiological landscape (Taglioni 2019). In the case of COVID-19, rationalisations of the situation are contested using argumentations based largely upon data-deterministic constructs such as hotspots, spatial and temporal lag, raw versus standardised rates versus case counts, covariates and confounding, and "the curve". Understanding the ways in which (geo)data and statistics are used to (de)construct argument and narrative is a key challenge not only for data literacy, but quite crucially for science communication and policymaking amidst crisis.

Ode to the Armchair Statistician

Dashboards and disease maps, in their unprecedented prevalence and prominence, expose a broad swath of the populace to maps and spatial data at a level of statistical complexity new to many, if not most. News media and governmental institutions sought to clarify uncertainties such as the difference between the absolute number of cases in a given area and its per capita rate, as epidemiological terminology such as "incidence" and "system capacity" became increasingly prominent in the public discourse. Seemingly rather suddenly, the general public was engaged in discussion and debate not solely about the lived experiences of illness (e.g., character and severity of symptoms, mounting stress on health care workers) and the politics of the state reaction (e.g., mask mandates, forced closures), but also concerning more abstract and intangible biostatistical constructs. Social media such as Twitter, Facebook, and Reddit quickly became inundated with armchair epidemiologists using maps and statistics to construct a broad variety of arguments relating to the sociopolitical re-action. These argumentations have taken forms ranging from direct interpretations of simple metrics (e.g., "the incidence rate in Berlin is higher than in Stockholm") to absurd false dichotomies (Theocharis et al. 2021) and meta-argumentations such as the comparison of metrics for pandemic monitoring and policy. For example, the following three metrics have featured prominently in social media and institutional media discourses and are often conflated and/or misunderstood. Each of these met-rics represents a different set of virological and epidemiological processes and fea-ture different assumptions, uncertainties, and implications regarding best practice:

- The number of new cases in a given area; this directly translates into load on the healthcare system and potential cumulative economic losses.
- The rate of new cases (incidence) in a given area; this provides a proxy for heuris-tically assessing the probability/risk that one might become infected.
- The areal density of new cases in a given area; this roughly proxies the odds of interpersonal contact with an infected person.

Temporality adds yet another layer of complexity. Whilst prevalence represents the number of active cases at a given point in time, incidence/mortality represent the number of new cases/deaths within a defined time period, e.g., seven days. The tem-poral denominator introduces a variety of challenges, such as incongruent time pe-riods and non-reporting days of the week differing by jurisdiction; for example, in many places patients are not tested and positive cases are not reported to central health authorities on weekends, resulting in a dramatic Monday spike (Bergman et al. 2020). Some jurisdictions report seven-day incidence rates, whilst others only provide monthly data or seven-day averages thereof. These differences are partic-ularly prominent when comparing data between various global regions (Riffe et al. 2021) and have led to confusion and erroneous interpretation in forums of expert and public discourse.

   No statistical construct has aroused more curiosity and speculation than *the curve*, the time series of cases and deaths whose rhythmic ebb and flow occasionally break into crescendo, demarcating a new *wave*. Once again, a force of nature is used to describe the epidemiological landscape, a metaphor betraying a sense of pow-erlessness as it echoes through the media, around dinner tables, and in WhatsApp groups worldwide. The imagery of a wave, the statistical artefact brought to life through human imagination, permeates the public (and even scientific) discourse, as metaphors are painted as a means of sense-making, rationalisation, and perhaps to some extent, coping (Taylor & Kidgell 2021; Stadlmeier et al. 2022). Through a Digital Humanities lens, we witness yet another example of how the digital footprint of the pandemic leaves tracks on the psychosocial and emotional terrain of the individual (Stadlmeier et al. 2022). Amongst interviewed participants, the narrative metaphor of the wave was evoked to convey a sense of looming inundation as persons anxiously monitored social media and dashboards, platforms for digital data as a harbinger of epidemiological, sociopolitical, and economic catastrophe (Stadlmeier et al. 2022).

Age- and sex-standardisation of epidemiological data is yet another new tool facing the untrained dashboard user. Briefly: in order to account for spatial variations in demographic structure (i.e., the age/sex pyramid varies geographically), biostatisticians employ a set of methods to estimate the *hypothetical* rate of incidence/prevalence/mortality in a given area, as if all areas had an identical age/sex pyramid. This effectively controls/corrects for age/sex differences in disease incidence, thereby allowing for comparison of demographically heterogeneous regions. In doing so, researchers reduce confounding and can thereby test for other suspected risk factors (e.g., socioeconomic deprivation, population density; Elliott & Wartenberg 2004). These can be challenging concepts even for those with some statistical education and training, especially when the method of standardisation (direct or indirect), the delineations of age/sex categories used in the calculation, the denominator population (regional, national, global, or fictitious), and the covariates selected for modelling vary immensely between institutions and studies. This raises many questions and merits a degree of criticality (and even scepticism) regarding the processes by which such modelling decisions are made and the factors influencing the modeller throughout.

As the researcher, epidemiologist, and amateur dashboard user engage with data, they are simultaneously engaged in continuous and iterative sense-making, searching for patterns, testing formal and heuristic/informal hypotheses, and navigating complex and interwoven assumptions. These processes are both statistical and socio-political, and provide the individual with a means of developing narrative and logics to assist with coping and decision-making amidst uncertainty. Are counts more important than rates? Is socioeconomic deprivation best measured using income, unemployment, educational attainment, or some other metric or combination thereof? If a combination, how should its constituent variables be weighted? As is often the case, space and place as cognitive objects for heuristic sense-making further complicate matters.

Waves and Wildfires

Since the first uncertain weeks of COVID-19's arrival in Europe, the map took a prominent role in the public discourse as users panned and zoomed in search of the next hotspot. As shades of orange and red appeared and spread across the political geometry like wine spilt on a Khotan rug, people once again drew on a metaphor of nature's might: COVID-19 was spreading like wildfire across the landscape (Kremer & Felgenhauer 2022; Semino 2021; Koch 2016; Koch 2005).

By providing a cognitive placial anchoring for the disease, the map enabled users not only to visually examine the spatiotemporality of COVID-19, but furthermore upon that basis to construct and challenge hypotheses regarding its epidemiology. For example, observation of spatiotemporal patterns in the first months of pandemic in Europe led many to postulate socioeconomic determinants; subsequent statistical analysis revealed a high degree of geographical non-stationarity and stochasticity (Kremer & Walker 2022; Chilla et al. 2022; Scarpone et al. 2020), demonstrating a significantly more complex picture than the public discourse would suggest. Certain regions experienced rapid emergence of clusters, whilst others appeared on the map to be unaffected. What could explain the difference? Narratives on social media pointed towards all manner of possible explanations: sociocultural, meteorological/climatic, religious, and political, to name but a few.

By drawing on experiences, stereotypes, and characteristics of places represented on the map, the user constructs theories to make sense of the observed data (Cöltekin et al. 2018; Koch 2011; Crampton 2010; Koch 2005; Krygier 2002). In this way, the map user/viewer actively (and perhaps to a certain degree subconsciously) searches for spatial correlations between the data as represented on the map and their own subjective interpretations and constructions of the aforementioned placial characteristics, factitious or fictional. For example, I recently led two geostatistical analyses of COVID-19 incidence rates in Germany and its crossborder regions (Chilla et al. 2022; Scarpone et al. 2020); while the accepted norms of scientific reporting prohibit open speculation and presentation of preliminary/exploratory analyses, the behind-the-scenes discussions and early statistical modelling efforts were in part informed by our team's knowledge and experience of the study area. We considered cultural and historical differences along Germany's north/south (e.g., cultural tendency towards interpersonal distancing) and east/west (e.g., prevalence of religious institutions and childcare facilities) axes in a qualitative manner, in our efforts to explain and fit statistical models to the observed geographical patterns.

Amongst the general public, and particularly in social media, geographical correlation plays a fascinating role in the construction and propagation of various speculative narratives concerning the pandemic and its causes. One of the more curious of these concerns an alleged spatial correlation between 5G data network masts and COVID-19 incidence (Flaherty et al. 2022). Just as statistical correlation is erroneously used to assert causal relationships with some degree of *quantitative authority*, so too does the map and the spatial correlation command a certain degree of authority and plausibility in non-critical public (and academic!) discourses. It remains an open question to what degree and with what characteristics do (pseudo-)scientific narratives become dominant discursive arguments in public spheres; the roles of (geo)data in these processes is one of many opportunities for geographic information science to expand beyond exclusively Cartesian mappings whilst embracing a Digital Humanities paradigm, and vice-versa (Kremer & Walker 2023; Dammann et al. 2021; Walker 2016).

That interactive digital maps and other data visualisations serve as powerful tools for exploration, sense-making, and argumentation has been well-understood long before the "dashboard pandemic" took root (Everts 2020; Andrienko et al. 2010; Andrienko & Andrienko 1999). However, the ubiquity of maps and geodata in discourse and policy and the degree to which non-expert publics have engaged with digital cartography amidst this pandemic illuminate important inroads for the Digital Humanities in contemporary geographic information science (GIScience). Just as researchers in the humanities seek to understand an artefact, whether digital or analogue, tangible or ethereal, contemporary or ancient, sacred or profane, in the context in which it was created, so too does rigorous GIScience praxis require that the geodata and the map be critically examined in light of their social, cultural, and political provenance (Harvey 2018; Wilson 2017), as the artefact itself reflects not only the materials and medium of its construction, but also the hand of the one who built it (*positionality*; Crampton & Krygier 2015; Wilson 2009; Monmonier 1991).

If we consider the Digital Humanities less as a transdisciplinary paradigm and more in terms of its methodological diversity and (functional) epistemological pluralism, new empirical techniques for knowledge production arrive at researchers' disposal. For example, semiautomated text processing techniques provide means for theory-informed, yet thoroughly applied social science (e.g., Kremer & Walker 2023; Moura de Souza et al. 2022). In established critical social sciences practice, one critically examines the source of an artefact, seeking to infer or divinate the source's motivations and biases, considering ways in which these might affect the artefact itself; for example, one might assert that public health organisations were motivated to freely and openly distribute COVID-19 incidence data as part of a strategy to inform the public about the risks of contracting the virus. To this end, the near-universal choice for cartographic representation was a graduated yellow-orange-red colour palette, signifying danger and thereby ascribing risk to areas with relatively high incidence rates. However, new approaches and methods from the Digital Humanities challenge us to depart from the traditional hypothesis testing framework, in which measurable differences between categories or ranges are analysed, and instead to focus on its *inversion*: what different discursive processes result in the *same*

artefact, and how do those processes differ? As the pandemic progressed and incidence rates continued to climb, the scale of hue shifted such that areas once painted
deep red were reduced to soft yellow, despite the fact that their incidence rates had
only continued to climb. The meanings of deep red and the epidemiological realities it represents continue to slide and transform with both the maximum incidence
rate in the geodata and the contextual backdrop of the geometric space being represented. The simple algorithm translating incidence rate to colour/hue is as such a
product of, and subject to, the decision-making of the cartographer and/or the organisation they represent (Crampton & Krygier 2015).

In a slightly more abstract example, consider the terms *hotspot* and *cluster*. In par-
lance, these terms describe a geographical concentration of cases or incidents; the
use of these terms in various public narratives and discourses would suggest that
they possess inconsistent or even primarily metaphorical meanings to ascribe illness to place (Lessler et al. 2017). Even within the stricter confines of spatial statistics, hotspots and clusters vary immensely in their definition and characteristics,
the implementation of which is largely at the behest of the analyst. Hotspots can be
interpolated surfaces based on the density of mapped points (e.g., kernel density
estimation; Walker et al. 2014), or they can be groupings of nearby areas with similar data values (e.g., Getis-Ord Gi* statistic; Getis & Ord 1992). Clusters encompass
a variety of heuristics and statistical metrics ranging from simple visual interpretation of point patterns to complex multivariate, multivariable, multilevel Bayesian
modelling of spatiotemporal datasets. Variety is not a problem, but a lack of transparency regarding how a hotspot or cluster is defined and calculated (which algorithm, which spatial function, what parameters, which distribution for inference,
etc. were used and, most importantly, why?) renders spatial epidemiology practice
something of a dark art.

It is neither novel nor particularly controversial to assert that maps and statistics are an art form – a means by which the analyst knowingly or unknowingly ex-
presses their positionality and reflects power structures and latent cultural artefacts
through the medium of data, algorithm, and visuality (Burns 2021; Thornton 2017;
Ash 2016; Koch 2011). The map's inherent visuality and its more elaborate historical forms render it easy to imagine as art. However, minus the visual element, so
too does the statistician express positionality, engage with subjectivities, and reflect
power structures and cultural artefacts. Under the banner of objectivity, scientific
reporting of statistical data requires methodological transparency and replicability
whilst simultaneously rejecting exploration of the analyst's and reporting institution's positionalities, subjective and qualitative decisions made during the analysis,
and intent. In this sense, the *black box* contains not only algorithmic unknowns (e.g.,
how outliers were defined and handled, or how a machine learning toolkit iteratively
splits a dataset), but also the analyst themself (e.g., why a heuristically relevant yet
non-significant variable was removed from a regression model). By inviting statis-

tics and geostatistics into the Digital Humanities, we can create space for a more transparent statistical practice, in which the quantitative artefact and the manner in which it is reported can be more deeply considered and critically examined amidst their sociopolitical and cultural backdrop.

Fisticuffs or Full Embrace

> Nature has established patterns originating in the return of events, but only for the most part. New illnesses flood the human race, so that no matter how many experiments you have done on corpses, you have not thereby imposed a limit on the nature of events so that in the future they could not vary.
> Gottfried Leibniz, 1703

Leibniz acknowledges and underscores the inherent uncertainties of disease epidemiology in a characteristically rationalistic tenor, describing the human body-object as subject to the stochasticity or chaos of nature. Rationalist modes of thought and *Occam's razor*-flavoured determinism and its progeny frequentist statistics continue to underpin, and in many ways define, contemporary western medicine and disease epidemiology (Miles 2012; Ashcroft 2005; Morabia 2004). By no means should we dismiss the remarkable advances in quality and duration of life that science-based medicine, epidemiology, and hygiene have brought about! But one may simultaneously recognise decades of scholarship in health geographies and the medical humanities that highlight long-standing issues stemming from the epistemological dominance of empirical positivism (Cole et al. 2014; Crawford et al. 2010; Kearns & Moon 2002; Kearns 1993). For example, decision-making concerning cancer treatments require that the physician and patient consider not only the risk of adverse outcomes, but also the psychological and emotional costs of chemotherapy, radiology, and/or resection surgery, including cultural attitudes, religious beliefs, power dynamics in the doctor-patient relationship, and even simply the logistics of travel to/from treatment centres (Finley et al. 2015; Walker et al. 2020b). Such subjective and highly variable characteristics resist deterministic modelling methodology and require detailed and deeply contextual means of qualitative analysis to inform policy and institutional/community response (Kenn & Packwood 1995; Davidson et al. 2008). This is as true of maps as it is of statistics, and the Digital Humanities invites those of us trained in traditional (geo)statistics and epidemiology to embrace uncertainty and subjectivity, not as a stochastic parameter in a cognitive model, but as a backdrop for the entire process of analysis from start to finish.

But what does this imply for the non-expert audience, the dashboard consumer? I argue that Digital Humanities approaches and methods focussing on discourses and narratives hold significant potential in this regard. The interweaving of genuinely relevant considerations with various degrees of conjecture within digital spaces for dialogue raises fascinating questions for both the Digital Humanities and public health, such as the ways in which scientific constructs are merged and melded with conspiracy theory and anti-state sentiment to propagate (dubious) narratives (Delafield-Butt & Trevarthen 2015; Guess & Lyons 2020). Here we see yet another intersection between questions in geographic information science and those for which the Digital Humanities are optimally positioned to address, specifically how data are mechanised and deployed within narrative construction. Indeed, as the general public became increasingly familiar with some of the tools and data used by health authorities, those tools have been instrumentalised to define and delineate the peri-pandemic discourse, often in ways that contradict or even actively seek to repudiate evidence-based information (Nyhan 2020). That said, the proportion (or incidence rate) of COVID-19-related misinformation on social media platforms appears to be rather low, despite having gained significant attention and notoriety (Cinelli et al. 2020b; Singh et al. 2020). A notable exception is YouTube, where researchers from Ottawa observed that 27.5% of the most viewed videos concerning COVID-19 contained disinformation relating to the virology and/or epidemiology of SARS-CoV-2 (Li et al. 2020). This raises additional questions about the roles of visuality and format in the audiences' assessments of plausibility, reliability, and trustworthiness (Evans et al. 2017), as non-expert publics attempt to navigate fact and fiction amidst a chaotic sea of sociopolitical ideologies and information of unknown provenance (Chou et al. 2021).

Petrichor

That curiously sweet scent of the violence above, the petrichor. Beginning only a few minutes into the storm and persisting long after the clouds had passed, this peculiar geochemical aroma left a ground-level trace of the storm's path across the landscape, an olfactory geographical footprint neither seen nor heard nor felt. Its pleasant aether nonetheless provided solace, and its presence left a lasting imprint of the storm in our mind and memory.

In the wake of the dashboard pandemic, one might optimistically expect to witness a public discourse more aware of critical cartography and (geo)statistical literacy. The disease map and the statistic serve not only as media for the dissemination of data, but also as tools and spaces for contesting views and knowledges (Kim 2015), even if those views and knowledges contradict dominant narrative or scientific fact. As social media and other informal networks continue to replace traditional forms for information sharing, questions of positionality and provenance must therefore be called to centre stage, not only by the political sceptic or armchair (geo)statistician, but by researchers and institutions of learning and knowledge production across the board.

Amidst the long-standing epistemological incongruencies of positivistic empiricism and constructivism/post-structuralism in medicine, health, and epidemiology (and certainly in medical and health geographies), we hear echoes of calls to intervention (Schuurman 2000; Wilson 2017) and increasingly urgent demands for hybridity and the pursuit of a middle-ground between hermeneutic phenomenology and deterministic reductionism. These calls need not only be heard by those concerned with theory, rather, they present important opportunities for applied (spatial) epidemiology, informed by methodological and conceptual progress in the Digital Humanities. In this sense, considering the spatial epidemiology of COVID-19 through a Digital Humanities lens leads us towards a more context-aware applied geostatistics, a situated spatial epidemiology (Moura de Souza, Kremer & Walker 2022; Walker et al. 2020c; Walker & Schuurman 2017). We are challenged to consider the (geo)data and their quantitative artefacts (e.g., p-values and hotspot maps) not as static and impartial summaries of a singular reality, rather as digital factualisations of complex sociocultural and deeply political narrative. This is bolstered greatly by the increasing prominence of geostatistical concepts and their instrumentalisations for producing Lefebvrian space (Pierce & Martin 2015), ultimately underscoring the need for a humanities-adjacent geostatistics that embraces the social, the cultural, and the situational.

References

Andrienko, G., Andrienko, N., Demsar, U., Dransch, D., Dykes, J., Fabrikant, S. I. et al. (2010). Space, time and visual analytics. *Int. J. Geogr. Inf. Sci* .24 (10), p. 1577–1600.

Andrienko, G., Andrienko, N. (1999). Interactive maps for visual data exploration. *Int. J. Geogr. Inf. Sci* 13 (4). p. 355–374. DOI: 10.1080/136588199241247.Ash, J. (2016). *The interface envelope: Gaming, technology, power.* Bloomsbury Publishing USA. Ashcroft, R. E. (2005). *Current epistemological problems in evidence-based medicine. Evidence-based Practice in Medicine and Health Care.* p. 77–85.

Bergman, A., Sella, Y., Agre, P., Casadevall, A. (2020). Oscillations in U.S. COVID-19 Incidence and Mortality Data Reflect Diagnostic and Reporting Factors. *mSystems 5* (4).

Brandl, M., Selb, R., Seidl-Pillmeier, S., Marosevic, D., Buchholz, U. Rehmet, S. (2021). Kontrolle eines COVID-19-Ausbruches im Landkreis Tirschenreuth, März bis Mai 2020. *Epidemologische Bulletin 12.*

Burns, Ryan (2021). Transgressions: Reflecting on critical GIS and digital geographies. *Digit. Geogr. Soc.* 2, p. 100011.

Chou W. S., Gaysynsky A., Vanderpool R.C., (2020). The COVID-19 Misinfodemic: Moving Beyond Fact-Checking. *Health Educ Behav,* 48(1). p. 9–13.

Cinelli, M., Cresci, S., Galeazzi, A., et al. (2020a). The limited reach of fake news on Twitter during 2019 European elections. *PLoS ONE 15*(6), e0234689.

Cinelli, M., Quattrociocchi, W., Galeazzi, A., Valensise, C. M., Brugnoli, E., Schmidt, A. L. et al. (2020b). The COVID-19 social media infodemic. *Sci Rep 10*(1), p. 16598.

Çöltekin, A., Janetzko, H., Fabrikant, S. (2018). Geovisualization. *Geogr Inf.Sci.,* 2018 (Q2), online. DOI: 10.22224/gistbok/2018.2.6.

Craig, W. J., Harris, T. M.; Weiner, D. (2002). *Community participation and geographic information systems.* Taylor & Francis. London, New York.

Crampton J. (2010). *Mapping: A critical introduction to cartography and GIS.* Chichester: Wiley-Blackwell.

Crampton, J. W., & Krygier, J. (2015). An Introduction to Critical Cartography. *ACME: An International Journal for Critical Geographies 4* (1), p. 11–33.

Crawford, P., Brown, B., Tischler, V., Baker, C. (2010). Health humanities: the future of medical humanities? *Mental Health Review Journal 15* (3), p. 4–10.

Dammann, F., Dzudzek, I., Glasze, G., Mattissek, A., & Schirmel, H. (2021). 14 Verfahren der lexikometrisch-computerlinguistischen Analyse von Textkorpora. In Glasze G. & Mattissek A. (Eds.). *Handbuch Diskurs und Raum: Theorien und Methoden für die Humangeographie sowie die sozial- und kulturwissenschaftliche Raumforschung* (p. 313 344).transcript. Bielefeld. Verlag.

Davidson, L., et al. (2008). Using qualitative research to inform mental health policy. *The Canadian Journal of Psychiatry 53*.3, p.137–144.

Deeg, A. (2021). Gottesdienst in ›Corona‹-Zeiten oder: Drei Variationen zum Thema Präsenz. *Evangelische Theologie 81* (2), p. 136–151.

Delafield-Butt, J. T., Trevarthen, C. (2015). The ontogenesis of narrative: from moving to meaning. *Front. Psychol.* 6. https://www.frontiersin.org/articles/10.3389/f psyg.2015.01157.

Elliott, P., Wartenberg, D. (2004). Spatial epidemiology: current approaches and future challenges. *Environmental health perspectives 112* (9), p. 998–1006.

Evans, S.K., Pearce, K.E., Vitak, J., et al. (2017). Explicating affordances: a conceptual framework for understanding affordances in communication research. *Journal of Computer-Mediated Communication 22* (1), p. 35–52.

Everts, J. (2020). The dashboard pandemic. *Dialogues in Human Geography 10* (2), p. 260–264.

Finley, C., Schneider, L., Shakeel, S., Akhtar-Danesh, N., Elit, L., Dixon, E., Lavis, J.,Abelson, J., Gauvin F.P, Schuurman, N., Walker, B.B. (2015). Approaches to high-risk, resource intensive cancer surgical care in Canada / CPAC. https://policycommons.net/artifacts/1199960/approaches-to-high-risk-resource-intensive-cancer-surgical-care-in-canada/1753079/.

Flaherty, E., Sturm, T., Farries, E., (2022). The conspiracy of Covid-19 and 5G: Spatial analysis fallacies in the age of data democratization. *Social science & medicine (1982)* 293, p. 114546. DOI: 10.1016/j.socscimed.2021.114546.

Fuchs, S.; Daniell, J. (2020). Corona Hotspots tagesaktuell & weltweit – Die Pandemiekarten des Karlsruher Risklayer Think Tanks zeigen, die Krise ist noch lange nicht vorbei – Campusreport am 23. Juni 2020: Karlsruhe. https://publikatione n.bibliothek.kit.edu/1000120433.

Getis, A. & J.K. Ord. (1992). The Analysis of Spatial Association by Use of Distance Statistics. *Geographical Analysis* 24(3). p. 189–206.

Guess, A.M., Lyons, B.A. (2020). Misinformation, disinformation, and online propaganda. Persily, N., Tucker, J.A. (eds.) *Social Media and Democracy: The State of the Field, Prospects for Reform* (p. 10–33). Cambridge University Press. Cambridge.

Jinyoung, I., Haemi, K., Miao, L. (2021). CEO letters: Hospitality corporate narratives during the COVID-19 pandemic. In *International Journal of Hospitality Management 92*, p. 102701.

Krygier, J.B. (2002). A praxis of public participation GIS and visualization. In Craig, W.J., Harris, T. M., & Weiner, D. (Eds.), *Community participation and geographic information systems* (p. 330–345). Taylor & Francis. London, New York.

Kearns, R., Moon, G. (2002). From medical to health geography: novelty, place and theory after a decade of change. *Progress in Human Geography* 26 (5), p. 605–625.

Kearns, R. A. (1993). Place and Health: Towards a Reformed Medical Geography. *The Professional Geographer* 45 (2), p. 139–147.

Keen, J., & Packwood, T. (1995). Qualitative research: case study evaluation. Bmj 311.7002, p. 444–446.

Kim, A. M. (2015). Critical cartography 2.0: From "participatory mapping" to authored visualizations of power and people. *Landscape and Urban Planning 142*, p. 215–225.

Kim, L. E., Leary, R., Asbury, K. (2021). Teachers' narratives during COVID-19 partial school reopenings: an exploratory study. *Educational Research 63* (2), p. 244–260.

Kitchin, R., Lauriault, T. P., McArdle, G. (2015). Knowing and governing cities through urban indicators, city benchmarking and real-time dashboards. *Regional Studies, Regional Science* 2 (1), p. 6–28. DOI: 10.1080/21681376.2014.983149.

Koch, T. (2005). *Cartographies of disease: maps, mapping, and medicine.* Esri Press.

Koch, T. (2011): *Disease maps. Epidemics on the ground. Chicago.* The University of Chicago Press.

Koch, T. (2016): Fighting disease, like fighting fires: The lessons Ebola teaches. *The Canadian Geographer / Le Géographe canadien* 60 (3), p. 288–299. DOI: 10.1111/cag.12258.

Kremer D., Felgenhauer T. (2022): Reasoning COVID-19: the use of spatial metaphor in times of a crisis. *Humanit Soc Sci Commun* 265 (9), p. 1–15.

Kremer D., Walker BB. (2023): Placing Wellbeing: Distant Reading Approaches for Exploratory Placial Data Analysis in Geographies of Health and Wellbeing. In Dammann F. & Kremer D. (Eds.), *Geographical Research in the Digital Humanities: Spatial Concepts, Approaches and Methods.* transcript Verlag. Berlin. (p. 121–142).

Leibniz, G. (1703). [Written correspondence to Jacob Bernoulli].

Lessler, J., Azman, A. S., McKay, H. S., Moore, S. M. (2017). What is a Hotspot Anyway? *The American Journal of Tropical Medicine and Hygiene* 96 (6), p. 1270–1273.

Li, HO-Y., Bailey, A., Huynh, D., et al. (2020). YouTube as a source of information on COVID-19: a pandemic of misinformation? *BMJ Global Health* 5: e002604.

Lucas-Gabrielli V., Eliot E. (2019): K comme Kilomètre. In Fleuret S., Gasquet-Blanchard C-, Hoyez A.C. (eds.), Abécédaire de la géographie de la santé: Dimension territoriale de la santé. Éditions Matériologiques. Paris

Mathew, N., Rumbidzai, C., Fungisai, M. (2022). Exploring factors enabling the spread of COVID-19: Narratives of health professionals in Harare, Zimbabwe. *Health & social care in the community* 30 (5), e2973-e2979.

Miles, A. (2012). Moving from a reductive anatomico-pathological medicine to an authentically anthropocentric model of healthcare: current transitions in epidemiology and epistemology and the ongoing development of person-centered clinical practice. *International Journal of Person Centered Medicine* 2.4, p. 615–621.

Monmonier, M. (1991), *How to lie with maps.* University of Chicago Press.

Morabia, A. (2004). *Epidemiology: an epistemological perspective. A history of epidemiologic methods and concepts.* Birkhäuser, Basel, p. 3–125.

Moura de Souza, C., Kremer, D., & Walker, B.B. (2022). Placial-Discursive Topologies of Violence: Volunteered Geographic Information and the Reproduction of Violent Places in Recife, Brazil. *ISPRS International Journal of Geoinformation 11 (10),* p.500.

Nekliudov, N. A.; Blyuss, O., Cheung, K. Y., Petrou, L., Genuneit, J., Sushentsev, N. et al. (2020). Excessive Media Consumption About COVID-19 is Associated With Increased State Anxiety: Outcomes of a Large Online Survey in Russia. *J Med Internet Res* 22 (9), e20955. .

Nerlich, B., Koteyko, N. (2012). Crying wolf? Biosecurity and metacommunication in the context of the 2009 swine flu pandemic. *Health & place* 18 (4), p. 710–717.

Nyhan, B (2020). Facts and myths about misperceptions. Journal of Economic Perspectives 34 (3), p. 220–236.

Paes-Sousa, R., Millett, C. Rocha, R., Barreto, M- L., Hone, T. (2020). Science misuse and polarised political narratives in the COVID-19 response. The Lancet 396 (10263), p. 1635–1636.

Pierce, J., Martin, Deborah G. (2015). Placing Lefebvre. Antipode 47 (5), p. 1279–1299. DOI: 10.1111/anti.12155.

Riffe, T. Acosta, E., Acosta, E. J., Manuel A. D., Alburez-Gutierrez, A., Altová, A. et al. (2021). Data Resource Profile: COVerAGE-DB: a global demographic database of COVID-19 cases and deaths. Int J Epidemiol 50 (2), p. 390–390f.

Rosenkrantz, L., Schuurman, N., Bell, N., Amram, O. (2021). The need for GIScience in mapping COVID-19. Health & place 67, p. 102389.

Scarpone, C.; Brinkmann, S. T., Große, T., Sonnenwald, D., Fuchs, M., Walker, B. B. (2020). A multimethod approach for county-scale geospatial analysis of emerging infectious diseases: a cross-sectional case study of COVID-19 incidence in Germany. Int J Health Geogr 19 (1), p. 32.

Schuurman, N. (2000). Trouble in the heartland: GIS and its critics in the 1990s. Progress in Human Geography 24 (4), p. 569–590.

Semino, E. (2021). COVID-19: A forest fire rather than a wave? Mètode Science Studies Journal 11, p. 5. https://www.redalyc.org/journal/5117/511766954022/html/.

Singh, L., Bansal, S., Bode, L., et al. (2020). A first look at COVID-19 information and misinformation sharing on Twitter. arXiv:2003, 13907v1. https://arxiv.org/abs/2 003.13907v1.

Stadlmeier A., Kremer D., Walker B.B. (2022). Experiences of place-bound sociality amidst the COVID-19 pandemic: A qualitative analysis of environment-related coping strategies. *Erdkunde 76* (3). DOI: 10.3112/erdkunde.2022.03.02.

Taglioni F. (2019). Z comme Zika. In Fleuret S, Gasquet-Blanchard C, Hoyez AC (eds.), Abédédaire de la géographie de la santé: Dimension territoriale de la santé. Éditions Matériologiques. Paris.

Taylor, C., Kidgell, J. (2021). Flu-like pandemics and metaphor pre-covid: A corpus investigation. Discourse, Context & Media 41, p. 100503. DOI: 10.1016/j.dcm.2021.100503.

Thatcher, J., Bergmann, L., Ricker, B., Rose-Redwood, R., O'Sullivan, D., Barnes, Trevor J. et al. (2016). Revisiting critical GIS. Environ. Plan. A 48 (5), p. 815–824.

Theocharis, Y., Cardenal, A., Jin, S., Aalberg, T., Hopmann, D. N., Strömbäck, J. et al. (2021). Does the platform matter? Social media and COVID-19 conspiracy theory beliefs in 17 countries. *New Media & Society*, 146144482110456.

Thornton, P. (2017). Geographies of (con) text: Language and structure in a digital age. *Computational Culture* 6.

Vialard L., Bochaton A., Charreire H. (2019). P comme Parcours. Fleuret S., Gasquet-Blanchard C., Hoyez A.C. (eds.), *Abédédaire de la géographie de la santé: Dimension territoriale de la santé*. Éditions Matériologiques. Paris.

Walker, B. B. (2016). Making connections in a tough data scene. *The Canadian Geographer/Le Géographe canadien, 60* (3), p. 285–287.

Walker B.B., Schuurman N. (2017). The pen or the sword: a situated spatial analysis of graffiti and violent injury in Vancouver, British Columbia. *The Professional Geographer 67* (4), p. 608–619.

Walker B.B., Schuurman N., Wen C.K., Shakeel S., Schneider L., Finley C. (2020a). Cancer resection rates, socioeconomic deprivation, and geographical access to surgery among urban, suburban, and rural populations across Canada. PLoS ONE 15(10), e0240444.

Walker B.B., Shashank A., Gasevic D., Schuurman N., Poirier P., Teo K., Rangarajan S., Yusuf S., Lear SA (2020b), The Local Food Environment and Obesity: Evidence from Three Cities. *Obesity 28*(1), p. 40–45.

Walker B.B., Moura de Souza C., Pedroso E., Lai R.S., Hunter P., Tam J., Cave I., Swanlund D., Barbosa K.G.N. (2020c). Towards a Situated Spatial Epidemiology of Violence: A Placially-Informed Geospatial Analysis of Homicide in Alagoas, Brazil. *Int J Environ Res Public Health 17* (24):9283.

Walker B.B., Brinkmann S.T., Große T., Kremer D., Schuurman N., Hystad P., Rangarajan S., Teo K., Yusuf S., Lear S.A. (2022). Neighbourhood greenspace and socioeconomic risk are associated with diabetes risk at the sub-neighborhood scale: Results from the Prospective Urban and Rural Epidemiology (PURE) Study. *J Urban Health.*

Walker, B. B., Schuurman, N., Hameed, S. M. (2014). A GIS-based spatiotemporal analysis of violent trauma hotspots in Vancouver, Canada: identification, contextualisation and intervention. *BMJ open 4* (2), e003642, DOI: 10.1136/bmjopen-2013-003642.

Wilson M. (2017). *New lines: Critical GIS and the trouble of the map.* University of Minnesota Press. Wilson, M.W. (2009). Towards a genealogy of qualitative GIS. In Cope M & Elwood S. (eds.), *Qualitative GIS: A mixed methods approach* (p.156–170). Sage. London.

Wilson, Matthew W. (2009). Cyborg geographies: towards hybrid epistemologies. *Gender, Place & Culture 16* (5), p. 499–516.

EVOLVING METHODS AND CRITICAL REFLECTIONS

Place and Space in Literature
Named Entity Recognition as a Possibility for Spatial Modelling in Computational Literary Studies

Mareike Schumacher, Marie Flüh & Julia Nantke

Abstract *In this chapter we discuss how Named Entity Recognition (NER) can be used in Computational Literary Studies to model spatial categories in narrative texts and historical letters. From a methodological perspective, we investigate the reliability of two models for automatic recognition of space in two different text types. In terms of a so-called domain adaptation – the optimisation of a digital method developed in one subject area for another subject area – we discuss possibilities and shortcomings of applying a method for computational spatial analysis to different research objects in Literary Studies. Regarding various philosophical and philological concepts of space, we assume that space is a multi-layered concept. Therefore, it can be divided into various sub-concepts that can be used to describe different phenomena like geographical places, action spaces or metaphorical space. The point of departure of our contribution is the translation of Humanities' concepts of space and place into machine-processable models. In applying these to different corpora we show that automatic space recognition with a model developed for fictional literary texts can also be made fruitful for non-fictional texts that are relevant to Literary Studies. We point at the shortcomings of such transmissions between different textual genres and historical epochs, too, because they provide relevant insights regarding differences in textual composition and research perspectives. Regarding the scope of this volume we investigate a text-based approach to space. We show that automation-based text mining developed to fit one domain or another always implements a certain conceptual understanding of the phenomenon in focus. It thus produces very different output data e.g., regarding what we conceive of when we talk about space. Although domain-specific implementations of Digital Humanities tools and methods are crucial for Computational Literary Studies we therefore argument that a broad conceptual foundation, that can also be brought back into other domains of spatial humanities, not only comes with using certain tools but also has to be reflected in its implications, advantages and disadvantages regarding the respective interest in knowledge.*

Keywords: Named Entity Recognition, Spatial Concepts, Literary Text, Letters, Domain Adaptation

Modelling Narrative Space in Novels and Letter Correspondences

In this contribution we concentrate on domain adaptation of a computational method, namely Named Entity Recognition (NER), for Literary Studies. NER is a machine learning method originating from Computational Linguistics. It is used to automatically annotate well-defined entities in texts. Common entity types that are determined by NER are persons, places and organisations (cf. Schumacher 2018). Applying NER to research objects in Literary Studies can support the analysis of huge text corpora and thereby help to gain insights into overriding structures of literary genres or literary-historical developments. In our study, we focus on two text types that are of equal interest to Literary Studies: Fictional (narrative) texts and non-fictional texts (letters). These two text types differ significantly regarding their conceptual foundation. Non-fictional letters are closer to the domain of origin of NER, which is non-fiction like articles in journals. Letters, as well as newspaper articles, can be described as functional, more pragmatic types of texts that are used by scholars as historical sources that provide information about former epochs, whereas fictional texts like literary narratives are usually considered and analysed from a more aesthetic point of view. Coming from Literary Studies and thus implying its research traditions in our study we need to take into account conceptual differences between a literary concept of space and the linguistic category of place (which is commonly implemented in Named Entity Recognition Tools, including administrative locations, physical places, pathways, buildings, and addresses) when we apply NER to our objects of research. At the same time, we try not to narrow down our conceptual foundation too much, so that the resulting model can still be transferred to other research settings. Therefore, in addition to Literary Studies approaches we consider studies dealing with space as a phenomenological unit coming e.g., from Philosophy or Culture Studies. How can literary space be conceptualised, modelled and operationalised for automatic annotation of spatial indicators at the surface of texts? How does this concept differ from a linguistic conception of place? What do we gain and what do we lose when analysing letters of interest to literary scholars using one concept rather than another? These are the questions we address in this study.

The relationship of Literary Studies to the analytical category of space is ambivalent. On the one hand, Lessing's Laokoon thesis of 1766 still has an effect today. In this thesis, he states that visual art is determined rather spatially, poetry rather temporally (cf. Lessing 1766). On the other hand, starting at least from the middle of the 20th century, there has been a tradition in Literary Studies focussing on spatial structures in literary texts. This research tradition is based on concepts of space developed e.g., by Bachelard (2001), Bakhtin (2008), Foucault (2005), Lotman (1973), and de Certeau (1988). What these approaches have in common is that they do not conceive of space as a stable category, but as a dynamic construction that is dependent on social and cultural activities (cf. Hallet/Neumann 2009: 13). While Bachelard, Foucault and de Certeau are more concerned with the relations of space(s) and social actions in general, Bakhtin and Lotman especially focus on space in literary texts. Based on these theoretical concepts there has been a lot of research concerning 'the question of space' in literature which was framed as part of the transdisciplinary spatial turn of the late 1990s (cf. Bachmann-Medick 2007; Frank et al. 2008). However, both in individual case studies (cf. Rippel 2016, Wilde 2016, or Hallet 2016, among others) and in narratological considerations of the spatial category (cf. Dennerlein 2008, Ryan et al. 2016), investigations that refer to larger text corpora remained absent or were merely postulated as desiderata for follow-up studies (as in Dennerlein 2008, for example). Thus, to date, there is no systematic corpus-based study on how space is represented in literature and thus reflected in this cultural form. Such a corpus-based approach would also make it possible to take into account cultural differences in literary representations of space in a systematic manner. The first step towards this desideratum is addressed by Mareike Schumacher (2022), who uses computational methods to systematically investigate places and spaces in German novels from the 18th to 21st century[1]. We take both the conceptual as well as the technical model developed by Schumacher as a crucial basis for the investigations of the study described in this article.

In this case study, we will focus on the conditions for success that go hand in hand with domain adaptation of the NER classifier for the detection of narrative space in novels and letters. To be able to discuss the possibilities for optimisation, we will test how well or poorly the model performs for the analysis of historical letters and examine the question of what insights emerge during the process with regard to spatial phenomena in fictional texts and letters.

Letters are considered part of and a commentary on an author's literary oeuvre as a whole. It is not uncommon for them to have literary and/or narrative elements, highlighting the aesthetic potential of the genre (cf. Matthews-Schlinzig et al. 2020, Joost 2013: 13) and illustrating the genre affinity between letters and mere

---

1   Vast concepts like space depend on cultural as well as historic settings. Although a large-scale comparative study ranging across different cultures would be highly interesting, the methodological framework used here is bound to a language and culture-specific approach. As Schumacher (2022) was the first to model and operationalise a concept of space based on Literary Studies to date there are no corresponding models which can be used on texts from languages other than German. Trained on texts from a relatively broad timespan the NER-model used here nevertheless can deal with some cultural variances resulting from the historic background of the narratives included in the training corpus.

fictional texts. Despite this inherent aesthetic value, however, letters are not narrative texts: Narrative passages in letters are found primarily in private correspondences (cf. Strobel 2020: 301), at the same time, private letters can do without fictional elements or for example business letters are often devoid of narrative elements. In terms of narrative, letters are a hybrid form, which can contain elements of (auto-)fictional narrative as well as non-fictional everyday narratives, in addition to communicative aspects (request, thanks, invitation, justification). Because of this genre-specific dual function, the letter is considered both a document with fictional potential and a historical-biographical document (cf. Matthews-Schlinzig et al. 2020; Depkat and Pyta 2021). Significant structural elements such as the indication of sender, recipient, destination, and place of origin of the letter characterise its medial specificity. Above all, places appear in different functions in address fields or letterheads as well as in the actual text of the letter, where it provides information, for example, about biographical stations, phases of life, or formative events that the writer experienced. Spatial categories play a major role in scholarly letter editions as they can be a key element for structuring the material. This is why places are relevant entities that are systematically marked throughout the entire corpus of scholarly editions. However, (place) registers in scholarly editions of letters have so far been created primarily based on very laborious manual annotations. An automated and transferable method for extracting specific entities is already under discussion (cf. Hildenbrandt/Kamzelak 2019; Ehrmann et al. 2021). A practical application has so far remained elusive but is currently developed in the course of the project Dehmel digital (cf. Nantke, Bläß and Flüh forthcoming).

Although the two philological subfields of analysis and exploration of letter networks deal with different questions, epistemological interests, and application scenarios, a research practice oriented towards a close reading of the text represents a common feature of both subfields. A second commonality is the relevance of the category of space as well as the desideratum of a (partially) automated procedure for the systematic recording of spatial phenomena across a larger text corpus. These common desiderata form the basis for the research study described below. In this context, we also discuss chances, limits, and conditions for success for the cross-domain transfer of a model for operationalising (literary) space.

Computational Literary Studies: Conceptual Design and Methods of Modelling Space

While it is not uncommon in Digital Humanities to adapt tools and methods from other fields of study, e.g., from Computational Linguistics or Social Sciences, it is rather rare to adapt tools from one very specific object of research (in this case novels) to another kind of text (in this case letters). In this study we can indeed profit from a tool – namely a classifier for the detection of space (cf. Schumacher 2021a) in narrative texts – which has already been optimised for the domain of narrative fiction, especially the analysis of novels, and develop it further. In this classifier, a conceptual model of space in novels containing six subcategories altogether is implemented (cf. Schumacher 2021a). One of these categories is 'place'. As this category is a common category of linguistic NER and relevant for research on narrative texts as well as on letters, we are able to compare the performance of the two tools. One is the domain adapted classifier for space in narratives, the other a NER-classifier trained for recognition and classification of entities in letters in the course of the project *Dehmel digital*.[2]

Before we turn to a comparative case study of space in narrative texts and letter networks, we will describe the conceptual model developed by Schumacher (2022) in more detail. We will especially focus on the question of which concepts of space were chosen to be of special interest for (Computational) Literary Studies and thus were implemented in the conceptual model. This conceptual model has been operationalised in order to be implemented in a machine learning tool, namely the classifier of narrative space. The output of this machine learning process – an algorithmic model – is able to automatically annotate literary space and classify words into spatial subcategories. As it has been trained on novels the performance of the classifier works best in the domain of narrative fiction, especially the genre of novels. The method used to automate annotations of spatial information in narrative texts and letters is based on Named Entity Recognition. As already mentioned above NER has been developed for linguistic research settings in order to automatically detect and classify entities such as place names, persons or organisations. The attempt to use methods of automatic information extraction for the indexing of literary texts has shown that NER is also suitable for the exploration of contents of literary texts under certain conditions (cf. Jannidis et al. 2015, Schumacher and Flüh 2020). A methodological and thereby also content-related added value arises when the modelling of spatial categories is developed further as part of the supervised learning process. Observing and documenting this process very carefully has proven to have a considerably high impact on research insights.

In principle, NER models can be adapted in a manual training process. It is possible to use the supervised learning procedure for the automation of detecting and classifying not only named entities but also other kinds of spatial information relevant to Literary Studies such as relations. This holds true not only for spatial categories but also for the automated recognition of gender stereotypes in different genres from different temporal contexts (cf. Schumacher und Flüh 2020, Schumacher 2021b). Not only considering two different genres of literature but with novels and letters two completely different kinds of texts, we show that in this case domain

---

2   For further information, see: https://dehmel-digital.de.

adaptation must be taken one step further towards a conceptual rethinking of annotation categories.

Spatial Concepts and a Model of Narrative Space

The Spatial Humanities as a subfield of Digital Humanities have already combined approaches from Geography with Humanities disciplines such as History or the study of Politics (cf. Schumacher 2022). In *Deep Maps and Spatial Narratives* Bodenhammer et al. (2015) showed how insights from narratology can be used to widen the scope of digital cartography. In her attempt to build up an atlas of literature Barbara Piatti (2008) brings together settings of narrative fiction with cartography. However, these approaches mostly include the use of geoinformation systems (GIS), which brings with it a concentration on the concept of place as a mapped entity (which we understand as a linguistic conception of place) and cannot easily be adapted to the literary concept of space we use here. Nevertheless, there have been attempts to further develop the research area of spatial narratology fundamentally brought forward by Katrin Dennerlein (2008). Gabriel Viehhauser and Florian Barth have already successfully implemented tools and methods originating from Natural Language Processing (NLP) to investigate space in narrative fiction (Barth and Viehhauser 2017, Viehhauser 2020, Barth 2022). It is this emerging digital spatial narratology we directly follow up on and which we like to contribute to with this study.

There are numerous approaches to the topic of space in literature, not the least because there is not the one, comprehensive and clearly defined concept of space. The most generic[3], and at the same time operationalisable, narratological model of space to date was presented by Dennerlein (2008). In this, space is defined as a place where literary characters can reside (cf. Dennerlein 2008: 209). In the model used here, this elastic concept of place (even wonder lamps become places from this perspective since it is literary possible to have djinns dwell in them) is countered with a concept of place that leads back to a geographical fixation of all that is referenced by place names and similar terms (cf. Schumacher 2022). In this case, then, a place is something where a character or a person can reside within a narrated world and which is uniquely, i.e., geographically (in relation to the regularities of the narrated or depicted world) situated within this world of reference[4]. In addition to wonder

---

3   By generic we mean widely usable inside the domain of literature, for example, for the analysis of different text genres.

4   This conception of place goes back to the cartesian differentiation between place and space (Descartes 2007) and is also used by Tuan (1977) who, although being a geographer, was widely recognised in Literary Studies.

lamps, moving objects such as vehicles fall outside our notion of place; erected tents that are larger on the inside than on the outside but are located at a geographical point in the storyworld, on the contrary, are places in this sense. However, a concept of place concretised in this way leads to the integration of far fewer aspects of literary space than in a broad concept of place. In order to take into account as many aspects of narrative space as possible in the modelling, the focus was extended from narratology to other fields of research within and outside Literary Studies. Both classical scientific concepts of space, such as absolute and relative space[5], as well as philosophical and cultural studies concepts were taken into account (cf. Schumacher 2022). The approach developed by Schumacher (2022) and followed by this study, is fundamentally pragmatic. All studies considered were questioned on whether or not they contained aspects that could be operationalised and used for computational analysis. At the same time, the focus lies on the study of texts. All aspects of production and reception of literature are therefore excluded (cf. Schumacher 2022). The same holds true for the scope of this paper. We concentrate on aspects that can be found on the linguistic surface and thus serve as an entry point into the interpretation of texts. This means that approaches dealing with narrative space as a creation of text as well as readers, such as the study of mental maps (cf. Ryan 2016, 75–101), are not taken into account.

As already stated above, at the centre of the conceptual model implemented in the classifier of space in narratives is the fundamental distinction between place and space, as it is quite common but by no means uniformly defined. Here, place is only one category of analysis among others that contributes to the literary representation of space. Space is a multidimensional entity and also a relatively diffuse concept since it is not conclusively clear how many dimensions belong to it. In some theories, for example, such as Einstein's spacetime (cf. Einstein 2006 and 2009) and Bakhtin's chronotopos (cf. Bakhtin 2008) time is considered the fourth dimension of space. In any case, not only mathematical-physical dimensions but also (cultural) levels of meaning play a role, such as aesthetics or social uses (cf. Schumacher 2022). Taking all these aspects of space into account, literary space has been modelled as a category system consisting of a total of six subcategories, which, depending on the concept of space and the research question, can also be split up and applied in smaller units (in this sense being a fuzzy set model), e.g., if a narrower concept of space is of importance for a consideration. The six categories of narrative space are: places, relations, relational verbs, descriptions of space, hints on spatial information and topoi (being thematic spatial units).

---

5   Most well known representatives surely have been Newton (absolute space) and Leibniz (relative space) – the correspondence between Clarke as representative of Newton (cf. Clarke [1]–[5] and Leibniz (cf. Leibniz 1714 and 1717 [1]–[5]) sheds light on the opposing positions. Later on Einstein (2009) also promoted the concept of space as relative quantity.

In addition to these subcategories of the theoretical concept of space, there are different levels of literary space that can be differentiated for every text. Three levels of literary space were given special consideration and were included in the modelling: space as a system of meaning, space as a literary theme, and space as a structural phenomenon of texts (cf. Schumacher 2022). The core of the considerations of literary space as a system of meaning is that many representations of place and space in narrative texts imply further meanings. This has often been referred to in Literary Studies as the metaphorical notion of space (cf. e.g., Ryan et al. 2017, 17, Ryan 2009, 420, Dennerlein 2008, 14), although spaces and places mentioned do often still play a role here along with the additional meanings.

Particularly prominent in this line of tradition is Lotman's approach, which is dualistic in nature and, for example, combines high situated places with positivity and low situated places with negativity (cf. Lotman 1973)[6]. However, if a character in a text stands on a mountain, he may have a positively occupied mental experience there, but he still stands (within the narrative world) on a mountain that has certain geographical features and is topologically fixed. That is why this kind of understanding of space also can be called semiotic or cultural space.

A completely different approach emerges when one considers spatial themes. Here, from the outset, it is not actually the entire space of a narrative text that is important, but only representations of space that work as literary motifs. Spatial themes are relatively clear-cut, often have a (literary) historical or genre-specific anchoring and at the same time a cultural level of meaning. On the one hand, spatial themes are related to semiotic assignments of meaning, but on the other hand, they can also influence narrative units and structures such as events or the plot. A typical spatial theme is the border motif, whose importance is already emphasised by Lotman (1973). Using the example of Odysseus' fight against his wife's suitors, Ryan et al. (2016) describe how borders and their openings contribute decisively to character direction and thus enable or prevent action (cf. Ryan et al. 2016). Other spatial themes include Foucault's heterotopias (cf. Foucault 2005) and Bakhtin's chronotopoi (cf. Bakhtin 2008).

Yet another approach is devoted to space as a structural phenomenon of texts. Here, classical narratological categories become particularly important, such as the distinction between story and discourse (cf. Chatman 1978), because here, on the one hand, the representation of space is analysed and, on the other hand, the functions that space can have in narrative texts, e.g., introducing readers to a setting, constituting an event together with (at least two) characters and action (cf. Dunn and Schumacher 2016), and the like.

---

6   So does Bachelard in his rather psychoanalytical reading of space in literature, combining the cellar and everything underneath the earth with fear and darkness and attics and everything high up with being clear and enlightened (cf. Bachelard 2001).

Left unconsidered in this conceptual model of narrative space are narratological approaches to the topic of space that have a reception-aesthetic focus and consider space as a phenomenon that emerges between text and reader. This includes considerations of the Possible Worlds Theory (cf. Ryan 2012), in which all non-manifest spaces are always considered along with the mention of spatial information manifest in the text. For the same reasons we also do not consider approaches to literary spaces based on mental maps (cf. Ryan et al. 2016, 75–101). Questions about the ontological status of spaces in fictional worlds in contrast to real-world space can therefore not be considered with the methodology applied and described here.

Figure 1: Six categories for the indication of narrative space developed in Schumacher (2022)

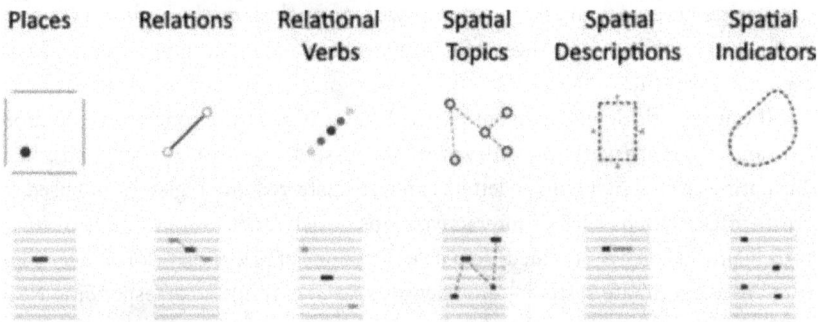

| Places | Relations | Relational Verbs | Spatial Topics | Spatial Descriptions | Spatial Indicators |

The resulting model is a fuzzy set of six spatial categories as seen in fig. 1 that differ in terms of explicitness with which they are indicated in narrative texts (cf. Schumacher 2022). More explicit categories belong to a narrower understanding of literary space whereas more implicit categories are of relevance for a wider understanding of space. As stated in Schumacher (2022), the model can be modified by using from one to all categories according to research interest and focus. In this study, we test transferability on one of the six concepts. As it is of core relevance for narrative texts as well as for letters we especially concentrate on the category of place here and only take into account the other categories to imply a possible future use for the digital scholarly analysis of letters.

In this case study, we draw on the text type letter comparatively, because here an automatic detection of spatial phenomena finds a very concrete application in the creation of registers and visualisations, which is a major task for projects with both, a DH-angle and a focus on the analysis of cultural artefacts such as historical letters. We assume that NER can be applied gainfully to automatic text analysis in both of the disciplines addressed here: while it continues the traditional literary examination of spatial phenomena and adds a digital, new variant to it, NER finds a very concrete and new application in the examination of digital letter networks.

As already mentioned, the established methods of exploration used when editing e.g. letters in order to produce scholarly editions include accurate manual annotation within the framework of a very time-consuming workflow. Referring to the ongoing research project *Dehmel digital*, we propose NER as part of a workflow that makes it possible to access and handle large manuscript corpora within the context of limited resources (funding, time, trained employees) that most scholarly edition projects face. Focussing on letters as a domain of interest for scholars of literature we find ourselves in between two research traditions. On the one side letters are – as stated above – not a narrative genre, but a non-fictional text type. The linguistic concept of place as location as implemented in traditional NER tools thus seems to be appropriate for the study of letters. On the other side, the letters focussed in this study are all written by authors and artists who often use narrative elements in their handwritten everyday communication as well. An analysis on the basis of a Literary Studies concept of place or even of narrative space altogether might be equally or even more fruitful.

The automatic detection of entities such as locations has a concrete application here and is part of a workflow with various processing steps that build on each other. The entities found in historical letters can be transferred into registers and used to create visualisations such as interactive maps or networks. From this perspective, place names – i.e., well defined, actual designations of places that can be clearly located in a coordinate system – are relevant spatial entities. A corresponding NER model for the computational annotation of place names, artworks, organisations, and persons that can be implemented in a pipeline for indexing large corpora of letters from around 1900 is being developed in the *Dehmel digital* project (cf. Bläß, Flüh, Nantke and Maus 2022). The project focuses on the digital indexing of the correspondence of Richard and Ida Dehmel. The couple corresponded with numerous relevant persons from the literary and cultural scene in Europe around 1900 and left behind a comprehensive correspondence network consisting of approximately 35,000 letters. In order to gain an overview of the extensive text corpus and to be able to (partially) automate its exploration, digital methods (including NER) of text analysis are used. In the turn of this comparatistic case study, we will test how this model performs for the automated detection of places in literary texts. Because of the shared historical context, we assume that general linguistic and stylistic similarities in terms of places in both text types are large enough to withstand domain adaptation. Besides this, we investigate to what extent the training data generated for the spatial model can be used for a post-training of the model developed specifically for the automatic annotation of letters, and vice versa. Thus, in addition to the conditions of success for domain adaptation, we also ask about those of transfer learning.

Method

For the automated recognition of named entities in German-language texts, free tools such as the German-language model (cf. Faruqui und Padó 2010) of the Stanford Named Entity Recognizer (cf. Finkel et al. 2005) or the NER feature of WebLicht[7] are available. Since these models lack relevant categories and the German language model trained on the basis of newspaper texts only achieves moderate results in entity recognition in literary texts (cf. Jannidis et al. 2015) or texts in general whose language usage is very different from that on which the training data is based on, it is obvious to train a model of one's own that does justice to the specifics of the selected texts or to adapt existing models to the respective text genre in the sense of a domain adaptation.

In adapting NER in the context of this chapter, we resort to the open-source software Stanford Named Entity Recognizer (StanfordNER) (cf. Finkel et al. 2005). The StanfordNER-Toolkit is frequently used to train or reuse genre-specific classifiers to annotate historical documents such as letters (cf. Ehrmann et al. 2021) and can be considered as a well-established tool for NER tasks. The software uses Conditional Random Field (CRF) algorithms (cf. Sutton and McCullum 2011), which enable context-sensitive entity recognition. This is an important prerequisite for our application scenario since we assume that spatial categories occur in more diverse, creative manifestations and contexts than is likely to be the case for non-fiction texts, for example. By using StanfordNER to train a classifier to detect spatial categories relevant to literary genres we stress the method so far that it cannot be called Named Entity Recognition in a narrow sense anymore. Even concentrating on the relatively explicit and concrete category of place, the classifier annotates much more than named entities. What turned out to be a huge advantage for the study of narrative texts might be disadvantageous for the genre of letters. To address this area of tension we developed the comparative research setting described in the following.

Training Data and Test Data

As annotated training data, text passages from 80 German-language novels from the 18th–21st centuries (320.000 tokens) were implemented in the classifier of narrative space (cf. Schumacher 2021a). The test corpus was not built by leaving out parts of the training corpus (as is a common technique in the evaluation of NER tools) but by choosing another eight novels from the 18th–21st century. For domain adaptation to letters, we added manually annotated text passages from the above-mentioned correspondence that are not in the test corpus (about 50.000 tokens). The NER model

---

7   For more information, see: https://weblicht.sfs.uni-tuebingen.de/weblichtwiki/index.php/
     Main_Page.

for historical letters contains four categories for the automatic annotation of places, artworks, persons and organisations. Representatives of these categories were annotated in a training corpus of about 400.000 tokens. A comparatively small part of the material base consists of letters from around 1900 that were digitised as part of the project *Dehmel digital*. In addition, the holdings of other digital scholarly letter editions were included. In total, the training corpus contains letters from the 18th, 19th and 20th centuries. In order to be able to evaluate the performance, text parts consisting of 3.000 to 5.000 tokens were excluded from the model training in each case. For domain adaptation to novels, we added manually annotated passages – 50.000 tokens in total – from the corpus of novels that are not in the test corpus.

The two classifiers used here were trained separately, one to detect narrative space and one for the analysis of letter correspondence networks, and have been tested on two kinds of test corpora. One contains excerpts from eight novels from the 18th to the 21st century (Core Corpus I thus containing two novels per century). The excerpts include 10.000 tokens taken from the beginnings of the novels. The other is made of six passages of letter correspondences (Core Corpus II) – Richard Dehmel's digitised correspondence with Stefan Zweig, Alfred Mombert and Peter Behrens, Ida Dehmel's correspondence with Emmi Marianne Gärtner and mixed correspondences of intellectuals from Berlin during the 18th and 19th century taken from the project *Letters and Texts: Intellectual Berlin around 1800*.[8] Each passage includes 3.000 tokens. Core Corpus I is used to test the performance of the classifier for place names trained on letters. Core Corpus II is used to test the classifier for space trained on novels. Core Corpora I and II are identical with the test corpus but are not included in the training corpora. For domain adaptation, according to our research object, the additional training data consists of parts of the novels not included in the test texts and parts of the correspondences the test texts were taken from (also not overlapping with the training data).

The test texts have been annotated manually and these annotations have been compared to the automatic annotation done by the adapted versions of the StanfordNER Classifier. The results have been documented per test text and the average has been calculated. This procedure nearly corresponds to the 'leave one out'-tests commonly done in Computational Linguistics[9] with the difference that we did not take out a percentage of the training data but chose additional data unknown by the classifier. In the following, we show the results generated with the conceptual model of literary space on novels and letters and compare them to those achieved by a conceptual model of place developed for the analysis of letters.

---

8   https://www.berliner-intellektuelle.eu/ (Access: 15.03.202).

9   Equally common is a cross validation procedure which usually tends to bring up slightly better results as the testcorpus is parted into equally large samples which are in turn taken as test data. In the end, a mean of those test results is calculated.

Case Studies and Findings

Automated Detection of Narrative Space in Novels

The novels taken as test texts were chosen randomly with the exception that we chose to pick one text by a male and one by a female author per century in order to strengthen the representation of women in the study of literature. The test texts as well as a text-specific overall F1-Score[10] can be looked up below in table 1.

Table 1: Performance of the Classifier for the detection of space in novels (trained on novels)

Century	Author	Title	Overall F1-Score	F1-Score of the category 'place'
18th	Therese Huber	Luise	66,4%	74,81%
18th	Friedrich Schiller	Der Geisterseher	79,44%	84,55%
19th	Lou Andreas-Salomé	Ruth	81,66%	88,73%
19th	Friedrich Spielhagen	Zum Zeitvertreib	76,18%	77,39%
20th	Franziska von Revent-low	Der Selbstmord-verein	76,24%	81,52%
20th	Kurt Tucholsky	Schloss Grips-holm	75,42%	78,57%
21st	Husch Josten	Das Glück von Frau Pfeiffer	76,94%	81,71%
21st	Saša Stanišić	Vor dem Fest	72,89%	73,18%
Average			75,65%	80,06

The average F1-Score of the classifier with all six spatial categories is 75,65%, the category of 'place' scores with 80,06%. As can be seen from the table and the average values, the accuracy of detection and classification of 'place' is always slightly higher than the overall values of the classifier with six spatial categories. This shows that 'place' is one of the most concrete and explicit categories of narrative space[11] (as shown in the description of the conceptual model above).

---

10   This weighted average combines precision as a calculation of how many of the automatic annotations are correct and recall as calculation of how many of the instances in the text falling into one of the categories of the classifier were annotated. The F1-score gives a good hint on the accuracy of the classifier.

11   'Relation' as an equally concrete and explicit spatial category shows similar results. Less explicit categories decrease in accuracy (cf. Schumacher 2022).

Automated Detection of Narrative Space in Historical Letters

Of course these results were reached on in-domain data. For our comparative case study, we needed to look at more data and also at categorical differences in the representation of space in letters. First, we tested the classifier based on the concept of literary space without adapting the training data to letters. We found that the overall F1-Score decreased by about 10% on average and the F1-Score for the detection of places went down about 4%. While the category of 'place' turned out to be more robust across domains than others, it is still striking that the variance of F1-Score for the specific samples of test data is very high. The difference between the novel with the lowest and the highest accuracy of place detection is 15%, the difference between the letter samples amounts to 30% (see tables 1 and 2).

Table 2: Performance of the Classifier (trained on novels) for the detection of space in historical letters

Century	Author	Receiver	Overall F1-Score	F1-Score of the category "place"
20th	Ida Dehmel	Marianne Gärtner	71,56%	80%
20th	Marianne Gärtner	Ida Dehmel	70,12%	82,17%
20th	Alfred Mombert	Richard Dehmel	61,36%	56,14%
20th	Berlin intellectuals	Berlin intellectuals	78,05%	60,22%
20th	Peter Behrens	Richard Dehmel	66,81%	86,24%
20th	Stefan Zweig	Richard Dehmel	74,34%	64,08%
Average			65,69%	76,15%

To optimise and stabilise the recognition of space and place in letters, we added about 50.000 manually annotated tokens taken from correspondences to the training corpus.

Table 3: Performance of the extended Classifier (trained on novels and letters) for the detection of space in historical letters

Century	Author	Receiver	Overall F1-Score	F1-Score of the category 'place'
20th	Ida Dehmel	Marianne Gärtner	74,66%	84,21%
20th	Marianne Gärtner	Ida Dehmel	75,57%	87,59%
20th	Alfred Mombert	Richard Dehmel	63,21%	68,85%
20th	Berlin intellectuals	Berlin intellectuals	60,54%	77,5%
20th	Peter Behrens	Richard Dehmel	70,17%	86,73%
20th	Stefan Zweig	Richard Dehmel	66,35%	78,63%
Average			68,42%	80,59%

As can be seen in table 3, the domain adaptation of the training corpus leads to a similarly high average in the detection of places as is reached in the domain of origin. In addition to that the variance sinks to a difference of 18,74% between the sample with the best and the one with the least F1-Score. Although we also reach better results on the other categories as before the overall F1-Score is way behind the 75% reached on novels. This can be interpreted as a hint for a conceptual similarity of 'place' in novels and letters while other expressions of space differ in the two text types.

Analysing Narrative Space in Letters

As we have seen from the test results above, it is quite easy to adapt a conceptual model implemented in a classifier to out-of-domain data. A relatively small sample of 50.000 tokens added to the training data can suffice to reach the same level of recognition and classification of the category of space as achieved with in-domain data and can improve the overall F1-score. By comparing the two series of tests one can also see that the representation of place in novels and letters differ significantly. What do we gain (and what do we lose) by using a comparatively complex conceptual model of literary space containing six categories altogether on letters? To answer this question, we will look deeper into the test data and analyse the automatically added annotations.

The annotations of the category 'place' included in the classifier of narrative space show how often places are explicitly named in letters. This includes all entities that can be unambiguously located in the coordinate system and that are suitable for transmission in registers. The first thing one notices when looking at the annotations of 'place' done by the classifier is that the two words which were annotated most often are 'hier' and 'dort', meaning 'here' and 'there'. Those two are closely followed by place names like 'Berlin', 'Heidelberg' or 'Bingen' (cf. table 4). Looking a bit closer at the annotations of this category one can roughly define three subcategories of the entities as shown in table 4. Most annotations of 'place' fall into the subcategory of 'concrete naming' (133 annotations) followed by 'abstract descriptions' (122 annotations). With 65 annotations 'adverbial references' are the least often but therefore the single words in this category show very high scores (as seen in table 4). The three categories seen in the table differ in terms of concreteness and abstractness (from the left column to the right column). As we do not use lemmatisation after applying the NER model the terms 'hier' and 'Hier' are not merged.

Table 4: Ad-hoc subcategories of 'place' annotations and the ten most frequently annotated words

concrete naming	abstract description	adverbial reference
Berlin (17)	Straße (6)	hier (28)
Deutschland (13)	Welt (6)	dort (18)
Hamburg (8)	Hause (5)	da (14)
Heidelberg (7)	Boden (4)	Hier (5)
Wien (7)	Haus (4)	
München (6)	Erde (3)	
Bingen (5)	Stadt (3)	
Blankenese (5)	Wohnung (3)	
Darmstadt (5)	Zimmer (3)	
Düsseldorf (4)	Adresse (2)	

Whereas concrete namings obviously are of interest for working with scholarly editions of letters and can easily be linked to standardised databases, used to create registers or create visualisations with geovis-tools, it is less common to take into account words like 'here' and 'there', which are shifters (a reflection on shifters from a narratological perspective can be found in Fludernik 2009). In this context, they can reference an opposite location depending on being used by one writer of a correspondence or the other. They can be seen as representatives for the epistemological interconnectivity, which highlight the network character of epistemological communications via letters. Additionally, adverbial references in letters and post-cards are used in reports on everyday life, travel plans or reading journeys (from 'here' to 'there) and refer to a movement in space that has actually taken place. When analysing correspondences from a Literary Studies point of view those small words can be of great interest. They show how often writers refer to their own positions (which could also manually be traced to a concrete place name) and how often they write about other unnamed places. The fact that 'here' is annotated more often in our test texts shows that these correspondences are conversations directed from the local point of view of the writer who frequently talks about what is going on in her or his close geospatial surroundings. Another subcategory of place that is covered by the classifier of narrative space, while it isn't covered by NER-Tools, is one that could be named 'abstract description' of places[12]. Those abstract descriptions can describe inner spaces as well as landscapes or single aspects of landscapes. The words 'room', 'flat' and 'house' are such generic terms. 'river' or 'seaside' are others. If a person in a letter or a character in a story is situated in a house or at the seaside it can be possible to locate them geographically in their world (be it a story world or the real world). For analysis, this means that if one's task is to describe places of location of characters or letter writing persons and show them on a map these generic terms can be a valuable piece of information. But entities in this second subcategory (generic descriptions such as 'fatherland', or 'nation') can also represent semantically charged spatial references that are suitable as gateways into text analysis but are not precise enough for register creation. In this respect, they can only be used in combination with a concretisation, i.e., the addition of supplementary information. This means that the results of the automatic annotation process help us to differentiate the 'spatial terminology' of our corpora with regard to different scholarly use cases in Literary Studies.

Moreover, the narrative space classifier not only annotates more kinds of terms as 'places' than NER-tools. It also features more spatial categories. On the technical side, the implementation of six spatial categories helps to improve the detection and classification of places. But is there also an added value of annotating more than just one spatial category for the literary study of letters? First of all, for the sample of about 18.000 tokens taken from six correspondences, one can state that relations and relational verbs (which are motion verbs as well as verbs describing sensory perception [cf. Schumacher 2022]) are the most frequently annotated spatial categories.

---

12   This term is related to Dennerleins (2009) category for 'generic names'.

Both categories tell a lot about motion. Questions like who has moved towards or from a place can be answered by looking at these annotations.

When comparing the finding that these relational categories are the most frequently annotated in the test sample with the findings of Schumacher (2022), one can state that independent of the kind of text – be it a novel or a letter – these categories are the most common for the representation of space. But the frequency of annotations of 'places' in novels and letters differ significantly. Whereas in novels 'places' are less frequently annotated than 'spatial hints' (cf. Schumacher 2022), in letters it is the other way around. Put in other words, in letters 'places' are more frequently named than objects or other bodies or body parts that serve as 'spatial hints'. It should be taken into account that the core corpus consists primarily of the texts of letters. Address fields, in which a frequent occurrence of places would not be surprising, are no elementary component and were therefore left out. The NER analysis provides empirical quantitative data which support the well-known assumption that places can be considered as a recurring theme in letters. Furthermore, it shows that a classifier based on a narrative concept of space can provide us with quantitative evidence on aspects of genre-specific use of spatial references when used in a comparative study like this one.

In order to compare the samples of our test texts, we pasted them all together forming a single text sample of about 18.000 tokens. As shown in the visualisation in figure 2, which is done with the annotation and analysis tool CATMA (cf. Gius et al. 2021), the different spatial categories are of different importance for the writers we are looking at.

Figure 2: Distribution of words annotated according to the six spatial categories of the space classifier in all six test samples

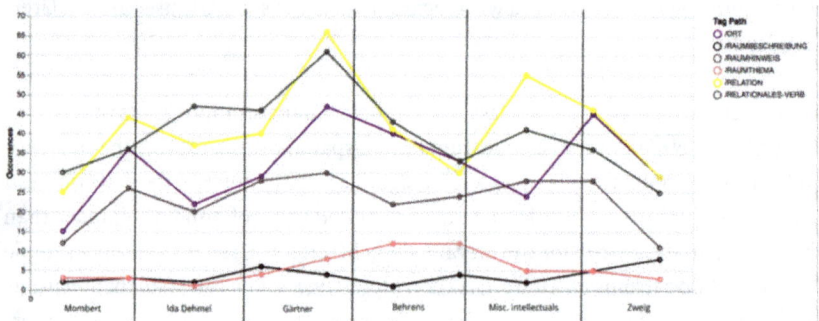

Without going into too much detail, we would like to highlight some phenomena, which show the benefits of taking more than one spatial category into account when analysing letters. The first thing which struck here is that Ida Dehmel most fre-

quently uses relational verbs in her correspondence with her niece Marianne Gärtner. The sample shows that motion spaces (in the sense of de Certeau 1988) are of
special relevance to Ida Dehmel's writing. This sample originates from a time span
when Emmi Marianne Gärtner was still very young. Ida writes to her about her life
with Richard Dehmel and above all, she organises holiday venues with her niece with
whom she shares a very loving personal relationship. Ida often asks Marianne to
visit her or writes about how nice the last visit of Marianne has been to her and her
husband. The second correspondance of Ida Dehmel and Marianne Gärtner stems
from a different period in time. Marianne Gärtner is a young woman now and Ida
Dehmel is often travelling with her husband to accompany him to invited talks or
similar events. This movement from one place to the other shows in the visualisation in figure 2 in which curves representing relations, relational verbs and places
are exceptionally high. In addition to that, the curve showing the number of mentions of words referencing 'spatial topics' rises up in this correspondence. This is
caused by the fact that Ida Dehmel frequently writes about the topos of travelling.
A similar topic causes the high frequency of mentions of 'spatial topics' in the next
sample, which shows the correspondence of Peter Behrens to Richard Dehmel. The
designer, architect and artisan frequently writes about exhibitions he is planning or
which have taken place and he also writes about his journeys. So, for his letters, the
heterotopic space (cf. Foucault 2005) of his exhibitions as well as the literary motif
of travelling become especially relevant.

Coming back to the question of what one can gain by using a classifier of narrative space when focussing on the domain of letters, we want to conclude with three
important interim findings.

First, we find that, whereas the linguistic notion of place includes mostly place
names, our (narrative) understanding of 'place' enhances this understanding e.g.,
with adverbial expressions (like 'here' and 'there'). In addition to adverbial expressions and concrete place names, generic place names like 'the seaside' are taken into
account. For scholarly editions, this means that these hints on sites at which the
writers might have been or were planning to go to could be included in disambigua-
tion and thereby also be linked with databases or be visualised with geospatial visualisation tools.

Second, we state that these generic place names and adverbial expressions can
be used for analysing the content and to enrich digital scholarly editions because
the use of words classified as belonging to a spatial category can be closely linked to
subjects of a conversation or show specific historically relevant chronotopoi like the
First World War.

Third and finally we would like to highlight that this shows that space is a complex multi-faceted concept in narrative texts and letters alike, while it is also possible
to spot differences in the composition of the 'spatial terminology' and with regard
to different use cases (analysis vs. edition). On the technical side, this behaviour is

also shown by the fact that the recognition and classification of spatial terms in non-fictional and fictional texts become better when using more than one category. However, this gain can also be considered as a loss of focus. In total 1.453 words have been annotated using the space classifier. Of those 1.453 tokens 320 have been classified as places and only a total of 133 words are place names that could be recognised as named entities. When the task is to search for these 133 mentions of place names ending up with more than 1.000 annotations is not a good solution according to the task.

Automated Detection of Places in Novels

Depending on the century in which the test texts were written, the NER classifier for the detection of place names, that was trained on letters, performs differently. Tested on the different texts listed in table 5, the average F-score is 87,31%. This performance has to be considered carefully, the high hit rate in the text of the 20th century is caused by the very low rate of place names in the set of test data in general.

Table 5: Performance of the classifier for the detection of places in historical letters

Century	Correspondence	F-Score for places
19th century	Daniel Sanders	92,04%
19th and 20th century (1888–1931)	Arthur Schnitzler	89,23%
20th century	Ida Dehmel and Simon Z. Coblenz	100%
20th century	Alfred Mombert/ Richard and Ida Dehmel	68,00%

In order to test how well or poorly the model trained on letters recognises locations in narrative texts, 10.000 tokens from narrative texts from the period between the 18th and the 21st century were manually annotated. These ground truth data were compared to those automatically annotated by the model trained on letters.

Table 6: Test of the model trained on letters for the detection of places in narrative texts

Century	Author	Title	Overall F1-Score (person, place, artwork, organisation)	F1-Score of the category "place"
18th	Therese Huber	Luise	70,27%	0,00%
18th	Friedrich Schiller	Der Geisterseher	51,85%	72%
19th	Lou Andreas-Salomé	Ruth	60,08%	85,71%
19th	Friedrich Spielhagen	Zum Zeitvertreib	39,14%	41,18%
20th	Franziska von Reventlow	Der Selbstmordverein	70,84%	0,00%
20th	Kurt Tucholsky	Schloss Gripsholm	55,25%	65,65%
21st	Husch Josten	Das Glück von Frau Pfeiffer	48,05%	50%
21st	Saša Stanišić	Vor dem Fest	66,07%	60,32%
Average			57,69%	46,85%

In this context, the right column is of particular interest, as the one left next to it also includes the recognition rate for the three other entity types. The F1-score varies greatly depending on the temporal context. The model achieves maximum values of 72 and 85% in the 18th and 19th centuries. The comparatively high hit rate can be explained by the fact that a large part of the training data comes from the 19th century. A look at the test data from the 20th century shows that in the excerpt from Reventlow's novel, a concrete place ('Pomerania') is mentioned only once in total. Similarly, in Huber's *Louise*, places are not named but abbreviated ('B,' 'S,' or '**', a phenomenon which is quite common for literary texts from this period and is therefore covered by the space classifier developed for this domain).

What do we learn from this from a technical perspective? Overall, the performance turns out to be rather poor which confirms the thesis that classifiers need to be trained domain-specifically to achieve good results. Fictional and non-fictional texts require a specific, genre-typical set of training data. Furthermore, it shows where further training data is needed to develop a generic model, which can be used diachronically and on different kinds of texts of interest for Computational Literary Studies. What does this tell us about spatial concepts in letters and narrative texts? Letters operate with a much more concrete concept of space than narrative texts. In order to be able to make agreements about personal meetings or joint projects, places must of course be named concretely. Otherwise, no communication can take place. This pragmatic characteristic is missing in narrative texts. This can also be seen in the low F-scores and confirms the thesis that transference of one NER model to a new domain is not fruitful without any kind of adaptation to its stylistic characteristics, no matter if both text types are from a similar time period or not. To validate our assumption that a significant improvement of the detection rate can be achieved by adding 50.000 domain-specific tokens to the set of training data and in order to be able to evaluate how the NER model made for letters reacts to an extension of its training data by novels we trained and tested a new model. This NER model consists of the training data from the *Dehmel digital* project and 50.000 additional tokens from the beginning of the novels listed below, manually tagged for place names.

In order to validate our finding that adding a comparatively small amount of training data (50.000 tokens) to the existing basis of training data suffices to improve the accuracy of automatic detection significantly, we tested the NER-model trained on 400.000 tokens taken from letters (19th and 20th century) and 50.000 tokens taken from novels (18th–21st century) on the Core Corpus II. Although the performance of the detection of 'place' is not as good as the one the classifier of narrative places shows on novels, table 6 shows that we were able to improve accuracy by about 9.54%.

The overall F1-score even improves by 16,47%. The slightly different research design of this machine learning training is also shown when comparing tables 3 and 6. As the training data of the NER-classifier focuses on data from the 20th century, accuracy is much higher for narrative texts from this timespan. The classifier for narrative space was pretrained on data of the 18th–21st century and thus does not show these differences on data from different time spans. In any case, it is important to keep in mind how the basic training data is assembled and which kind of additional training data is best to adapt a model to one's specific object of interest.

Table 7: Test of the extended model trained on letters for the detection of places in narrative texts

Century	Author	Title	Overall F1-Score (places, persons, artworks, organisations)	F1-Score of the category "place"
18th	Therese Huber	Luise	88,61%	0,00%
18th	Friedrich Schiller	Der Geisterseher	57,89%	76,92%
19th	Lou Andreas-Salomé	Ruth	75,56%	90,09%
19th	Friedrich Spielhagen	Zum Zeitvertreib	67,43%	18,18%
20th	Franziska von Reventlow	Der Selbstmordverein	95,96%	100,00%
20th	Kurt Tucholsky	Schloss Gripsholm	64,29%	74,63%
21st	Husch Josten	Das Glück von Frau Pfeiffer	78,13%	46,15%
21st	Saša Stanišić	Vor dem Fest	65,73%	45,16%
Average			74,16%	56,39%

Conclusion

Coming from Literary Studies and especially the emerging digital spatial narratology we brought together a conceptual model of space deeply rooted in non-Digital Humanities research traditions and the method of Named Entity Recognition coming from Computational Linguistics. We showed that it can be fruitful to implement such operationalisations of theoretical approaches into machine learning tools. However, the space classifier which was trained on a corpus being very homogenous in terms of genres included but quite broad when it comes to the historical time span texts originate from, could not be used on the genre of letters without further adaptation. Nevertheless, our study could show that letters, that are of special interest for Literary Studies as a chimeric genre, can be analysed using either a narrative concept of space or a linguistic notion of place. Taking into account that the study of literature is bound to the analysis of fictional texts, which brings with it that concepts used for interpretation may differ significantly from those used in other disciplines like Linguistics, our study identifies some crucial aspects of domain adaptation as they appear in Computational Literary Studies:

(1) Concepts as e.g., a linguistic or a narrative notion of space clearly show in the output of a computational analysis.
(2) Both research areas we compared in this study – computational literary studies and scholarly editions – can profit from a conceptual change in point of view. A linguistic notion of space can be applied to literary texts as well as a narrative understanding of place can be used to analyse and enrich a digital scholarly edition of letters.
(3) Applying just any classifiers available can lead to a mess of data and moreover to a loss of focus. Nevertheless, it can be fruitful to use and combine different approaches to the respective research subject, especially when dealing with multifaceted concepts like space.

However, the central task we deal with in this paper – domain adaptation not only with specific training data but also through the implementation of different conceptual foundations, one of them closely referring to non-Digital Humanities scholarship – might be transferred to other research settings. To the Spatial Humanities, we add a non-GIS-based approach dealing with different conceptual understandings of space as an interpretive category and show how they can fruitfully be used through implementation in machine learning tools according to very specific research domains.

The various experiments in this article hint at commonalities and at the same time highlight differences between the conceptualisation of space in the two text types novels and letters. Especially the comparison of the results of the different classifiers using domain-specific training data or not shows how domain adaptation can significantly improve the automatic detection of textual elements that belong to the category of place. We showed that both the analysis of letters on the basis of a concept of narrative space as well as a rather linguistic conception of places can be made fruitful depending on the respective research goal. Critical success factors of domain adaptation are the optimisation of a classifier for a specific genre or text as well as a conceptual background that suits one's specific research interest. When a generic classifier is found that conceptually meets the research focus it can suffice to add a comparatively small amount of training data to adapt a machine learning model. This is already illustrated by our tests with the CRF algorithms and it should be even more valid for transformer models like BERT. However, an extensive test series as done in this comparison can reveal the special focus of a classifier. Therefore, it is advisable to do such tests before using a machine learning classifier for analysis in Computational Literary Studies.

On the content side, we emphasise the importance of theoretical and conceptual modelling during the process of machine learning, which is very domain-specific. Using a conceptual model containing a complex category system can reveal interesting aspects about how space is referenced in letters and which spatial features are of special relevance to certain writers and/or historical eras. However, when focussing on a very specific aspect of space like place names such a classifier will certainly produce too much data. Comparing the performance and outcome of a classifier for narrative space with a NER system, we show that the linguistic concept of place implemented in standard NER classifiers differs considerably from the literary concept of space. While it is quite easy to adapt classifiers trained on different material for the detection of places in a new text type, this doesn't hold true for more abstract categories of references to space. A more complex literary concept of space cannot be transferred to the analysis of letters without both an algorithmic and a theoretical conceptual adaptation, which means that it is not sufficient to add domain-specific training data but that it is also necessary to work on the ontology used. We thus conclude that spatial modelling in Computational Literary Studies always needs to include a theoretically based conceptual foundation and an open technical and data-driven training process with extensive test series. Both should be fitting the individual research focus in the field of application.

References

Bachelard, G. (2001). *Poetik des Raumes* (Ungekürzte Ausg., 6th Ed.). Fischer Taschenbuchverlag.

Bachmann-Medick, D. (2007). "Spatial Turn". In: Doris Bachmann-Medick: *Cultural Turns. Neuorientierungen in den Kulturwissenschaften*. Rowohlt. Reinbek bei Hamburg: p. 284–328.

Bachtin, M. (2008). *Chronotopos* (1st Ed.). Suhrkamp. Frankfurt am Main.

Barth, F. (2022). Von der literaturwissenschaftlichen Theorie zur maschinellen Erkennung: Operationalisierung von Raumentitäten und Settings. In Horstmann, J. & Fischer, F. (Eds.), *Digitale Verfahren in der Literaturwissenschaft*. Textpraxis.

Barth, F. & Viehauser, G. (2017). Digitale Modellierung literarischen Raums. Konferenzabstracts DHd2017 Bern. Digitale Nachhaltigkeit. http://www.dhd2017.ch/wp-content/uploads/2017/03/Abstractband_def3_%20März.pdf%20 [Accessed 24.2.2020].

Benz, M. & Dennerlein, K. (2016). Zur Einführung. In: dies. (Hrsg.): Literarische Räume der Herkunft. Fallstudien zu einer historischen Narratologie. Narratologie Band 51 (p.1–19). De Gruyter. Berlin/Boston.

Bläß, S., Flüh, M. & Nantke, J. (2022). Literatur als Praxis: Neue Perspektiven auf Brief-Korrespondenzen durch digitale Verfahren. In Horstmann, J. & Fischer, F. (Eds.), Digitale Verfahren in der Literaturwissenschaft. Textpraxis.

Bodenhamer, D. J., Corrigan, J., & Harris, T. M. (2015). Deep Maps and Spatial Narratives. Indiana University Press. Bloomington.

Certeau, M. de (1988). Praktiken im Raum. In: (Ed.) Kunst des Handelns. Aus dem Franz. v. Roland Voullié. Merve. Berlin.

Chatman, S. B. (1978). Story and discourse. Cornell Univ. Press. Ithaca. http://gso.g bv.de/DB=2.1/PPNSET?PPN=011286377 [Accessed 6.11.2019].

Clarke, S. [1]. "Dr. Clarke's First Reply". In: Ders.: A Collection of Papers, Which passed between the late Learned Mr. Leibnitz, and Dr. Clarke, In the Years 1715 and 1717. London. https://web.archive.org/web/20120528124834/http://w ww.newtonproject.sussex.ac.uk/view/t exts/normalized/THEM00227 [Stand 6.11.2019].

Clarke, S. [2]. "Dr. Clarke's Second Reply". In: Clarke, S.: A Collection of Papers, Which passed between the late Learned Mr. Leibnitz, and Dr. Clarke, In the Years 1715 and 1717. London. https://web.archive.org/web/20120528124517 /http://www.newtonproject.sussex.ac.uk/view/t exts/normalized/THEM00229 [Stand 6.11.2019].

Clarke, S. [3]. "Dr. Clarke's Third Reply". In: Clarke, S.: A Collection of Papers, Which passed between the late Learned Mr. Leibnitz, and Dr. Clarke, In the Years 1715 and 1717. London. https://web.archive.org/web/20120524180657/http://ww w.newtonproject.sussex.ac.uk/view/t exts/normalized/THEM00231 [Accessed 6.11.2019].

Clarke, S. [4]: "Dr. Clarke's Fourth Reply". In: Clarke, S.: A Collection of Papers, Which passed between the late Learned Mr. Leibnitz, and Dr. Clarke, In the Years 1715 and 1717. London. https://web.archive.org/web/20120524180539/http://ww w.newtonproject.sussex.ac.uk/view/t exts/normalized/THEM00233 [Accessed 6.11.2019].

Clarke, S. [5]: "Dr. Clarke's Fifth Reply". In: Clarke, S.: A Collection of Papers, Which passed between the late Learned Mr. Leibnitz, and Dr. Clarke, In the Years 1715 and 1717. London. https://web.archive.org/web/20101211174753/http://ww w.newtonproject.sussex.ac.uk/view/te xts/normalized/THEM00235 [Accessed 6.11.2019].

Dennerlein, K. (2008). Narratologie des Raumes. De Gruyter. Berlin.

Depkat, V. & Pyta, W. (2021). Briefe und Tagebücher zwischen Literatur- und Geschichtswissenschaft. In Depkat, V. & Pyta, W. (Eds.), Briefe und Tagebücher zwischen Text und Quelle. Berlin.

Descartes, R. (2007; 1644). Die Prinzipien Der Philosophie. Unverändertes eBook der 1. Aufl. von 2007. https://dx.doi.org/10.28937/978-3-7873-2041-7 [6.11.2019].

Dunn, S. & Schumacher, M. (2016). Explaining Events to Computers: Critical Quantification, Multiplicity and Narratives in Cultural Heritage. Digital Humanities Quarterly 010(3).

Einstein, A. (2006). Raum, Äther und Feld in der Physik. In: Dünne, J. and Günzel, S. (Eds.) Raumtheorie. Suhrkamp. Frankfurt am Main.

Einstein, A. (2009). Über die spezielle und die allgemeine Relativitätstheorie (24. Aufl.). Springer. Berlin Heidelberg. https://doi.org/10.1007/978-3-540-87777-6.

Ehrmann, M., Hamdi, A., Pontes, E.L., Romanello, M. & Doucet, A. (2021). Named Entity Recognition and Classification on Historical Documents: A Survey. CoRR abs/2109.11406.

Faruqui, M. & Padó, S. (2010). Training and Evaluating a German Named Entity Recognizer with Semantic Generalization, KONVENS. Sarbrücken. https://puma.ub.uni-stuttgart.de/bibtex/16475c614f540914d7300f477009d829 [Stand: 24.4.2021].

Finkel, J. R., Grenager, T. & Manning, C. (2005). Incorporating Non-local Information into Information Extraction Systems by Gibbs Sampling. Proceedings of the 43nd Annual Meeting of the Association for Computational Linguistics. Michigan. p. 363–370.

Fludernik, M. (1991). Shifters and deixis: Some reflections on Jakobson, Jespersen, and reference. Semiotica, 86 (3–4). DOI:10.1515/semi.1991.86.3-4.193.

Foucault, M. de (2005). Die Heterotopien. Der utopische Körper. Zwei Radiovorträge. Suhrkamp. Frankfurt am Main.

Frank, M., Gockel, B., Hauschild, T., Kimmich, D. & Mahlke, K. (2008). Räume zur Einführung. Räume. Zeitschrift für Kulturwissenschaften 2, p. 7–16.

Gius, E., Meister J. C., Meister, M., Petris, M., Bruck, C., Jacke, J., Schumacher, M., Gerstorfer, D., Flüh, M. & Horstmann, J. (2021). CATMA (6.3.0). Zenodo. https://doi.org/10.5281/zenodo.5015305.

Hallet W. & Neumann, B. (2009). Raum und Bewegung in der Literatur. Die Literaturwissenschaften und der Spatial Turn. transcript Verlag. Bielefeld.

Hallet, W. (2016). Die Re-Semiotisierung von Herkunftsräumen im multimodalen Migrationsroman. In: Benz, M., & Dennerlein, K. (Eds.), Literarische Räume der Herkunft. Fallstudien zu einer historischen Narratologie. Narratologia 51 (p. 337–357). De Gruyter. Berlin/Boston.

Hildenbrandt, V. & Kamzelak, R. S. (2019). Persönliche Schriften: 'Scalable Reading' für Briefe, Tagebücher und Notizen. In Nutt-Kofoth, R. & Plachta, B. (Eds.), editio 33/2019, p. 114–129.

Jannidis, F., Reger, I., Weimer, L., Krug, M., Toepfer M., & Puppe, F. (2015). Automatische Erkennung von Figuren im deutschsprachigen Roman. DHd2015. Von

Daten zu Erkenntnissen. Konferenzabstracts. http://gams.uni-graz.at/o:dhd20 15.abstracts-gesamt [6.11.2019].

Joost, U. (2013). 'Chatoullen ..., welche den vertrauten Briefwechsel ... enthielten'. Die Erschließung großer Briefkorpora der Goethezeit. Probleme, Aufgaben und Möglichkeiten. In Bohnenkamp, A. & Richter, E. (Eds.): Brief-Edition im digitalen Zeitalter. De Gruyter. Berlin/Boston.

Leibniz, Gottfried Wilhelm (2014; 1714). Monadologie Und Andere Metaphysische Schriften. Meiner Verlag. Hamburg https://dx.doi.org/10.28937/978-3-7873-211 7-9 [6.11.2019].

Leibniz, G. W. 1717[1]. Mr. Leibnitz' First Paper Being an Answer to Dr. Clarke's First Reply. In: Clarke, S. (Ed.) A Collection of Papers, Which passed between the late Learned Mr. Leibnitz, and Dr. Clarke, In the Years 1715 and 1717. London. https://web.archive.org/web/20120528124843/http://www.newtonproject. sus ex.ac.uk/view/t exts/normalized/THEM00226 [6.11.2019].

Leibniz, G. W. 1717[2]. Mr. Leibnitz' Second Paper Being an Answer to Dr. Clarke's First Reply. In: Clarke, S. (Ed.) A Collection of Papers, Which passed between the late Learned Mr. Leibnitz, and Dr. Clarke, In the Years 1715 and 1717. London. https://web.archive.org/web/20120528124759/http://www.newtonproject. sussex.ac.uk/view/t exts/normalized/THEM00228 [6.11.2019].

Leibniz, G. W. 1717[3]. Mr. Leibnitz' Third Paper Being an Answer to Dr. Clarke's Second Reply. In: Clarke, S. (Ed.) A Collection of Papers, Which passed between the late Learned Mr. Leibnitz, and Dr. Clarke, In the Years 1715 and 1717. London. https://web.archive.org/web/20120528124510/http://www.newtonproject. sussex.ac.uk/view/t exts/normalized/THEM00230 [Stand 6.11.2019].

Leibniz, G. W. 1717[4]. "Mr. Leibnitz' Fourth Paper Being an Answer to Dr. Clarke's Second Reply. In: Clarke, S. (Ed.) A Collection of Papers, Which passed between the late Learned Mr. Leibnitz, and Dr. Clarke, In the Years 1715 and 1717. London. https://web.archive.org/web/20120524180739/http://www.newtonproject. sussex.ac.uk/view/t exts/normalized/THEM00232 [Stand 6.11.2019].

Leibniz, G. W. 1717[5]. Mr. Leibnitz' Fifth Paper Being an Answer to Dr. Clarke's Second Reply. In: Clarke, S. A Collection of Papers, Which passed between the late Learned Mr. Leibnitz, and Dr. Clarke, In the Years 1715 and 1717. London. https://web.archive.org/web/20120524180620/http://www.newtonproject .sussex.ac.uk/view/t exts/normalized/THEM00234 [Stand 6.11.2019].

Lessing, G. E. (1766). Laokoon oder über die Grenzen der Malerei und der Poesie. ht tp://www.zeno.org/nid/20005265576 [Accessed 17.12.2020].

Lotman, J. (1973). *Die Struktur des künstlerischen Textes*. Suhrkamp. Frankfurt am Main.

Matthews-Schlinzig, M., Schuster, J., Steinbrink, G., Strobel, J. (2020). Vorwort. In dies (Eds.): *Handbuch Brief. Von der Frühen Neuzeit bis zur Gegenwart. Band 1: Interdisziplinarität – Systematische Perspektiven – Briefgenres*. De Gruyter, XI–XIV. Boston/Berlin.

Nantke, J., Bläß, S., Flüh, M., & Maus, D. (2022). Best of Both Worlds – Zur Kombination algorithmischer und manueller Verfahren bei der Erschließung großer Handschriftenkorpora. In *DHd 2022 Kulturen des digitalen Gedächtnisses. 8. Tagung des Verbands "Digital Humanities im deutschsprachigen Raum"* (DHd 2022), Potsdam. https://doi.org/10.5281/zenodo.6328113.

Piatti, B. 1973– (2008). *Die Geographie der Literatur Schauplätze, Handlungsräume, Raumphantasien*. Wallstein. Göttingen.

Rippl, C. (2016). Raum der Herkunft, Ort des Erzählens. Zum Phänomen der andersweltlichen Herkunft im Roman der Frühen Neuzeit. In Benz, M. & Dennerlein, K. (Eds.), *Literarische Räume der Herkunft. Fallstudien zu einer historischen Narratologie. Narratologia 51*. De Gruyter. Berlin/Boston.

Ryan, M.-L. (2009). Space. In Hühn, P. (Ed.), *Handbook of narratology*. Walter de Gruyter Berlin (Narratologia). New York.

Ryan, M.-L. (2012). Possible Worlds. In Hühn, P. et al. (Eds.), *The Living Handbook of Narratology*. Hamburg. http://www.lhn.uni-hamburg.de/article/possible-wo rlds [Accessed 16.03.2022].

Ryan, M.-L., Foote, K., & Azaryahu, M. (2016). *Narrating Space/Spatializing Narrative*. The Ohio State University Press. Columbus.

Schumacher, M. & Flüh, M. (2020). m*w – Figurengender zwischen Stereotypisierung und literarischen und theoretischen Spielräumen. Gendersterotype und -bewertungen in der Literatur des 19. Jahrhunderts. In Schöch, C. (Ed.), *DHd 2020 Spielräume: Digital Humanities zwischen Modellierung und Interpretation. Konferenzabstracts* (p. 162–167). DOI: 10.5281/zenodo.3666690.

Schumacher, M. (2021a): *Raum-Classifier (kompatibel mit StanfordNER) (v1.0.0)*. Zenodo. https://doi.org/10.5281/zenodo.4992662.

Schumacher, M. (2021b). *StanfordNER Gender-Classifier (1.0)*. Zenodo. https://doi.org/ 10.5281/zenodo.5555952._

Schumacher, M. (2022). *Orte und Räume im Roman – Ein Beitrag zur digitalen Literaturwissenschaft*. J. B. Metzler. Berlin, Heidelberg.

Strobel, J. (2020). Narratologie des Briefs. In: Strobel, J.:Matthews-Schlinzig, M.S., Schuster J.& Steinbrink, G. (Eds.), *Handbuch Brief. Von der Frühen Neuzeit bis zur Gegenwart. Band 1: Interdisziplinarität – Systematische Perspektiven – Briefgenres* (p. 300–322). De Gruyter. Boston/Berlin.

Sutton, C. & McCullum, A. (2011). An Introduction to Conditional Random Fields. In *Foundations and Trends in Machine Learning 4* (4), p. 267–373.

Tuan, Y.-F. (1977). *Space and Place. The perspective of experience*. Minneapolis: University of Minnesota Press.

Viehauser, G. (2020). Zur Erkennung von Raum in narrativen Texten. In Reiter, N., Pichler, A. & Kuhn, J. (Eds.) *Reflektierte algorithmische Textanalyse* (p. 373–390). De Gruyter. Berlin.

Wilde, S. (2016). 'Wo gehen wir denn hin?' 'Immer nach Hause'. Zu Funktion und Be-
deutung des Herkunftsraums in Friedrich von Hardenbergs Heinrich von Of-
terdingen. In Benz, M. & Dennerlein, K. (Eds.), *Literarische Räume der Herkunft.
Fallstudien zu einer historischen Narratologie.* Narratologia 51. De Gruyter. Berlin/
Boston.

The Knowledge Graph as a Data Sculpture: Visualising Arts and Humanities Data with Maps, Graphs, and Sets over Time

Florian Windhager, Saminu Salisu, Johannes Liem & Eva Mayr

Abstract *Division of labor structures not only societal operations on a large scale, but also academic theory and practice: Scholarly tribes are trained to work and look at different things – and to cultivate distinct perspectives to that end. However, by establishing their domain-specific points of view, they also provide each other with concepts, tools, theories – and recently also visualisation techniques – to interpret complex subject matters from multiple perspectives.*
Starting from the case of cultural collections, we explore the question of how to represent such rich historical assemblies (e.g., of images, texts, and other cultural artifacts) in newly synoptic ways. By drawing together multiple visualisation perspectives, we sketch out a multi-dimensional modeling framework ("PolyCube"), which connects map, set, and graph-based views with multiple time-based encodings. This strategy of information integration allows not only to spatialise the many data dimensions of cultural collections in a coherent fashion, but also to do so with a wide range of other data and topics from arts and humanities domains. Exemplarily, we show how biographical data about historical individuals can be translated into novel shapes of time.
Tellingly, such a cross-disciplinary endeavor has become possible only due to recent developments at digital intersections (i.e., in fields such as Digital Humanities, data science or information visualisation), where the digitisation and parametrisation of formerly divided domain perspectives allows for novel exchanges on a leveled digital playing field. In this context, the indispensable views of geography meet a wide variety of 'non- geographic spatialisation techniques' (cf. Skupin & Fabrikant, 2003) and can merge into new kinds of "bigger pictures" to both incorporate and transcend traditional epistemic divisions.

Keywords: Arts and Humanities Data, Knowledge Graph, Visualisation, Space-Time-Cube, Collection Visualisation, Biography Visualisation, Distant Reading, Digital Humanities, Digital History

Introduction

When modelling and visualising arts and humanities topics, most roads eventually lead to geography.[1] To substantiate such a generic statement, one could point to numerous anecdotal evidence or more systematic philosophical voices[2] but also to the complex and 'ill-disciplined' nature of many arts and humanities topics themselves. Theoretical reflections of such topics can start *anywhere* – i.e., from very diverse perspectives or disciplinary points of view – to eventually also touch upon aspects of *geo-spatial* locations, movements, aims, or relationships – and then move on to other aspects.

The largely language-based approach of most arts and humanities disciplines to model their subject matters descriptively or theoretically allows scholars to easily interconnect these multiple perspectives by sequential chaining. Text-based approaches to the construction of complex representations connect words and concepts along the lines of scholarly prose – and use conjunctions to stitch together larger units of meaning (sentences, paragraphs, texts, hypertexts). Texts then are used to connect, contrast, and comprise multiple analytical perspectives, answering manifold questions, such as what, who, with whom, why, how, when, or *where*. These syntactic rules seem hardly worth mentioning. For any possible topic, we expect capable authors to combine required perspectives (e.g., topic or actor-oriented, relational, causal, historical and geographical perspectives) and thus convey a 'bigger picture' of their chosen subject matter.

Recent times have brought about new ways to encode digitised information – not only verbally but also visually. In addition to realistic pictures (photo and video), information abstractions, such as diagrams and interactive visualisations, have become established tools able to convey multiple perspectives on complex subject matters in a wide range of fields between journalism, media, research, and education. In the arts and humanities, visualisations provide a plurality of novel views, including "generous" and "distant" views at large archives and aggregates of cultural activity (Jänicke et al., 2015; Whitelaw et al., 2015). Obviously, cartography and geospatial visualisations play a major role in this regard. But how does the well-established geospatial point of view combine and connect to newer essential visualisation perspectives? How do we connect a geographic perspective (e.g., on cultural or his-

---

1   This paper originated in the context of a reflection on new intersections between Digital Humanities and geography.

2   In his lectures on physical geography, Immanuel Kant elaborated on the general conception that human reason structures information either geographically, chronologically, or systematically. We meet our own knowledge thus organised in a systematic fashion (i.e., what would be called "conceptual", "theoretical", or "discursive" today), in historiographic, time-oriented sequences, or as spatial tableaux and geographic constellations (Werlen, 1993).

torical actors or objects) to a taxonomic or set-based point of view, to a relational network perspective, and how do we enrich these representations with temporal or historical information? Or put in geographers' words: How do we intertwine geographic maps with the rich panoply of "non-geographic spatialisations" (cf. Skupin & Fabrikant, 2003)?[3]

In the following, we sketch out a synoptic approach to visualising arts and humanities topics that was developed with a specific focus on the *integration* of multiple visualisation perspectives. In it, geography plays a vital role, but so do other non-geographic mapping techniques, including set diagrams, network graphs, and multiple representations for the historical data dimension. While we developed this framework with specific regard to cultural collections, an unlimited array of subject matters in the (digital) arts and humanities could benefit from similar representation approaches. We illustrate the applicability of this synoptic modeling and visualisation method by means of a current research project on the visual analysis, communication and curation of cultural heritage information. In addition, we sketch out a future scenario where arts, humanities and history experts could lead interested audiences into a growing garden of both aesthetically and cognitively appealing data sculptures for the purpose of multimodally (i.e., verbally *and* visually) mediating the Digital Humanities' growing knowledge graph.[4]

Digital & Distant Perspectives on Cultural Materials

The digital transformation has not only changed our current means of writing, but it is also transforming cultural archives by 'duplicating' or 'mirroring' texts and other cultural objects of the past (see Kaplan & di Leonardo, 2020; Maaz, 2020). To document their richnees and make them available on the web, countless heritage institutions are engaged in the creation and growth of a digital layer of their stocks, which comes with genuine new qualities and actionable affordances. In addition to new ways of accessing and processing this layer, digital methods allow us to literally look at things anew, and to strengthen visual sensemaking strategies on various levels. Regarding textual materials, for instance, we can still follow their lines and chapters on screen ("close reading"), yet also utilise additional data analytical

---

3   For an exemplary overview, see the "Data Visualisation Catalogue" (https://datavizcatalogu e.com/).

4   In this article, the term "data sculpture" refers to data visualisations which deliberately include a third dimension to raise both the temporal expressiveness and attraction power of flat visualisation designs (Windhager et al., 2020). More specifically, we reflect on the three-dimensional and interactive rendering of such visualisations on graphical displays, as opposed to their possible embodiment in physical space (Bentz et al., 2022; Zhao & Vande Moere, 2008).

perspectives to parse, query, recognise, analyse, question, model, and visually represent whole collections of textual sources in unforeseen, "distant" or freely scalable ways. The associated use of *visual-analytical* methods then enriches our understanding of complex cultural subject matters with diagrammatic representations. They provide "computer-supported, interactive, visual representations of abstract data to amplify cognition" (Card, 1999), and thus foster new kinds of insights into "massive, dynamic, ambiguous, and often conflicting data" (Cook & Thomas, 2005, p.4).

While Digital Humanities projects have not created equally massive data collections as other fields, such as engineering or the natural sciences yet, they have started to translate a wide range of historical phenomena into event-based datasets and to connect them as larger historical knowledge graphs (cf. Kaplan & di Lenardo, 2017; 2020). Working their ways into our text-based archives, technologies of natural language processing extract structured data from historical sources as semantically categorised entities and data points together with multiple types of attributes (e.g., events with specific geotags, but also timestamps, categorical tags, individual tags, as well as links to other entities and events). Extracted entities then are linked to known entities and controlled vocabularies in factual knowledge bases (such as Geonames, WikiData or DBpedia) to identify and validate them – and to leverage existing data and knowledge for their interpretation (Ehrlinger & Wöß, 2016, Oldman & Tanase, 2016). With their focus on the historical dimension, knowledge graphs in humanities and history fields model temporal change as a "fourth dimension" of our three-dimensional, present-day world and thus incrementally build up a 4D twin model of our world and its past (Kaplan & di Lenardo, 2017, 2020). For such data collections, technologies of "distant reading" or "distant viewing" prove their value, as they frequently leverage formal or statistical data analysis methods together with visualisation techniques (e.g., maps, networks, set diagrams, or timelines) to make macroscopic patterns for various subject matters visible, which remain hidden to the close readers of individual texts.[5]

However, when engaging in the visual analysis of such complex arts and humanities data, scholarly or public audiences rarely get to see their multidimensional richness (or the richness of the underlying knowledge graphs) in a synoptic way. Commonly, visualisation tools require their users to selectively cut into the complexity of such data to highlight and project particular aspects (e.g., the geo-spatial origins

---

5   For richly illustrated windows into the field of text visualisation and "distant reading" technologies, see Jänicke et al. (2015) or Kucher et al. (2015), with the latter providing an interactive browser at https://textvis.lnu.se/. "Distant viewing" technologies, on the other side, focus on the formal or statistical analysis of visual materials (such as images, photographs, films) – and they pair equally well with methods of data visualisation (e.g., Arnold & Tilston, 2019; Windhager et al., 2018a, Zaharieva et al., 2011).

of selected entities), while neglecting other facets and data dimensions. To represent more dimensions visually, *coordinated multiple views* have been proposed, which allow to establish a plurality of individual perspectives side by side and to interact with them in a coordinated way (Dörk et al., 2018; Roberts et al., 2019). However, such faceted displays entail a variety of downsides on their own, including a lot of visual work on the user side, the splitting of users' attention and a significant amount of visual complexity (Baldonado et al., 2000; Windhager et al., 2018b). Faceted or multiple views allow us to see and sample partial insights, while hindering us to see a coherent bigger picture – to say nothing of a larger historical context. If analysts want to overcome this "schizo-pictorial" state of affairs, they have to reassemble and reconnect the partial impressions from multiple views in their heads, which turns out to be a demanding cognitive task (Windhager et al., 2018b).

The PolyCube Framework of Visualisation for Arts & Humanities Topics

To provide a more integrated and interdisciplinary approach for the analysis of event-based arts and humanities data, we recently introduced the PolyCube visualisation framework (Windhager et al., 2020). As a web-based visualisation system, it draws together multiple visualisation methods and perspectives to convey a bigger picture for complex, time-oriented data, and to support synoptic exploration of the data, as well as navigation between particularistic perspectives for expert and casual users alike. The system provides:

- multiple spatialised (i.e., geographic and non-geographic) overview perspectives (including a map-based, a category-based, and a network-based view) implemented as coordinated views side-by-side, which the user can blend in or out on demand,
- multiple temporal perspectives to choose from (including a space-time cube representation (STC), a juxtaposed, an animated and a colour-coded view),
- close-up access to single events or objects on demand, together with
- animated canvas transitions, supporting the switching between various temporal perspectives.

In the area of cultural collection visualisation, we demonstrated the analytical options of this system with two case studies (Windhager et al., 2020), including the Charles W. Cushman photography collection (Indiana University, 2007), and a collection of influential movies, based on cinematic references (Spitz & Horvat, 2014).[6]

---

6   For an interactive demo of these two case studies, see: https://danubevislab.github.io/poly
      cube/cga2020/.

Objects of cultural collections are frequently specified by multiple metadata entries, such as place and time of origin, class of object (e.g., object type, content type, topic, genre, or style), or by various types of relations between objects. The PolyCube system allows users to import their own data with a web-based spreadsheet template[7] and to engage in the synoptic visual analysis of these data dimensions. For that matter, the system starts with a setup of three coordinated space-time cubes to investigate the time-oriented composition of geographical, categorical and relational collection data as three-dimensional data sculptures (Fig. 1) – and to seamlessly transition to three alternative perspectives on the temporal data dimension (Fig. 2), based on animated space-time cube transformations (Fig. 3).

Figure 1: Three parallel views of the PolyCube system, providing a map-based, a category-based and a network-based space-time cube perspective (from left to right), together with a close-up view on a selected photograph of the Cushman photography collection (left hand side).

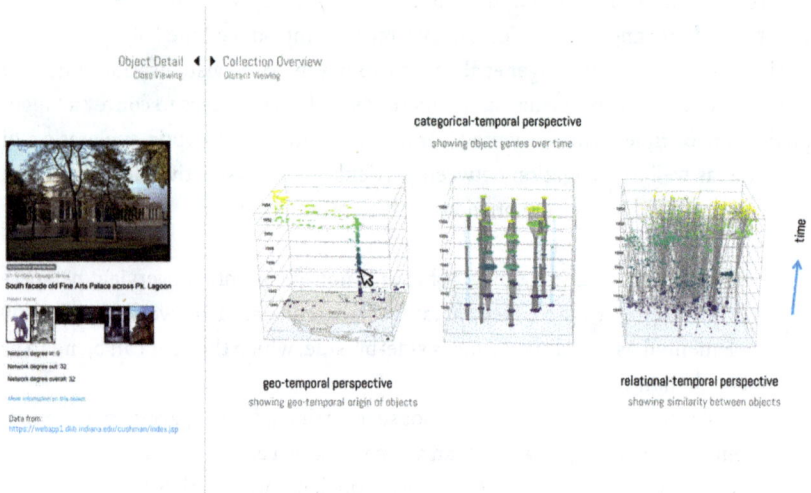

---

7   See the specification in the corresponding GitHub repository: https://github.com/danubevi slab/polycubeViews.

Figure 2: *Three alternative views on time, including a colour-coded superimposition view (a), an animated view (b), and a juxtaposition or data comic perspective (c).*

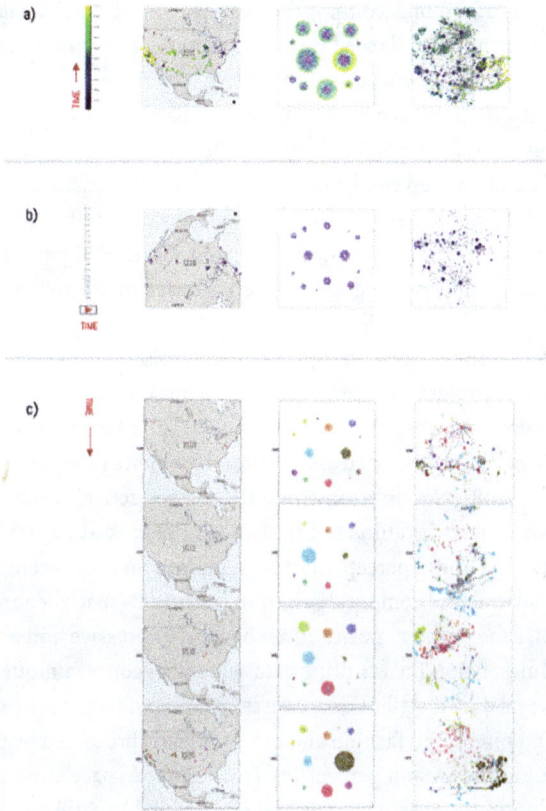

Figure 3: *Animated transitions between the PolyCube system's four alternative views on time, based on space-time cube operations.*

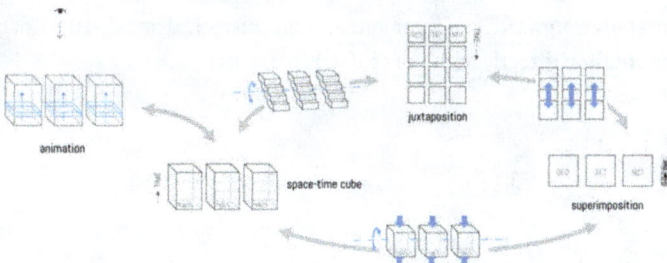

With this systemic design approach we fully approve the established rationale that "one view is not enough" to depict cultural complexity (Dörk et al., 2017), but also argue for overcoming the resultant problem of fragmented and incoherent visualisation plurality (Windhager et al., 2018b; 2020). We contend that research into visual-analytical operations of decomposition (cf. the roots of Greek *'analuin'* – cutting or loosening things up) be balanced by the development of 'visual-synthetical' design strategies, which deploy so-called coherence techniques to better support humanists' reasoning operations across commonly separated data dimensions, scales and perspectives (Windhager & Mayr, 2022). While such macroscopic frameworks always allow the user-driven reduction to one- or two-dimensional points of view (such as a flat, geographic perspective only), we consider their main benefit to lie in their synoptic potential, such as in the drawing together of geographical, taxonomical, relational, and historiographical perspectives into novel perceptual joint ventures.

While the three-dimensional design of data sculptures (Fig. 1) comes with some downsides (e.g., visual clutter or perspective distortion), we consider the space-time cube concept's perceptual and cognitive benefits to far outweigh these costs – especially if multiple other (undistorted and uncluttered) views on time are made available (Mayr et al., 2018). Not only can space-time cubes actively interconnect these different temporal views by animated transitions (Bach et al., 2017) but they also provide a uniquely balanced perceptual representation for spatio-temporal data, by encoding both spatial and temporal origin to "position" (spatial coordinates to x- and y-positions, time to the z- position) as the most expressive and effective visual variable (Mackinlay, 1986). The resulting data sculptures convey unique perspectives on spatio-temporal data distributions, constellations and patterns in a perceptually even-handed and integrated fashion and can be directly processed by the combined faculties of volume and Gestalt perception. Furthermore, space-time cubes provide an intuitive solution for a) spatio-temporal scalability, b) spatio-temporal navigation, and c) spatio-temporal aggregation.

Figure 4 shows how the volumetric dimensions of space-time cubes can be freely adjusted and scaled to appropriately frame the smallest or largest spatio-temporal datasets. In all the resulting frames, a specific information spatialisation sets the visual analytical scene on the base plane (x- and y dimension), while the time axis commonly points upward, and interconnects the "historical imagination" or chronological orientation directly with the spatial representation.

Figure 4: Space-time cubes can scale "from home to globe, and from day to lifetime" (Häger-strand, 1970).

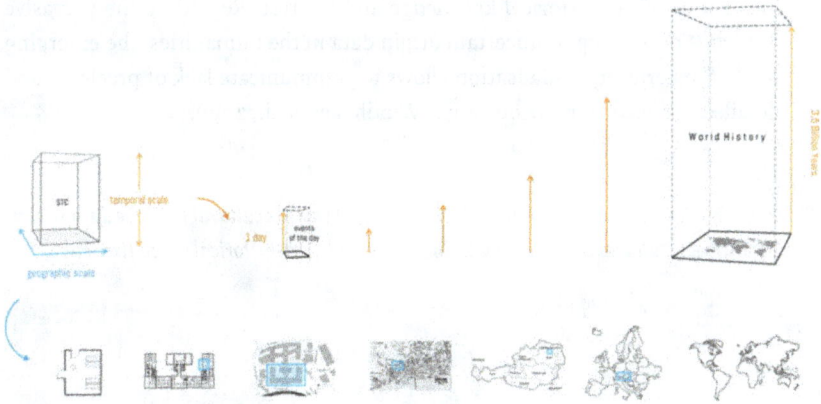

a) From a mental models perspective (Liu & Stasko, 2010; Windhager & Mayr, 2022), navigating historical and geo-spatial information spaces usually requires the mental combination of a map-based schema (which we usually look at orthogonally), and of representations of chronological sequences which are commonly visualised in a linear, timeline-based fashion, read from left to right. In the space-time cube framework, the structure of both representations is preserved, but interconnected orthogonally: Moving forward in time equals the pursuit of an upward trajectory, moving back in time equals a downward shift, while spatial navigation equals the established horizontal movements within existing mental maps.[8]

b) This freely scalable framework does not only allow for the visualisation of selected cultural datasets (such as the exemplary photography collections depicted in Fig. 1), but also to aggregate the representation of collections from different geo-historical regions. Figure 5 shows with a conceptual drawing how a large-scale space-time cube can visually integrate any number of cultural (sub)collections, by assigning them to their geo-temporal coordinates in a larger 3D scatter plot. As such, the framework acts like an effective generator of data-driven big pictures or sculptures of cultural history, and aside from the basic geo-temporal localisation of objects and collections in a collective frame of reference – similar to a shared mental model – it facilitates (art) historians' navigation (whether for their own reasoning operations or for the purpose of knowledge communication) between the densely packed patches or generative clusters

---

8   With Tversky (1993) and Liu & Stasko (2010) we do not assume a veridical nature of visualisation-based mental maps or mental models, but that they vary in cognitive quality, structural consistency, and practical utility.

of cultural creation events, between anomalies and outliers, and also between gaps or structural holes, which signify both the lack of cultural activity or the limitations of art-historical knowledge and interest. Regarding the pervasive challenge of missing or uncertain origin data in the humanities, the emerging field of uncertainty visualisation allows to communicate lack of precision and detailed knowledge in various ways (Windhager et al., 2019).

Figure 5: Geo-temporal aggregation and localisation of various cultural heritage data sets (e.g., of different cultural collections) within a large-scale, art-historical space-time cube.

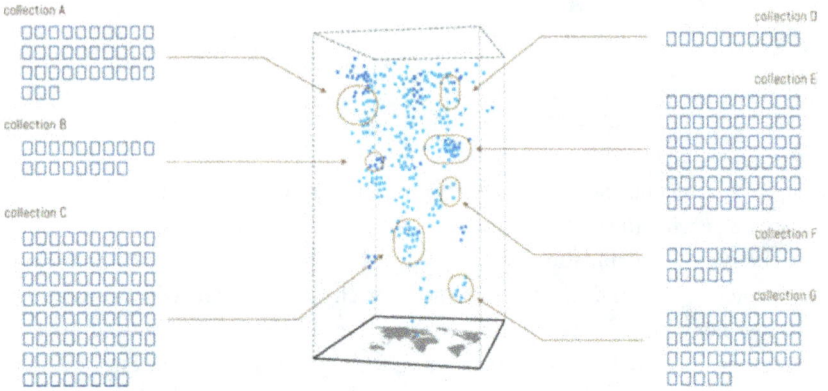

Connecting Geo-Temporal and Diagrammatic Space-Time

While geo-temporal representations are of undeniable value for various situations of knowledge creation and communication, they do not exhaust the representational opportunities and affordances that complex cultural data offers by any means. Recently, a rising number of advanced digitisation efforts results in relational and contextual models of cultural information, shortly referred to as knowledge graphs (Vavliakis et al., 2012). Figure 6 shows main components of cultural knowledge graphs floating in geo-temporal space (left) where they can be visualised in their various spatio-temporal constellations. The right side, on the other hand, shows how all these elements can also be transferred into time-oriented visualisations (here again with a space-time cube) which make use of diagrammatic foundations, such as set-based layouts, or force-directed network layouts.

Figure 6: Basic components of knowledge graphs can be transferred from a geo-temporal frame of reference (left) into various diagrammatic-temporal frames of reference, so that data structures and patterns that would remain invisible to geo-based analyses can be visually analysed.

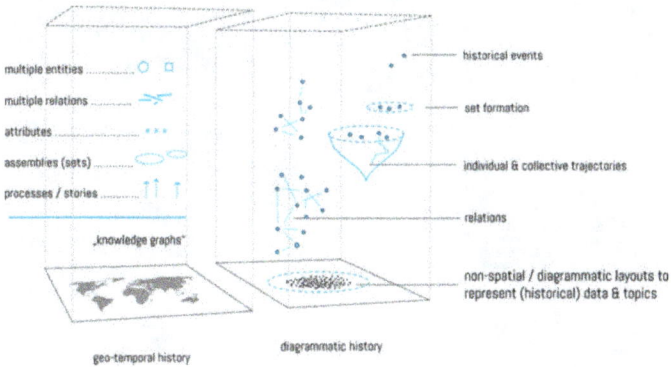

Exemplarily, figure 7 shows how collective historical entities (such as groups, organisations, institutions, societies, schools, movements, parties, religions, opinions, ideas, ideologies, theories, customs, practices, memes, styles, genres, etc.) can be transferred from the geographers' primordial frame of reference (where many collective entities are often scattered) to a space-time cube utilising a set diagram instead of a map as a base layout. When visualising the temporal trajectories of such sets (time axis again pointing upwards), the temporal "hull" of such sets is drawing flow patterns into the vertical historical dimension, and any change of the size or structure of the set (due to addition or subtraction of entities or subsets) creates basic evolutionary patterns (right), which can be read and interpreted by our gestalt perception as elementary "shapes of time" (Kubler, 1962; Salisu et al., 2019). The vertical-historical concatenation of these basic patterns allows to visually represent the complex organic trajectories of social and cultural phenomena in a data-driven fashion (see Fig. 1, centre).[9]

---

9   Obviously, the actual heuristic quality of all the outlined visual representations relies on – and directly varies with – the quality (density, reliability, structuration) of historical data – which is the crucial bottleneck for all DH approaches to visualisation and modelling (Windhager et al., 2019).

Figure 7: *Set-based representation of assemblies of things (left) whose collective set-trajectory (blue) represents the evolution of such sets over time. The angles (<) of such set-trajectories creates a number of evolution patterns (right), which can be read as various collective dynamics – from group emergence to decline.*

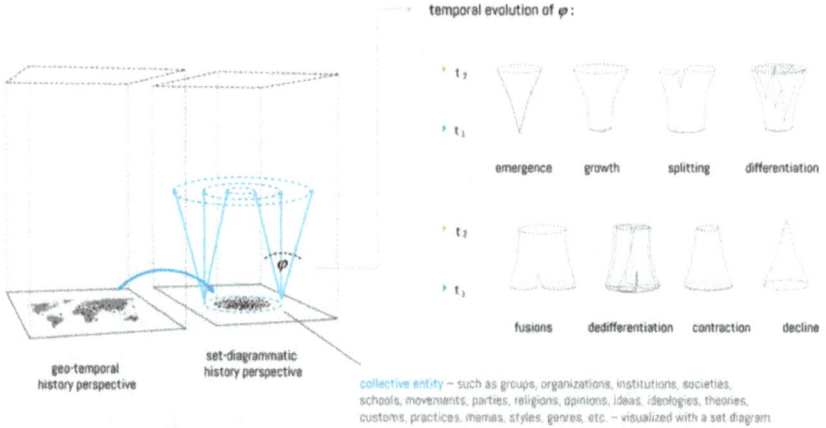

temporal evolution of φ:

emergence   growth   splitting   differentiation

fusions   dedifferentiation   contraction   decline

geo-temporal
history perspective

set-diagrammatic
history perspective

collective entity – such as groups, organizations, institutions, societies, schools, movements, parties, religions, opinions, ideas, ideologies, theories, customs, practices, memes, styles, genres, etc. – visualized with a set diagram

Another prominent visual-analytical perspective on historical data and topics are *network-analytical* views, which are oftentimes based on force-directed layouts. While the time-oriented visualisation of dynamic networks remains a notable challenge (Beck et al., 2017), space-time cubes can also accommodate all kind of relational-temporal data. Figure 8 (left) shows how this perspective is able to maintain a non-temporal, aggregated network perspective (view from above), but also allows to observe temporal developments and temporal subgraphs from a lateral perspective, to gain insights on various levels of temporal structuration. With this relational-temporal perspective, all kinds of graph-based modelling approaches to arts and humanities topics (Ahnert et al., 2020) could be connected and potentially integrated into the synoptic PolyCube framework (Fig. 8, right, Federico et al., 2011) – including directed, acyclic graphs with branching or hierarchical structures, such as genealogical trees, or even set-based trees (Fig. 10, bottom, centre left and right).

Figure 8: Utilisation of space-time representations for the visualisation of relational-temporal data.

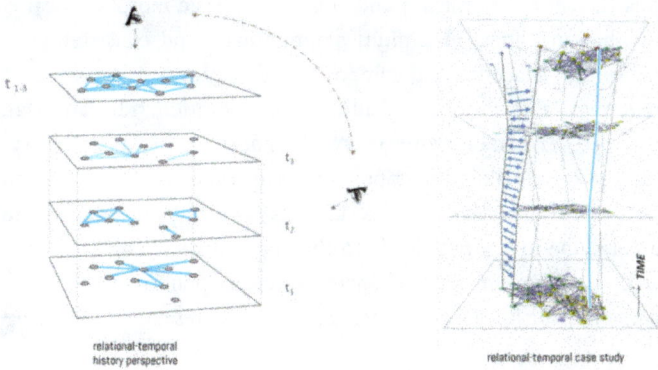

relational-temporal
history perspective

relational-temporal case study

The open and adaptive nature of the polycubistic visualisation framework also allows to reframe existing visualisations with relevance for cultural and historical analyses. Looking at 24 critical dynamics and trends of modern culture in terms of a socio-economic, environmentally situated system, Steffen and colleagues (2015) depict the "great acceleration" that characterises socio-economic and earth system trends in the Anthropocene. While they have originally visualised these trends with 24 synchronised line graphs, Figure 9 shows how they can be regrouped in a circular fashion, to draw the sprawling shape of a dramatically expanding radar chart into diagrammatic space and time (Windhager, 2018).

Figure 9: Reframing the socio-economic trends of the Anthropocene (Steffen et al., 2015) in the polycubistic framework.

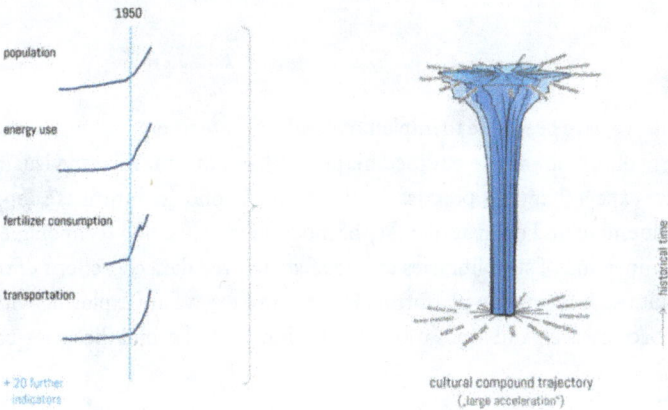

1950

population

energy use

fertilizer consumption

transportation

+ 20 further
indicators

cultural compound trajectory
("large acceleration")

historical time

It is guiding hypothesis of our developments that a wide portfolio of arts and humanities topics could benefit from the availability of multi-spatiotemporal visualisations (Fig. 10). By utilising and connecting basic morphological elements (such as points and lines) in a multi-diagrammatic and consistently time-oriented, framework, collective and composite trajectories (e.g., of actor networks, institutions, political territories, and all kinds of innovation, translation, and modernisation processes) can be aggregated and rendered visible as polymorphic data sculptures. The topic-tailored juxtaposition of geo-temporal and diagrammatic-temporal representations for complex datasets (as for instance illustrated with a tripartite PolyCube in figure 1) leads to the appearance of combinatorial "meta-shapes", which offer more comprehensive, interdisciplinary pictures of cultural-historical phenomena for the augmentation of various research or teaching tasks.

Figure 10: Outlook on a whole spectrum of data-driven morphologies, using space-time cube projections to make a variety of historical and conceptual phenomena visually accessible for research, teaching and public communication.

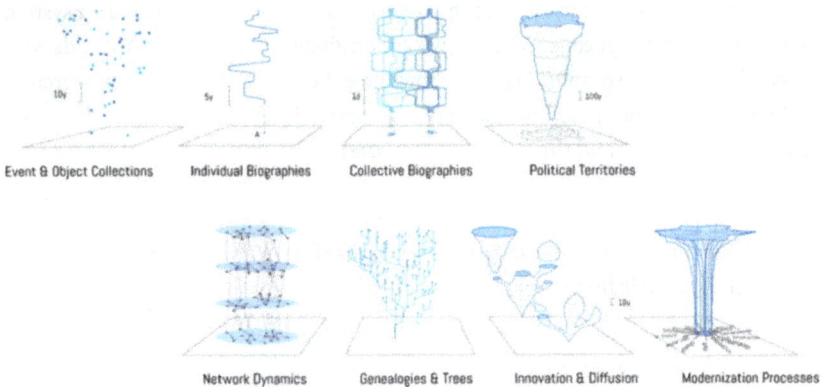

Event & Object Collections Individual Biographies Collective Biographies Political Territories

Network Dynamics Genealogies & Trees Innovation & Diffusion Modernization Processes

While we have been able to implement and evaluate interactive visualisations as proofs of concept for all the outlined map-based and diagram-based visualisations above, we expect that their practical value and their concrete future use depends on the development and open availability of modular visualisation technologies – and on the connection of such libraries to larger, structured data collections of transnational cultural information platforms. For that matter, we are exploring with a current H2020 research and innovation action[10] how to go beyond the event-based vi-

---

10 In/Tangible European Heritage — Visual Analysis, Curation and Communication (https://intavia.eu).

sualisations of cultural collection data (Fig. 1 and Fig. 10, top left) and combine such representations with the depiction of linked actor and object biographies (Fig 10, top centre left and centre right).

Visual Analysis, Curation and Communication of In/Tangible Cultural Heritage (InTaVia)

Most digitisation initiatives in the cultural sector focus either on tangible or on intangible aspects of cultural heritage, thereby splitting up the focus on tangible artefacts (such as paintings, documents, or technological artefacts) from historically related entities (such as creators, contributors, institutions, art schools, etc.). The project InTaVia brings back together digitised information on tangible cultural heritage and related intangible cultural heritage – in our case, stories on the lives of historically relevant actors and their related cultural objects. While information on artefacts has been digitised by different GLAM institutions and aggregated on platforms like Europeana.eu, biographical information has been traditionally preserved in textual form as nationally organised biographical lexica. Within the last several years, these texts were digitised and transformed into structured machine-readable prosopographical data (e.g., actor A was born in year Y at place P, and related to institution I), which allows linking to related other information. By harmonising and interconnecting sources and data formats of intangible and tangible heritage (cf. Fokkens & ter Braake, 2017), InTaVia assembles an integrated cultural knowledge graph, which interlinks national prosopographical databases (starting with those from Slovenia, Austria, the Netherlands, and Finland) with related objects from Europeana. Thereby, a rich relational graph of in/tangible cultural heritage data can be explored and communicated – if users in fact can access this knowledge graph and make use of it easily, which we consider to be a research and development challenge of its own.

To make such a complex knowledge graph with multiple types of historical entities (such as objects, actors, places, events, or institutions), attributes and relations accessible to interested expert users, InTaVia develops a visual analytics studio, which also integrates the PolyCube approach. Polycubistic visualisations of traces and trajectories thus can make the movements of historical entities visually accessible in geographic, categorical and relational space-times (Mayr et al., 2019). As a proof of concept from an earlier investigation, Figure 11 shows how the known movements of historical persons in geographic space thus can be visually remediated as expressive data sculptures, to be compared and inspected with further visual-analytical perspectives.

Figure 11: Visual remediation of individual biographies as geo-temporal data sculptures (Mayr & Windhager, 2018).

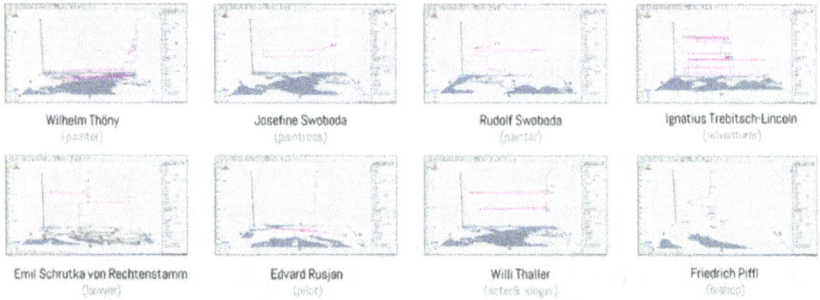

By aggregating individual trajectories, we will also explore how to model and visualise different collective trajectories and histories, from art schools and cultural institutions to cities and regions (Fig. 10, top right). In addition to these visualisations, a separate module will foster storytelling with cultural data, to share cultural hi/stories in an engaging and accessible form with a wide range of non-expert target audiences from areas such as education, journalism, or cultural tourism.

Towards Digital History as Polymorphic and Discursive Data Sculpting

We started our reflection with a reconstruction of how arts and humanities scholars commonly create language-based representations in writing. By the lines of their scholarly prose, they connect the subjects, predicates, and objects of their attention to sentences, paragraphs, chapters, and texts – and they provide "bigger pictures" of complex topics by a) interconnecting multiple investigative perspectives within their own texts and b) by connecting their own texts with other texts, whether to confirm, augment, or contradict related work in the larger intertextual networks of academic discourse.

The proceeding digitisation of cultural materials and their increasing assembly into knowledge graphs is currently providing experts and non-expert audiences with a newly structured and interconnected medium and mode of information (Vavliakis et al., 2012). This source, however, also requires novel representation methods to become human-readable and accessible for various questions, and to become comprehensible and usable for all sorts of activities between contemplation, analysis, and communication. Arguably, cultural and (art-)historical knowledge graphs largely result from text recognition and natural-language processing initiatives, directed to our print-based libraries and book collections. Their complex interconnections and network structures – built of large amounts of subject-predicate-object triples – thus do not only mirror (parts of) the conceptual and (inter)textual networks contained by our books and libraries (Auer et al., 2018) but arguably also the conceptual hypergraphs and mental models in our minds (Castro & Siew, 2020).

It is the guiding hypothesis of learning psychology that well-designed "external representations" (i.e., textual or visual representations) can dramatically support and enhance the creation of "internal representations" (i.e., of mental models or cognitive structures) and all related reasoning activities especially for things at the complex side of the human experience spectrum (Hartley & Barnden, 1997; Schnotz & Kürschner, 2008). It is the corresponding operating principle of visualisation research and development to design interactive, graphical representations of external complexities to augment and amplify internal model creation, inspection, and interpretation (Card et al., 1999; Liu & Stasko, 2010; Windhager & Mayr, 2022). However, when it comes to the visual representation of our growing knowledge graphs – whether cultural or not – it is our own guiding hypothesis that a graph-based or network-analytical perspective alone is not enough (Hartley & Barnden, 1997; Hills & Kennett, 2021). To the contrary, we consider accessible representations of knowledge graphs to require novel interconnections of existing visualisation methods in larger "visual-synthetical" design settings, and to leverage all kinds of "coherence techniques" to that end (Windhager & Mayr, 2022). In this context, the PolyCube framework exemplifies one specific design strategy, which we hope to become complemented, revised, criticised, confirmed, contradicted, or challenged by numerous other macro-syntactical visualisation design strategies, which go beyond one-dimensional data portraits and find new combinations of orchestrated, perspectival plurality. It is our assumption that only such designs will allow to (re)assemble complex objects, hyperobjects, and historical matters of concern from a synoptic point of view, which otherwise remain hidden for the fragmented and mono-disciplinary modelling endeavours and the early-stage technologies of reductionist visualisation design (Latour, 2008).

Speaking of discursive operations in the arts and humanities, we know most of their subject matters are at the centre of controversial discussions, of a multi-faceted discourse, and of larger interpretive debates. Arts and humanities scholars interpret symbolic and cultural materials, and they do so commonly in a text- or language-based fashion, which frequently prefers a polylogic, open-ended discourse. Guiding notions of efficiency, precision and problem-solving thus are often set aside for the sake of interpretative openness, novelty, provocation, critique, theoretical diversity, and a dynamic unfolding of plural perspectives (Drucker, 2011). Whatever the specific area of application – we should not expect such a contested pluriverse of interpretations ever to translate into uncontested data and visualisations. On the contrary – these foundational debates deserve their own representation techniques so that visualisations can become an integral part of discursive and critical sense-making procedures. On the one hand, this requires open visualisation systems, which allow for distributed and competing settings of multilateral data curation and interpretation (van Ruymbeke et al., 2017). On the other hand, it seems necessary to make critical and adversarial standpoints and interpretations visible in the representations themselves (Solli et al., 2018). This would allow to utilise the outlined framework not only for the creation and communication of agreed-upon data sculptures, but also for their collective critical edition, annotation, and ongoing revision. As such, historiographical and present-day controversies can migrate from the realms of academic prose into the hybrid worlds of graphical displays, to be contemplated, curated, taught, and engaged with on a polycontextual, multimodal basis.

References

Ahnert, R., Ahnert, S. E., Coleman, C. N., & Weingart, S. B. (2020). *The Network Turn: Changing Perspectives in the Humanities*. Cambridge University Press.

Arnold, T., & Tilton, L. (2019). Distant viewing: analyzing large visual corpora. *Digital Scholarship in the Humanities 34*. (Supplement_1), i3–i16.

Auer, S., Kovtun, V., Prinz, M., Kasprzik, A., Stocker, M., & Vidal, M. E. (2018). Towards a knowledge graph for science. *Proceedings of the 8th International Conference on Web Intelligence, Mining and Semantics*, p. 1–6.

Bach, B., Dragicevic, P., Archambault, D., Hurter, C., & Carpendale, S. (2017). A descriptive framework for temporal data visualizations based on generalized space-time cubes. *Computer Graphics Forum 36* (6), p. 36–61.

Baldonado, M. Q. W., Woodruff, A., & Kuchinsky, A. (2000). Guidelines for Using Multiple Views in Information Visualization. *Proceedings of the Working Conference on Advanced Visual Interfaces*, p. 110–119. doi.org/10.1145/345513.345271.

Bates, M. J. (2007). What is browsing-really? A model drawing from behavioural science research. *Information Research-an International Electronic Journal*, 12(4).

Beck, F., Burch, M., Diehl, S., & Weiskopf, D. (2017). A taxonomy and survey of dynamic graph visualization. *Computer Graphics Forum 36* (1), p. 133–159.

Bentz, I., Gfrereis, H., Hildenbrandt, V., Mayr, E., Offenberg, E., Tropper, E., & Windhager, F. (2022). Daten im Raum – Visualisierungen und Physikalisierungen im Medium Ausstellung. In M. Geierhos: DHd2022, Book of Abstracts. doi.org/10.5281/zenodo.6304590.

Card, M., Mackinlay, J., & Shneiderman, B. (1999). *Readings in Information Visualization: using vision to think*. Morgan Kaufmann.

Castro, N., & Siew, C. S. (2020). Contributions of modern network science to the cognitive sciences: revisiting research spirals of representation and process. *Proceedings of the Royal Society A*, 476 (2238), 20190825.

Dörk, M., Pietsch, C., & Credico, G. (2017). One view is not enough. High-level visualizations of a large cultural collection. *Special Issue of Information Design Journal*, 23 (1), p. 39–47.

Drucker, J. (2011). Humanities approaches to graphical display. *Digital Humanities Quarterly*, 5 (1). Ehrlinger, L., & Wöß, W. (2016). Towards a definition of knowledge graphs. *SEMANTiCS (Posters, Demos, SuCCESS)*, 48(1–4), 2.

Federico, P., Aigner, W., Miksch, S., Windhager, F., & Zenk, L. (2011). A visual analytics approach to dynamic social networks. *Proceedings of the 11th International Conference on Knowledge Management and Knowledge Technologies*, p. 47:1–47:8. ACM. New York.

Fokkens, A., & Ter Braake, S. (2017). Connecting People Across Borders: A Repository for Biographical Data Models. *Biographical Data in a Digital World (BD 2017)*, pp. 83–92.

Hägerstrand T. (1970). What about people in regional science? *Regional Science Association Papers XXIV*: 7– 21.

Hartley, R. T., & Barnden, J. A. (1997). Semantic networks: visualizations of knowledge. *Trends in Cognitive Sciences*, 1(5), p. 169–175.

Hills, T. T., & Kenett, Y. N. (2021). Is the mind a network? Maps, vehicles, and skyhooks in cognitive network science. *Topics in Cognitive Science*.

Hogan, A., Blomqvist, E., Cochez, M., d'Amato, C., Melo, G. D., Gutierrez, C., ... & Zimmermann, A. (2021). Knowledge graphs. *ACM Computing Surveys (CSUR)*, 54(4), p. 1–37.

Indiana University (2007). Charles W. Cushman Photograph Collection. https://webapp1.dlib.indiana.edu/cushman/index.jsp.

Kaplan, F., & di Lenardo, I. (2017). Big data of the past. *Frontiers in Digital Humanities* 4, 12. Kaplan, F., & di Lenardo, I. (2020). The advent of the 4D mirror world. *Urban Planning 5*, 307.

Kucher, K., & Kerren, A. (2015). Text visualization techniques: Taxonomy, visual survey, and community insights. In *2015 IEEE Pacific Visualization Symposium (PacificVis)*. IEEE. https://textvis.lnu.se/. pp. 117–121.

Latour, B. (2008). A cautious Prometheus? A few steps toward a philosophy of design (with special attention to Peter Sloterdijk). *Proceedings of the 2008 annual international conference of the design history society* p. 2–10.

Liu, Z., & Stasko, J. (2010). Mental models, visual reasoning and interaction in information visualization: A top-down perspective. *IEEE transactions on visualization and computer graphics*, 16 (6), p. 999–1008.

Maaz, B. (2020). *Das gedoppelte Museum*. Köln: Walther König.

Mackinlay, J. (1986). Automating the design of graphical presentations of relational information, *ACM Transactions on Graphics (Tog)* 5 (2), p. 110–141.

Mayr, E., Salisu, S., Filipov, V. A., Schreder, G., Leite, R. A., Miksch, S., & Windhager, F. (2019). Visualizing Biographical Trajectories by Historical Artifacts: A

Case Study based on the Photography Collection of Charles W. Cushman. Paper presented at *the 3rd Conference for Biographical Data in a Digital World (BD 2019)*, Varna. https://doi.org/10.17605/OSF.IO/E62X4.

Mayr, E., Schreder, G., Salisu, S., & Windhager, F. (2018). Integrated Visualization of Space and Time: A Distributed Cognition Perspective. https://doi.org/10.3121 9/osf.io/agvhw.

Mayr, E., & Windhager, F. (2018). Once upon a spacetime: Visual storytelling in cognitive and geotemporal information spaces. *ISPRS International Journal of Geo-Information 7* (3), 96.

Oldman, D., & Tanase, D. (2018). Reshaping the knowledge graph by connecting researchers, data and practices in ResearchSpace. *International Semantic Web Conference*. Springer, Cham. (pp. 325–340).

Roberts, J. C., Al-maneea, H., Butcher, P. W. S., Lew, R., Rees, G., Sharma, N., & Frankenberg-Garcia, A. (2019). Multiple Views: Different meanings and collocated words. *Computer Graphics Forum 38*(3). p. 79–93. https://doi.org/10.1111/cgf .13673.

Salisu, S., Mayr, E., Windhager, F., Filipov, V., Leite, R. & Miksch, S. (2019). Shapes of time: Visualizing set changes over time in cultural heritage collections. *EuroVis 2019 – posters*. Eurographics. (p. 45–47).

Schnotz, W., & Kürschner, C. (2008). External and internal representations in the acquisition and use of knowledge: visualization effects on mental model construction. *Instructional Science 36* (3), p. 175–190.

Solli, A., Mäkitalo, Å., & Hillman, T. (2018). Rendering controversial socioscientific issues legible through digital mapping tools. *International Journal of Computer-Supported Collaborative Learning 13* (4), p. 391–418.

Spitz, A., & Horvát, E. Á. (2014). Measuring long-term impact based on network centrality: Unraveling cinematic citations. *PloS one 9* (10), e108857.

Thomas & Cook (2005). *Illuminating the Path: The Research and Development Agenda for Visual Analytics*. National Visualization and Analytics Ctr.

Tversky, B. (1993). Cognitive maps, cognitive collages, and spatial mental models. *European conference on spatial information theory*. Springer, Berlin, Heidelberg. p. 14–24.

Van Ruymbeke, M., Hallot, P., & Billen, R. (2017). Enhancing CIDOC-CRM and compatible models with the concept of multiple interpretation. *ISPRS Annals of the Photogrammetry, Remote Sensing and Spatial Information Sciences 2*, p. 287–294.

Vavliakis, K. N., Karagiannis, G. T., & Mitkas, P. A. (2012). Semantic Web in cultural heritage after 2020. *Proceedings of the 11th International Semantic Web Conference (ISWC), Boston, MA, USA*, p. 11–15.

Werlen, B. (1993). Gibt es eine Geographie ohne Raum? Zum Verhältnis von traditioneller Geographie und zeitgenössischen Gesellschaften (Human Geographies without Space? The Relationship between Traditional Geography and Late-Modern Societies). *Erdkunde*, p. 241–255.

Whitelaw, M. (2015). Generous interfaces for digital cultural collections. *DHQ, 9*(1).

Windhager, F. (2018, November). Gaia Dissociative Identity Disorder. Visualizing Contrarian Regimes in the Struggle for Geopolitics. *Exhibition of the Study Group on the Critical Zone*, Hochschule für Gestaltung, Karlsruhe (HfG), DE.

Windhager F., & Mayr, E. (2022, forthcoming). Mental Models and Visualization. In M. Chen et al. (eds.), *Visualization Psychology*. Springer. New York.

Windhager, F., Federico, P., Schreder, G., Glinka, K., Dörk, M., Miksch, S., & Mayr, E. (2018a). Visualization of cultural heritage collection data: State of the art and future challenges. *IEEE transactions on visualization and computer graphics 25* (6), p. 2311–2330.

Windhager, F., Salisu, S., Schreder, G., & Mayr, E. (2018b). Orchestrating Overviews. A Synoptic Approach to the Visualization of Cultural Collections. *Remaking Collections. Special Issue of the Open Library of the Humanities 4* (2), p. 1–39. https://doi.org/10.16995/olh.276.

Windhager, F., Salisu, S., Leite, R. A., Filipov, V., Miksch, S., Schreder, G., & Mayr, E. (2020). Many Views Are Not Enough: Designing for Synoptic Insights in Cultural Collections. *IEEE Computer Graphics and Applications 40* (3), p. 58–71.

Windhager, F., Salisu, S., & Mayr, E. (2019). Exhibiting uncertainty: Visualizing data quality indicators for cultural collections. *Informatics 6* (3). Multidisciplinary Digital Publishing Institute, pp. 29.

Zaharieva, M., Mitrović, D., Zeppelzauer, M., & Breiteneder, C. (2011). Film Analysis of Archived Documentaries. *IEEE MultiMedia, 18* (2), p. 38–47.

Zhao, J., & Moere, A. V. (2008). Embodiment in data sculpture: a model of the physical visualization of information. *Proceedings of the 3rd international conference on Digital Interactive Media in Entertainment and Arts*, p. 343–350.

Acknowledgements

This work was partly funded by a grant from the Austrian Science Fund (FWF), project No. P28363-24 and the H2020 research and innovation action InTaVia, project No. 101004825. We want to thank colleagues of both projects for their invaluable contributions and Nicole High-Steskal for a revision of this manuscript.

Placing Wellbeing: Distant Reading Approaches for Exploratory Placial Data Analysis

Dominik Kremer, Blake Byron Walker

Abstract *In the context of the spatial turn in humanities, place-related data and geovisualisations are used frequently to provide deeper insights in broad variety of domains ranging from spatio-temporal traces of historical persons or objects to spatial visualisation of complex scenes and environments. For this purpose, in a practice of mapping, data are often projected to the ubiquitous 2-dimensional artefact of the map. In addition to the well-researched suggestive power of this artefact to reveal (contested) truths, this approach features severe conceptual limitations, particularly when individual perspectives on space and place are brought into consideration. Tim Cresswell argues that "[w]e do not live in landscapes – we [just] look at them"!*

Theory-guided social science practice is well-suited to describe the impacts of digital artefacts and processes, but remains insufficient for facilitating rapid data screenings on a larger-than-case-study scale. Pattern recognition alone presently serves only as a complement to such inquiry, rather than a standalone solution optimised for qualitative data screening and analysis. In this paper, we make first steps towards a scalable solution by demonstrating the utility of semi-automated, theory-informed text mining approaches for offering complementary insights compatible with traditional qualitative methodologies from the social sciences.

In calling for a scalable, text-based, multi-perspective analysis of data representing different conceptualisations of space and place in the health geographies domain, we derive a process model of earlier contextual spatial analysis and empirical discourse analysis. In a second step, we provide examples for an integrated model enhanced by different digital methods, used to produce knowledge that would otherwise go undetected. We comparatively evaluate the outcome of our proposed process model based on earlier studies and derive a research agenda for a general use of those methods in the Digital Humanities.

Keywords: Text Analysis, Phenomenology, Placial GIS, Distant Reading

Introduction

Analysis of placial data can provide deeper insights in a broad variety of domains within Spatial Humanities if conflicting individual conceptualisations of space and place cannot be reified in a simple map. Examples range from spatial imaginations of spatial stages in literature (see Schumacher et al. in this collection) to meanings ascribed to individual spatial trajectories of persons or objects (see Windhager et al. in this collection). Particularly in the context of health geographies and the qualitative turn (Kistemann 2016), one of the most important contributions of theory-guided social sciences is their ability to reveal the impacts of (spatially constructed) social inequalities on human wellbeing (Smith/Easterlow 2005). To extend this goal from traditional conceptualisations focussing on biomedical and physical health into newer domains underscoring mental and social health, environment must be framed not simply as an outside world external to the human body, rather as a subjectively experienced and interpreted landscape where individual differences of a given place at a given time vary widely and are contingent to socialisation, individual preferences, and individual needs (Kistemann 2016). In other words, "[w]e do not live in landscapes – we look at them" (Cresswell 2004, S. 10f). By using this phenomenological approach of being inside the world, mental health geographies have enabled researchers to overcome the spatial trap (Lippuner/Lossau 2004) of Cartesian maps. This is particularly useful in light of the prominence of maps and visualised geodata, as they compete to illustrate and convey the alleged 'true' state of the COVID-19 pandemic, operationalised and leveraged by stakeholders ranging from state authorities to local news media to non-expert publics (see Walker in this collection). A large number of persons engaged these media as a mode of sense-making whilst suffering under isolation measures and fears of an uncertain future (Stadlmeier et al. 2022). Crucial in this regard are the decades of phenomenological theory enabling a switch of perspectives without a loss of conceptual resolution nor methodological power.

In sum, a study in that area shares a fundamental deficit with other disciplines from Digital Humanities: despite the significant potential unlocked by contemporary phenomenology, theory-guided social science practice suffers from an inability to facilitate rapid data screenings on a larger than case-study scale. This limitation is highlighted especially in times of a public crisis, when their timely contribution to the public debate is needed most! In this context, the question arises: how can well-known methods and approaches from the Digital Humanities realm be used to scale-up contemporary health geographies based on a phenomenological perspective? When the Digital Humanities approach is a holistic and hermeneutic one (Jannidis et al. 2017), pattern recognition alone will only act as complement, not as a solution fitted to interpret data. In this paper, we demonstrate the utility of semiautomated, theory-informed text mining approaches for offering complementary insights compatible with traditional qualitative methodologies.

We first show the outstanding value of social theory for Health Geographies (Kistemann 2016), outlining how the linguistic turn in cultural geography was necessary for methodological development to analyse competing productions of space (Dammann 2021) and illuminate potential synergies between Health Geographies and language-based analysis. In a second step we call back to earlier process models from contextual spatial analysis (Kremer/Walker 2022) and empirical discourse analysis (Keller 2010, Mayring 2016, Flick 2017) to propose for an integrated process model providing rapid insights on coping strategies and mental health in times of public crisis. Relying on our previous works (Moura de Souza 2022, Kremer/ Felgenhauer 2022), we demonstrate how the integrated model is used to produce knowledge that would otherwise have been missed. In a final step, we comparatively evaluate the outcome of our proposed process model based on these earlier studies and derive a research agenda for a general use in Digital Humanities.

Analysing Geographies of Wellbeing

Contemporary Health Geographies have eschewed geo-deterministic approaches in favour of dynamic process models focussing on the interaction between individuals in their socio-cultural contexts and the environment (Kistemann 2016). As such, both health and disease are framed as (psycho)social constructs contingent to the individual's perspective and embedded social norms/values (Antonovsky 1979). The term *therapeutic landscapes* is used in this sense to capture the individual, their environment, and the experiential and subjective interplay. These refer not simply to the accumulation of physical objects and features in a given site, rather, they are formed and shaped by social and affective resources bound to those sites and varying for different viewers. Wellbeing in the sense of a salutogenetic (instead of a pathogenetic) approach thus results from a complex and individual state of consciousness bound to place (Trojan und Legewie 2001).

This approach closely resembles the paradigmatic shift from mapping physical space with defined features and attributes to individual places that are the product of individual sense-making in psychosocial, sociopolitical, and cultural contexts associated with emotions and meaning (Cresswell 2004). In this sense, places are differentiated from spaces (spatial features and geodetic delineated objects) in that they are experiential, emotional, and subjective, and as such, are the key objects that connect human beings to their environment (Relph 1976). Places and the individual and socially-mediated expectations of places therefore play an important role in health and wellbeing in a manner that is epistemologically and methodologically differentiated from environmental health. Places are part of our geographically mediated identities, or place-identities (Lengen 2016). Places as semantic units can even provide this expectation if the place itself has never been visited before: feelings of foreignness and insecurity as well as relaxation and wellbeing.

If individual places (as opposed to positivistically defined spaces) are the base of a deeper analysis of human wellbeing in Health Geographies, methodology turns from spatial analysis of geodata to the analysis of social interaction at, and communication about, places. Suitable data covers interviews and protocols of self-reported health (White et al. 2021). Partially, this resembles the general linguistic turn in Cultural and Political Geography (Glasze 2021). For example, local and regional identities, nationalist ideologies, geopolitics, and imaginations of global development depend on stable discursive structures. Geography's perception of discourse theory and methodology has correspondingly intensified since the beginning of the 21st century. Discourse theory and analysis made a profound contribution to our current understanding of how language, society, and politics are intertwined (e.g., Kendall and Wickham, 1999; Chilton 2004; Wodak and Chilton, 2005). Weichhart and Weixlbaumer (1988) and Shortridge (1985) demonstrated that place-images prove to be very stable and independent from material changes in the "real world". Thus, sociocultural concepts are more likely to shift in spatial reference than their associated semantics. One example from the health domain is the analysis of the use of spatial metaphor to explain and govern the COVID-19 pandemic (Kremer/Felgenhauer 2022; Walker, in this collection).

In addition to an examination of political structures and socioeconomic inequalities, Health Geographies are interested in a detailed analysis of how individual sense-making of places is (re)produced and socially mediated in the context of human health and disease. This approach, loosely attached to the concept of symbolic interactionism (Keller 2016) can help to identify measures to rearrange therapeutic places and landscapes to the needs of public health (Bell et al. 2018). Discourse theory and analysis were originally seen as a counterpart to the perspective of cognitive linguistics. However, in the current linguistic discussion "discourse" and "individual sense-making" are no longer to be treated as mutually exclusive theoretical approaches. Instead, connections between experiential cognitive structure and the external societal context are increasingly explored (Hampe 2017). This opens qualitative analysis of interview data on self-reported health for distant reading approaches from the Digital Humanities and social sciences (Moretti 2013).

Implementing Qualitative Text Analysis

While Dammann et al. (2021) provide a thorough introduction for the use of basic lexicometric methods in cultural geography, Kremer (2018) proposes a generic approach for phenomenological place-related modelling in the specific context of city tourism. Other than methods from computational text analysis (Jurafsky 2009) or computational grounded theory (Nelson 2017, Berente/Seidel 2014*, see also Evans/Acedes 2016*) both do not aim at implementing machine learning approaches, but instead to carefully integrate methods generating additional results into conventional qualitative workflows in an exploratory manner. As an important consequence, results produced can be compared to existing theoretical frameworks in the field, in a more consistent manner than computational approaches that are difficult to explain within conceptual frameworks of the social sciences.

Accordingly, in a next step, we extract common workflows of qualitative text analysis to identify their potential for the analysis of individual sense-making in the context of Health Geographies. In doing so, we largely rely on the methodological framework for qualitative social research set up by Flick (2017). Flick frames the research process as an open one: structures (of the social world) appear step by step when working with the text data collected in an explorative manner. As more and more data is available digitally, even the process of data compilation contains an option for assistance systems supporting the filtering and selecting data for further analysis. Beside social theory providing the ground for a later comparison of results with expectations, unbiased analysis of the data is key for the discovery and production of new findings. Flick recommends an iterative approach: starting with in-vivo-codes, i.e., concepts that are stated explicitly in the text data, differences and context markers are extracted by the researcher and inform both, stepwise aggregation of concepts to codes as well as the (filter and) selection process of the next chunk of data. Flick explicitly names switching methods between exploration steps as valid means for producing new results. This research process is largely compatible with Mayring (2016). Main component is the break-up of texts in an open coding approach to identify key categories and their relationships with the goal of thorough analysis of the (social) contexts of individual action. Like Flick, Mayring proposes to use stepwise selection and aggregation in this process. However, despite explicitly naming methods of computer-aided categorisation both authors do not propose methods to assist and scale the research process itself and not only organising it digitally. Table 1 shows a simplified workflow model of the traditional process of qualitative text analysis.

Table 1: The traditional process of qualitative text analysis (adapted from Mayring 2016)

Workflow step	description
Sample selection	After choosing a specific corpus, a sampling technique (worst case manual search) is defined to obtain material to be analysed
Theoretical framing	Defining the perspective and conceptual framework in which knowledge is produced and interpreted
Definition of units of analysis	Key concepts are identified that provide information on the research question while looking at the data
Analysis	Analysis is performed summarising, explicating and structuring data
Interpretation of results	Binding back obtained results to the theoretical and conceptual framework chosen

Enabling the Process – Three Flavours

Recent methodological approaches in health geographies call for an integration of more (theory-based) context to data analyses (Kremer/Walker 2022, see Walker in this collection). Vice versa, digitally enabled processes of explorative qualitative text analysis can help to identify key concepts and their relations on larger corpora in a shorter amount of time, thus stabilising scientific findings from social studies. In essence, this can be done in at least three ways in congruence with the traditional process model introduced above: (1) filtering by keyword, (2) extraction of language use patterns and (3) explorative relation mining based on cooccurrences.

Basically, we rely on the large number of linguistic methods that have been already adapted to the needs of social sciences (Scholz, 2018). As recommended by Stefanowitsch (2007), we propose an iterative approach for the stepwise exploration of the data in congruence with the requirements of qualitative text analysis. In a first step, texts can be scanned for patterns in the microcontext, e.g., specific lexicalised word sequences or frequently cooccurring terms (Hilpert, 2007) to gain insights about the prominence of specific concepts. An example is to search for occurrences of the term 'war' to look for metaphors of fight in a study on disruptive products in a specific market.

Bubenhofer (2009, 2015) proposes to look for recurring language usage patterns in the environment of specific search terms. In his approach, language usage patterns are defined by collocations, i.e., an exact sequence of a specific number of words. These ordered sequences can be generalised to skip-grams and conc-grams (Cheng et al. 2006) to reflect syntactical variances or circumpositions in grammatical structures. These language usage patterns can include part of speech tags as variables, e.g., by setting the third constituent to a proper noun in general. An example of is to look for a pattern like:

<COVID>+<$,>?<KOKOM>?<NE|NN>+

Where <COVID>+ covers one or more search terms associated with the COVID-19 pandemic, <$,>? none or one comma, <KOKOM>? none or one comparative particle, e.g. 'like' or 'as' followed by one or more (proper) nouns. Of course, those grammatical structures are language dependent and have to be fine-tuned for any language in the study corpus. The current example is an efficient way to look for metaphors of analogy associated with the COVID-19 pandemic in the German language (Kremer/ Felgenhauer 2022). Also, all grammatically valid rearrangements have to be considered.

Other than collocations or skip-grams, cooccurrences generalise form a specific word sequence by considering all terms in a certain context window (e.g., a sentence or a paragraph) to be collocated (Evert, 2009). Basic representation is a set or list of lemmas occurring in the chosen context window (Jurafsky and Martin, 2009). Mining concept relations (e.g., Haarmann, 2014) is possible on that level by comparing mutual association between all co-occurrent terms at that level. One very simple metric that is easy to understand and thus easy to integrate in qualitative analysis workflows is association rule mining (Hipp, 2000). As asymmetric cooccurrence measure it allows for an assessment of the confidence of cooccurring terms with respect to all of their single occurrences respectively.

Figure 1 illustrates the process using a simplified fictional example (see Moura de Souza et al. 2022): "We live in Hamburg. We find Hamburg to be a nice city. Our cat is with us in Hamburg. The cat ran away to Berlin." After selecting the nouns 'cat', 'city', 'Berlin', and 'Hamburg' from a text corpus, the occurrences of each word are counted. 'Cat' occurs in two sentences, 'city' in one, 'Berlin' in one, and 'Hamburg' in three. Association rules are then computed based on asymmetric cooccurrences: because 'cat' occurs alongside one of the three occurrences of 'Hamburg', the term 'Hamburg' points with an estimated confidence of 0.33 to the context of 'cat'. However, as 'Hamburg' occurs in only one of the two occurrences of 'cat', the term 'cat' is bound to the context of 'Hamburg' with an estimated confidence of 0.5.

Figure 1: Example graph built from association rules

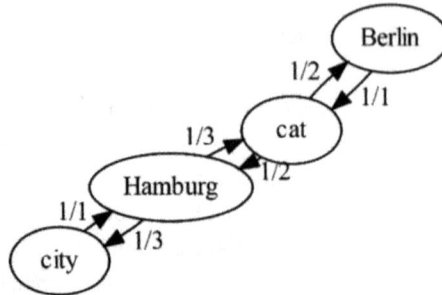

In essence, the extracted association rules provide in-sights into significant bindings from noun-terms to their context-terms. In the example, 'Hamburg' is bound to 'city' with low confidence, as it cooccurs only in 1 of its 3 occurrences. Vice versa, 'city' is bound to 'Hamburg' with high confidence, as it only occurs in this context. Of course, results must not be interpreted at such low frequencies. Minimal term frequency and minimal confidence level thus form the parameters of this analyse that can be readjusted according to the corpus. Further, more than random cooccurrences can be accessed via Log Likelihood Ratio (e.g., Kolesnikova 2016). As associations are represented as rules pointing from one term to another, annotated with confidence, association rules define a graph representing the semantic network of context bindings of a specific text fragment which allows for further inference (e.g., application of centrality measures, see Elo 2022).

Table 2: Digitally enhanced model of qualitative text analysis

Workflow step	Digital support of workflow step
Sample selection	Sample selection can be supported by any filter mechanism, e.g., a search term list
Theoretical framing	(ontological consistency)
Definition of units of analysis	Identified key concepts can be formalised to filter their occurrences in the preselected sample
Analysis	Structuring data is the main advantage of automated text analysis. To a limited degree, also summarising is supported (e.g., Allahyari et al. 2017Q).
Interpretation of results	Interpretation of the results as scientific sense- making is completely up to the qualitative researcher

Table 2 shows how the workflow of table 1 can be assisted by digital methods. Remember that it is not our desire to solve steps automatically, but to help the qualitative researcher to accelerate and complement their findings. According to the three options identified, filtering for search terms or language use patterns can assist the process of sample selection. Structural analysis or even summarising can aid the actual analysis process.

The only additional precondition is that key concepts are formalised in a way that makes them available for automated processing alongside the data. Even the theoretical framing might profit from ontological consistency checks in the future. Only the interpretation of the results as an act of scientific sense-making is completely up to the researcher.

Results from first Evaluations

The proposed process model has been evaluated in two recent publications (Moura de Souza et al. 2022 and Kremer/Felgenhauer 2022). This allows for an assessment of the advantages and disadvantages of our approach. In both publications, we used the quantitative extensions to complement our qualitative findings.

Moura de Souza et al. (2022) identified spatial conceptualisations of unsafety in Recife, Brazil. 12 qualitative interviews were conducted with different stakeholders confronted with everyday unsafety in Recife, e.g., police, physicians and teachers. All of them were asked about their biographical background and to reflect on places which they associate with unsafety. After that a map showing recent events of gun shootings was shown to the interviewees to provoke reactions and comparisons with individual experiences. After a complete qualitative analysis had been done, we used association rule mining on the interview data to obtain additional insights that we might have overlooked otherwise.

Over all, maps were not prominent as sources for assessing unsafety on an everyday basis. Instead, participants used a combination of three sources: (1) reports from their individual network of trusted colleagues, family, or friends; (2) prominent TV shows like Cardinot, which act as an information multiplier by soliciting, synthesising, and selectively disseminating VGI via social media; and (3) local knowledge from various sources redistributed through social media. Accordingly, our context analysis revealed the personal background in which the interviewees were confronted with unsafety. Since the police officers were involved in fighting drug trade in the metropolitan area Recife, it became evident that they often mentioned place names in connection with drug-related violence (figure 2).

Figure 2: Association rule graph of cooccurrents of crime named by police members

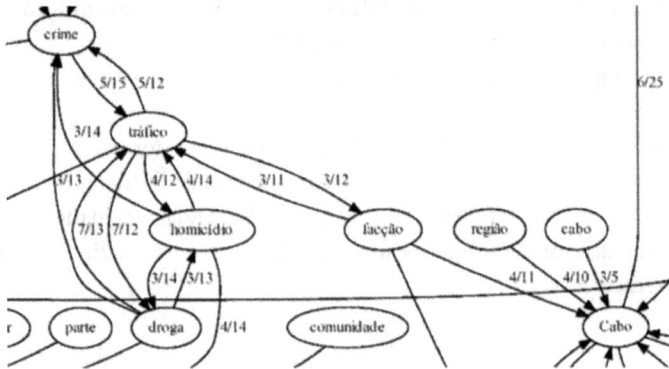

Even more interestingly, interviews with local residents revealed the level of spatiality unsafety is ascribed to. Embedded within our theoretical framing in phenomenological place geography like proposed in the beginning, unsafety proved to form an over-complexe problem that can not be attributed easily to specific place names (even less to spaces), rather to vague high-level regions instead (figure 3). Also, naming public transportation as unsafe, everyday sense-making might not be bound to places but also to types of mobility (Cresswell 2006). In combination with the (social) media sources of the participants, we learned that unsafety is not needed in a high spatial resolution, but rather in a high temporal resolution on an everyday basis within a network of trust, a task not supported by current map services at all.

Figure 3: 'regiao', 'bairro', and 'area' as spatial concept in the concept of unsafety

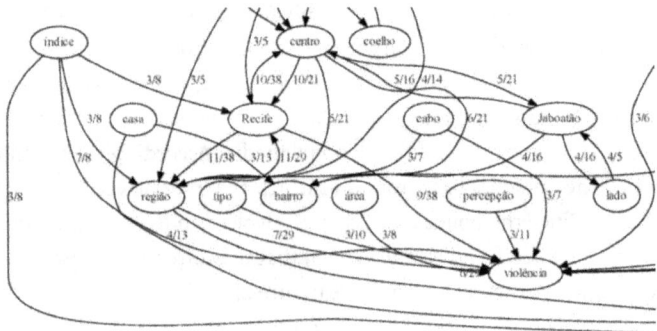

Kremer/Felgenhauer (2022) used the proposed framework to identify spatial metaphors in early narratives of the COVID-19 pandemic in public media. Crises discourses are well known to make use of spatial metaphor for several purposes. In general, the pandemic forms a *capsular place* not attached to any specific location (Bissell, 2021). War metaphors are very productive, both indicating a connotation of seriousness and urgency (Semino, 2021) and calling for defensive actions and victory conditions (Chapman and Miller, 2020). Especially in the beginning of the COVID-19 pandemic, common defensive tactics of *othering* known from reactions to other diseases like AIDS (Craig, 2020) were applied to attach the disease to racial or regional attributes (see also Kremer, 2020). But other than spatial metaphors used in the context of diseases like cancer (*spread*), the war on COVID seems to be primarily structured temporally (*waves*, see Craig, 2020). Semino (2021) proposes to discuss the alternative metaphor of *fire fighting* that involves deliberate application of measures.

After conducting a qualitative pre-study, we were able to identify different pattern of spatial metaphor in the corpus on COVID-19:

- Toponyms: Toponyms like Wuhan, Ischgl or New York were used to identify hotspots (a metaphor of its own) of the pandemic
- Containerisation & Spatialisation: Spatial generalisation of toponym to surrounding regions was used to identify areas with increased risk in narratives. Othering was used then to infer which regions and places do not belong to those regions and are thus not directly affected.
- Naturalisation & Natural disaster: By framing the pandemic as wildfire, tsunami or wave the rapid and uncontrollable manner of the developing pandemic is highlighted.
- Personification (or metonymy, see Littlemore 2015): By framing the pandemic as person, intentions and possible counteractions can be derived.

These early findings were then used to explore the corpus further. For this purpose, indicators consisting of term lists or language usage patterns were defined that act as filters (see section 4). All of these filters were then applied programmatically on all sentences of the corpus that contained a term indicating a reference on the COVID-19 pandemic. Figure 6 shows all used filters. In a second step, we explored intermediate results any time by applying association rule mining. Hypotheses derived were then compared with the original sentences that qualified for one of the filters applied.

Table 3: Filters applied by term list or skip-grams

Search pattern	Type of analysis	Condition
Personification	Structural collocation	Part of speech tag sequence equals <COVID>[1]+<VVFIN>[2]+ or <VVFIN>+<COVID>+
Toponym	Named entity recognition	Named entity tag equals 'LOC'
Spatialisation	Search term list	['Grenze', 'Region']
Naturalisation	Search term list	['Epizentrum', 'Hotspot', 'Sturm', 'Tsunami', 'Welle']
Analogy	Structural collocation	Part of speech tag sequence equals <COVID>+<$,>?<KOKOM>?<NE\|NN>+ or <NE\|NN>+<$,>?<KOKOM>[3]?<COVID>+

As in Moura de Souza et al. (2022), we were able to look at the granularity of toponyms after having extracted them automatically. Interestingly, most prominent use of toponyms was associated not primarily with places of high incidence values, but more to the level of political action (e.g., 'Berlin'). As immediate coordinated responses were only possible on the national and supranational level, spatial containers (e.g., 'Italy', 'Germany', 'Europe') dominated the use of toponyms. Tracking hotspots, boulevard media showed a higher tendency to pin the COVID-19 pandemic to specific place names than high-quality journalism. We were able to show that specific place names (e.g., 'Ischgl') were often used as an external source of infections and as a reason to reject local responsibility.

As a pattern not pre-informed by our qualitative exploration of the data, interestingly, patterns analogy revealed a number of ad hoc framings of the pandemic. Consistent with metaphors of natural disasters, we found 'wildfire', but also 'fire accelerator' as a metaphor indicating the catalytic function of the pandemic under specific socio-economic conditions. More abstractly, the pandemic was framed as a challenge or thread, in two cases metaphorically framed as 'Sword of Damocles'.

Places in Texts: A General Framework?

Our framework has proven to ease investigation of a number of questions in Health Geographies. Textual data representing self-reported health, open interviews or secondary corpora can help to identify previously unnoticed challenges or implications for social and public health. At the same time, binding this type of analysis in a specific theoretical framework – a phenomenological one in the case of Health Geographies – requires careful integration of digital methods. When looking at places produced by sense-making of individuals and not at essentialist outside spaces, a traditional spatial data analysis would not have provided congruent results for our perspective. In the query for suitable methods, Digital Humanities provided the perfect middle ground to overcome both traditional qualitative text analysis that has only been represented in software as well as computational approaches that "bypass human coders altogether" (Krippendorff 2004, 259). This holds even more for a phenomenological setting in which individual human sense-making is key to a deeper understanding of the needs of society. A real step ahead in scaling and complementing qualitative research must thus align itself with the research process and workflows.

The framework explored in our explorative studies revealed structural as well as singular knowledge that we might have overlooked otherwise. Filtering for language usage patterns was not only far more efficient than looking up manually, generic patterns like analogy proved to reveal additional contexts of individual sense-making that might have escaped us in a manual coding process. Structural analysis of interviews and news media by association rule mining enabled the secondary analysis of the spatial granularity and context in which specific health-related phenomena – urban unsafety and the situation of a pandemic respectively – are negotiated in everyday discourses and narratives. In both cases, this analysis led to scrutinising the research perspective itself. While our initial perspective was a spatial (or placial) one, both phenomena – unsafety as well as the pandemic – proved to have an essential temporal dimension on an everyday scale that pushed vague spatial components into the mere function of narration for the purpose of sense-making. Unsafety is only vaguely attributed on a neighbourhood level whereas public transportation can be regarded as unsafe while local inhabitants look for updated information on very short temporal scales. Toponyms in tellings of the pandemic were used to address the level of political negotiation and counter-action more than the level of actual transmission and incidences. At the same time, place names were used to push the effects of the pandemic outside the scope of established habits and routines. Even the spread of the virus itself was framed by fast-running natural processes like wildfires or waves.

Of course, as we used rough indicators, our current approach still produces a lot of false positives when looking for language usage patterns and of course not all instances of a phenomenon under investigation were detected, but we were able to trim down the sheer amount of text by magnitudes while offering a complementary perspective on the data. As association rule mining requires a certain level of frequency and confidence to act as structural exploration of the data, our instrument used was not sensitive enough to reveal interesting speech acts at the scale of the individual. At the same time, identifying structural patterns on corpus level will result in semantic networks too large to explore. We can report best experiences when combining association rule mining with preset filters that reveal the structure of the semantic context of the result set. We can also report that all methods used were easy to communicate to the research partners familiar with qualitative coding only.

Conclusion

The conceptual shift in Spatial Humanities from objectivist space to individual places has opened a new powerful conceptual perspective carried by phenomenology that has not been nearly explored nor digitally enabled yet. We argue that well-known methods from language processing in Digital Humanities can help both accelerate and complement traditional qualitative text analysis when integrated carefully into established research workflow. In our understanding, Digital Humanities does not mean that processes that have been established before are not represented digitally. Nor does it mean that established workflows are completely replaced by automated recognition. In essence, we call for a dedicated Digital Humanities approach that aligns methodological innovation and exploration both with established theoretical perspectives and research workflows.

In our contribution, we first analysed traditional workflows of qualitative text analysis and then identified possible enrichments by methods from the Digital Humanities. We report from two earlier studies that made use of the framework. In both cases, complementary and well-aligned integration of additional computer-aided steps into the traditional workflow of qualitative text analysis proved to provide additional insights of the research question under investigation. As integrating association rule mining is partially experimental, we can report that we obtained best results when applying it to prefiltered corpora. At the same time a big advantage of the approach is that its results were very easy to communicate to our research partners only familiar with qualitative research.

Recently, in health geographies there has been the proposal of a process model for the careful consideration of context while conducting spatial analysis (Kremer/Walker 2022). In this paper, we extend this for the support of a specific conceptual and theory-based framework while using language-based methods well known from the Digital Humanities. A further integration of the two approaches will help to enhance and solidify recent methodological developments not only in geographies of health and wellbeing but in Spatial Humanities in general.

References

Allahyari, M., Pouriyeh, S., Assefi, M., Safaei, S., Trippe, E. D., Gutierrez, J. B., & Kochut, K. (2017). Text summarization techniques: a brief survey. *arXiv* preprint arXiv:1707.02268.

Antonovsky, A. (1979). *Health, stress and coping*. San Francisco: Jossey-Bass Publishers.

Bell, S. et al. (2018). From therapeutic landscapes to healthy spaces, places and practices: A scoping review. *Social Science and Medicine, 196*, p. 123–130.

Berente N, Seidel S. (2014): Big Data & Inductive Theory Development: Towards Computational Grounded Theory? *Proceedings of the Americas Conference on Information Systems*, 20th, Savannah. AIS Electronic Library (AISeL), https://core.ac.uk/reader/301361940.

Bubenhofer, N. (2009). *Sprachgebrauchsmuster: Korpuslinguistik als Methode der Diskurs- und Kulturanalyse*. De Gruyter, Berlin/New York.

Cheng, W. et al (2006). From n-gram to skipgram to concgram. *International Journal of Corpus Analyitics, Volume 11*, issue 4, p.411–433.https://doi.org/10.1075/ijcl.11.4.04che.

Chilton P. (2004). *Analysing Political Discourse. Theory and Practice*. Routledge, London

Cresswell, T. (2004). *Place: a short introduction*. Black.

Cresswell, T. (2006). *On the move: Mobility in the modern western world. Taylor* & Francis.

Dammann, F., Dzudzek, I., Glasze, G., Mattissek, A., & Schirmel, H. (2021). 14 Verfahren der lexikometrisch- computerlinguistischen Analyse von Textkorpora. In Glasze, G., Mattissek, A. (eds.), *Handbuch Diskurs und Raum* (p. 313–344). transcript Verlag.

Elo, K. (2022). A Text Network Analysis of Discursive Changes in German, Austrian and Swiss New Year's Speeches 2000–2021. *Digitial Humanities Quaterly, 16* (1). http://www.digitalhumanities.org//dhq/vol/16/1/000598/000598.html.

Evans, J. A., & Aceves, P. (2016). Machine Translation: Mining Text for Social Theory. *Annual Review of Sociology, 42*(1), p. 21–50, https://doi.org/10.1146/annurev-soc-081715-074206.

Evert S. (2009). Corpora and collocations. In Lüdeling A., Kytö M. (eds) *Corpus Linguistics. An International Handbook*, de Gruyter, Berlin, p. 1212–1248.

Flick, U. (2017). *Qualitative Sozialforschung: Eine Einführung*. 8. Aufl., Hamburg: Rowohlt.

Gebhard, U., & Kistemann, T. (2016). *Landschaft, Identität und Gesundheit. Zum Konzept der Therapeutischen Landschaften*. Springer, Wiesbaden.

Glasze, G., & Mattissek, A. (Eds.). (2021). *Handbuch Diskurs und Raum: Theorien und Methoden für die Humangeographie sowie die sozial-und kulturwissenschaftliche Raumforschung* (Vol. 11). transcript Verlag.

Haarmann B. (2014). *Ontology On Demand. Vollautomatische Ontologieerstellung aus deutschen Texten mithilfe moderner Textmining-Prozesse*. epubli GmbH, Berlin.

Hampe B. (2017). Embodiment and Discourse: Dimensions and Dynamics of Contemporary Metaphor Theory. In Hampe B (ed) *Metaphor. Embodied Cognition and Discourse*. Cambridge University Press, Cambridge, p. 3–24.

Hipp J., Güntzer U., Nakhaeizadeh G. (2000). Algorithms for association rule mining – a general survey and comparison. *ACM sigkdd explor newsl* 2(1), p. 58–64.

Hilpert M. (2007). Keeping an eye on the data: Metonymies and their patterns. In Stefanowitsch A., Gries S.T. (eds.), *Corpus-based approaches to metaphor and metonymy* (Vol 171). (p. 123–151). de Gruyter, Berlin.

Jannidis F, Kohle H., Rehbein M. (Eds.). (2017). *Digital Humanities. Eine Einführung*. J.B. Metzler, Stuttgart.

Jurafsky D., Martin J.H. (2009). *Speech and Language Processing: An Introduction to Natural Language Processing, Speech Recognition, and Computational Linguistics*. 2nd edition. Prentice-Hall, Upper Saddle River.

Kendall G., Wickham G. (1999). *Using Foucault's Methods*. SAGE, London/Thousand Oaks/New Delhi. Kolesnikova, O. (2016). Survey of word co-occurrence measures for collocation detection. *Computación y Sistemas*, 20(3), 327–344.

Keller, R. (Ed.). (2010). *Handbuch Sozialwissenschaftliche Diskursanalyse*: Forschungspraxis (Vol. 2). 4th edition. Springer-Verlag. https://doi.org/10.14361/978383945 9584-021.

Kremer D. (2018). *Rekonstruktion von Orten als sozialem Phänomen: Geoinformatische Analyse semantisch annotierter Verhaltensdaten* (Vol. 30). University of Bamberg Press, Bamberg.

Kremer, D., Felgenhauer, T. (2022). Reasoning COVID-19: the use of spatial metaphor in times of a crisis. Humanities and Social Sciences Communications, 9(1), 1–15.

Kremer D., Walker B. (2022). Geodaten quantitativ, aber kritisch analysieren: die Methode der explorativen räumlichen Datenanalyse am Beispiel von COVID-19 in Brasilien. In Dammann F., Michel B. (Eds.), *Handbuch Kritisches Kartieren*. (p. 307–324). Bielefeld.

Lengen, C., (2016b). Place Identity. Identitätskonstituierende Funktionen von Ort und Landschaft. In U. Gebhard, & T. Kistemann (Eds.), *Landschaft – Identität – Gesundheit. Zum Konzept der Therapeutischen Landschaften* (p. 185–199). Wiesbaden: Springer VS.

Lippuner, R. & Lossau, J. (2004). In der Raumfalle. Eine Kritik des spatial turn in den Sozialwissenschaften. DOI: 10.14361/9783839402160-003.

Littlemore J. (2015). *Metonymy*. Cambridge University Press, Cambridge.

Mayring, P. (2016). *Qualitative Inhaltsanalyse. Grundlagen und Techniken*. 13. überarb. Aufl. Beltz.

Operationalising Territories in 16th-Century Europe: A Critical Reflection on Spatial Concepts

Ramona Roller

Abstract *Why did some places become protestant whereas others remained catholic as a result of the European Reformation? To find large-scale patterns across these places, I operationalise the territory of a ruler, since, in the 16th century, he was the one choosing the denomination for his subjects. However, operationalisation is challenging because territories were complicated structures. In this article, I critically discuss the operationalisation of territories. I identify the main historical characteristics of territories and describe how they could be optimally operationalised. I show that the implementation of this optimal approach is currently infeasible due to data scarcity and a large number of assumptions. As an alternative, I present a simplified operationalisation based on vectorised surface geometries. Despite its historical inaccuracy, I show that this simplified operationalisation enables ecologically valid interpretations of neighbourhoods and the analysis of small localities for which the corresponding ruler and his denomination are unknown. The article highlights the need for a diversity of operationalisations and proposes future directions on how data should be gathered to improve the historical representations of territories.*

Keywords: Operationalisation, Reformation, Holy Roman Empire, Map Vectorisation, H-GIS

Introduction

The adoption of Protestantism during the European Reformation is associated with many societal changes, including state formation (Reinhard 1999, Schilling 1986), economic output (Weber 1930), literacy (Becker/Woessmann 2009), secularisation (Cantoni et al 2018), and national identity (Watling 2001, Zachhuber 2020). Due to this wide-ranging impact, it is relevant to ask why some places back then became protestant whereas others remained catholic. To find large-scale patterns across these places, quantitative methods can be used, which require operationalisation.

That is, we have to translate abstract concepts from our question, such as 'place' or its 'denomination', into measures.

However, operationalisation is challenging since concepts are ambiguous and appropriate data are often scarce. In this article, I critically discuss the operationalisations required for the above question of why places became protestant. I argue that point-specific representations of places that are interconnected by power relations between princes and subject to geographic spillovers captures the historical concept best. Since a lack of data and a large number of assumptions prevent the practical implementation of this 'optimal' operationalisation, I present a simplified one based on vectorised surface geometries.

The resulting data are publicly available and can be used to study the impact of geo-political space on socio-economic processes during the Reformation. As such, this article enhances quantitative studies in historical sociology and economic history. Moreover, I describe the steps to generate these spatial data from maps in detail (see Appendix). This documentation provides a hands-on guide for practitioners and should encourage wider use of spatial data in the Digital Humanities. By conceptualising the spatial representation of 16th-century territories, this article provides a theoretical contribution to the perception of space during the Reformation, which is relevant for historiographical research.

In the 16th century, the main political structure in Central Europe was the Holy Roman Empire (HRE), a lose amalgamation of hundreds of territories, each ruled by a prince and held together by the emperor. The prince imposed his denominational choice onto his subjects, whereby he could choose among Catholicism and several protestant denominations, such as Lutheranism, Zwinglian-Reformed, or Calvinism (Harrington/Walser Smith 1997). Although this practice only became official law with the Peace of Augsburg in 1555, princes already practiced it in the decades beforehand and the emperor often tolerated it. The large number of individual denominational decisions by the princes makes the HRE a good use case for statistical analyses.

Addressing the question of why places became protestant during the Reformation is challenging for two reasons: the outcome variable and the unit of analysis are ill-defined. First, the outcome variable is ill-defined because it is unclear when a place is considered to be protestant. Although the prince officially chose the denomination for his subjects, in practice the situation was more complicated. Tolerant princes often allowed the simultaneous practice of several denominations (e.g., Strasbourg), whereas the subjects of less tolerant princes practiced unofficial denominations underground (e.g., Baptists in Zwinglian-Reformed Zürich). Moreover, this denominational situation was highly dynamic due to frequent political changes (e.g., Electoral Palatinate)[1]. Since data on these denominational ambiguities, let alone on numbers of practitioners per denomination and place, do not exist, we adopt a simplifying assumption for this article: The denomination of a place equals the official denominational choice of the prince[2] for which data exist.

Second, given the assumption above, the unit of analysis in our question is ill-defined because it is unclear which places were affected by the denominational choice of a prince. These affected places must be those that are under the rule of the prince and therefore are part of the prince's territory. But how can we measure this territory, i.e., operationalise it?

The aim of this contribution is to provide a critical guide for the operationalisation of territories in the 16th century. I identify the main characteristics that describe the historical nature of territories and suggest how to operationalise them if resources were not restricted. I present an alternative operationalisation which represents territories as surface geometries and show how even historically inaccurate assumptions can add value to empirical analyses. The article highlights the need for a diversity of operationalisations and proposes future directions on how data should be gathered to improve the historical representations of territories.

Territories in the 16th Century

The territory of a prince defines the geographic area under his rule. To operationalise territories, I first capture their historical characteristics and later try to measure these. The closer the measure matches the main aspects of the historical situation with respect to our question of interest, the higher the validity of our operationalisation, i.e., we measure what we are supposed to measure. I emphasise that the focus lies on the *main* historical characteristics rather than *any*, because operationalisation should reveal the essence of a territory rather than negligible characteristics.

Historiographical research has identified three characteristics of territories in the 16th century that I consider relevant for the question of why territories became protestant. First, territories are point-specific. Places and localities are the constituents of territories rather than the connecting space in-between (Gotthard

---

1   The Electoral Palatinate became Lutheran in 1556, Calvinist in 1563, Lutheran again in 1576, Calvinist again in 1583, and after some changes in the context of the Thirty Years War, catholic again in 1622 and afterwards.

2   Although the political situation on religious matters was unclear in the 16th century (Cantoni 2012), imperial statements encouraged princes to demonstrate leadership in the denominational choice. For example, the final declaration of the Diet of Speyer (1526) says that princes should 'behave in religious matters as they may hope and trust to answer before God and his Imperial Majesty'. The Peace of Augsburg passed this statement to liability stating that 'Whose realm, whose religion'.

2003). Travel reports reveal that the affiliation of a place to a prince is unambiguously known in the population, whereas the space between places remains unmentioned. This prince-to-place mapping existed independent of the size of the place or power of the prince: affiliations were known from small villages to large towns and from lords to electors.

Second, territories are dependent on power-relations between princes. The rights of a prince not only depended on his own status (e.g., weak count vs powerful elector) but also on political dependencies with other princes. Powerful princes could impose their denominational choice onto their territories, but weaker princes often waited and copied the choice of more powerful ones (Cantoni 2012, Roller et al. 2022). Different types of dependencies further differentiated the influence among princes. For example, in bailiwicks, princes only had as much power as their protecting power granted them.[3] Condominates were shared territories of several princes, often brothers, who inherited land together.[4] Feudal relations existed between princes where one prince had to provide parts of his subjects' harvest or military support to another prince in exchange for protection.[5]

Third, territories are subject to spillover effects between their neighbours. Since trade was concentrated locally (Epstein 2013), trade routes between neighbours increased information exchange, and religious practices could easily spillover from one territory to another. In contrast to power-relations, spillovers are a geographic property and not necessarily related to power. For example, imperial knights provided bishops in neighbouring Bamberg despite being equally powerful as the city council (Ninness 2011). However, in practice, power relations often influenced spillovers between neighbours leading to entangled dependencies between territories (Cantoni 2012, Roller et al. 2022).

Despite these three main characteristics, the picture of historical territories is incomplete. Other factors have been proposed to have shaped territories, such as stem duchies, biased historical sources, and discrepancies between written and practiced law. However, I currently lack evidence to understand their precise impact.

Consider the case of stem duchies. Originating from old Germanic and Celtic tribes, four stem duchies were introduced in the 6th century to help Merowingian kings govern their large Franconian Empire (Swabia, Bavaria, Saxony, Lorraine)[6] (Schneidmüller 2000, Tacitus 1877). They represented divisions of the population

---

3   E.g., many Swiss Kantons were bailiwicks of the Habsburgs in Austria.

4   E.g., the municipality of Kürnbach in the south-west of Germany was a condominate between the landgrave of Hesse-Darmstadt and the Duke of Württemberg.

5   E.g., feudal knights along the Rhine obtained feuds from the Elector of the Palatinate and from the Duke of Württemberg.

6   After the Karolingian times Franconia was added as a fifth stem duchy.

based on ethnic, judicial, military-political, and cultural similarities[7] (Goetz 1981: 35), and even after their dissolution (mainly in the 13th century), shaped geo-political decisions during the Reformation, such as the formation of political alliances[8] and the formation of imperial circles.[9] Given that stem duchies shaped regional identities, their uniting power may have worked across the affiliation between territories and princes in the 16th century. For example, if two territories had been part of the same stem duchy, their subjects may have rather been attracted by former shared traditions than manners imposed by their current princes.

In addition, the historiographical view on territories is biased since it is based on travel reports from mostly rich individuals and neglects the perspective of the immobile part of the population who actually experienced the rule of the prince (Gotthard 2003). Last, discrepancies between written and practiced law may also reshape the historiographical view on territories, since historical sources tend to focus on the official aspects of law and neglect how it was executed in daily life.

In summary, historiographical research has revealed three main characteristics of territories: point-specific, shaped by power relations, and by geographic spillovers. Yet, the precise historical nature of territories remains unclear or inaccessible. This vagueness is not specific to the study of territories, but applies to all abstract concepts, whether historical or modern. Due to this vagueness, an operationalisation can never fully capture the real-world concept but always simplifies it.

The 'Optimal' Operationalisation

Based on the main characteristics of territories identified above, I formulate requirements for an 'optimal' operationalisation. That is, what should optimal measures look like that capture the historical notion of territories. I critically discuss to what extent this operationalisation can be realised in practice. My findings show that the proposed operationalisation is only ostensibly optimal: it requires many assumptions, data sets which are not available yet, and similar to historiographical

---

7   People in the same stem duchy shared a common language, tribal law, structure of the army, tribal gatherings, and traditions.

8   For example, alliances formed between cities (Swabian Leagues (1331, 1376, 1488)), between peasants (Swabian, Franconian), and between imperial knights (Swabian and Franconian 'Ritterkreise').

9   Imperial circles were administrative groupings of several territories to organise military defense and collect taxes. In 1500, six imperial circles were created (Bavarian, Franconian, Saxon, Swabian, Upper Rhenish, Lower Rhenish-Westphalian), which were extended in 1512 by the Austrian, Burgundian, and the Electoral Rhenish Circle, and modified by splitting the Saxon Circle into the Lower and Upper Saxon Circle.

research itself, does not capture the full complexity of historical territories. Hence, this 'optimal' operationalisation is currently infeasible for practical usage.

Requirements of the 'optimal' operationalisation

Point-specific. The constituents of territories were places and localities, rather than the space in between. To capture this property, towns and villages should form the unit of analysis of a territory. Princes are mapped onto these places if they are identified as the ruling entity for that place (Fig. 1a). Bipartite networks[10] are suitable to represent this relational nature of territories. Nodes correspond to princes and places, and binary edges to affiliations with territories. Historical travel reports and the 'German Cities Book' (Deutsches Städtebuch) could serve as sources for this mapping (Butzbach 1918, Dussler 1968, Faber 1923, Keyser/Stoob 1939–1974, Kiechel 1866, Klenner 1751, Vincentz 1918). In the best case, there is a one-to-one mapping of a place to a prince.

Power relations between princes. Territories were shaped by power-relations between princes. The power of prince A over a place C depended on the relation of prince A with another prince B (e.g., feudal relation, condominate princes). In contrast to the point-specific property, rule is no longer binary, but continuous. Princes can share power and weaken/strengthen each other's power. We can extend the network representation of the point-specific property to also include relations between princes that influence the prince-place relations, (Fig. 1b). Biographies of princes (Edel 1999, Grimm 1953, Schubert 1961) and case studies of territories (Schindling/Ziegler 1989–1995, Wolgast 2014) could serve as sources for prince-prince relations and their impact on prince-place relations.

Spillovers between places. Territories were subject to spillovers between their neighbours. The power of prince A over a place C depended on the relation between place C and place D. We can extend the network from the power-relations property by accounting for relations between places that influence prince-place relations (Fig. 1c). Many options exist to define relations between places, i.e., defining neighbourhoods, such as geographic distance or connections via trade routes. Studies on cities (Keyser 1939–1974), transport networks (Becker et al. 2020), and political alliances (Wurpts et al. 2018) could serve as sources for place-place relations and their impact on prince-place relations.

---

10   A bipartite network connects two types of nodes, such as actors and films, genes and proteins, or princes and places. In contrast, a unipartite network only comprises one type of node. Bipartite networks can be projected onto unipartite networks, such as actors starring in the same film, genes contributing to the same protein, or princes ruling over the same place.

Figure 1: *Operationalising territories based on three main historical charac-teristics*

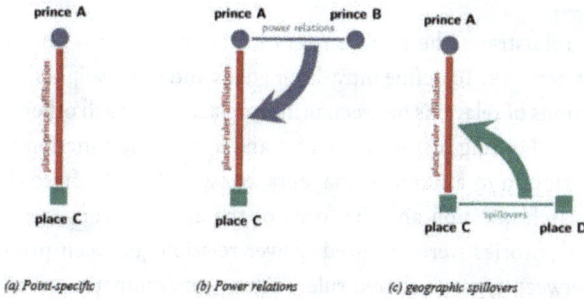

(a) *Point-specific*   (b) *Power relations*   (c) *geographic spillovers*

Figure 2: *Schematic representation of the 'optimal' opertionalisa-tion as multi-layer network*

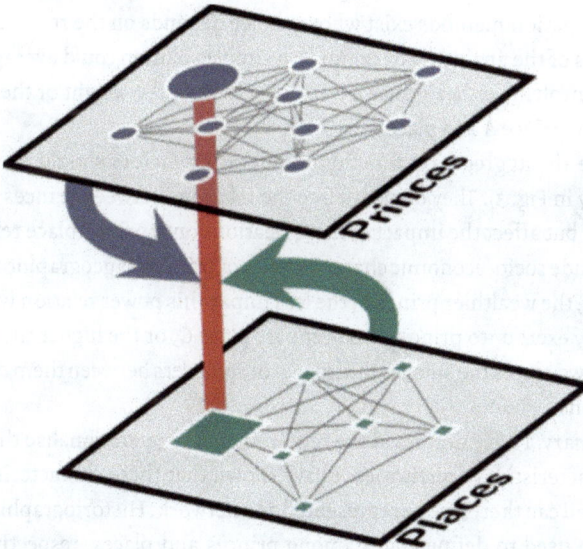

If all required information was available and resources were not constrained, the 'optimal' operationalisation of territories could be represented as a multi-layer network (Fig. 2). In the first layer, nodes correspond to princes and edges to power relations (e.g., condominates). In the second layer, nodes correspond to places and edges to neighbourhood relations (e.g., geographic distance). Intra-layer edges quantify the strength of power relations and of spillover effects, respectively. Inter-layer edges indicate whether a prince exerts power over a place. Their weights indicate the amount of this power and depend on edges between princes and between places. All edges connecting one prince and several places define the prince's territory.

Figure 3 illustrates the requirements for quantifying the constituents of the multi-layer network. To define intra-layer edges and their weights, historiographical descriptions of relations between princes, places, and each other are quantified. This requires choosing historical sources and a mapping function from the qualitative description to a number (magenta arrow in Fig. 3). These choices depend on the research question and the focus of the analysis. For example, if political aspects of territories were captured, power relations between princes could distinguish between types of shared rule, such as condominates or bailiwicks. But if also religious aspects of territories were considered, sources on denominational similarities between princes should also be included.

To define the power of a prince over a place, one has to combine the effect of inter-prince and inter-place relations (yellow arrow in Fig. 3). That is, the weights of intra-layer edges have to be aggregated to yield the weights of inter-layer edges. Several aggregation methods exist whose choice depends on the research question and the focus of the analysis. For example, a simple solution could average all intra-layer edges involving either prince A or place C to yield the weight of the inter-layer edge between prince A and place C.

To refine the aggregation function, moderating factors should be considered (green arrow in Fig. 3). They do not define the relations between princes and places, respectively, but affect the impact of these relations onto prince-place relations. Examples, include socio-economic characteristics of princes or geographic landmarks. For example, the wealthier prince A, the less impact his power relation with another prince B may exert onto prince's A power over place C, or the higher the mountains separating two places the smaller the impact of spillovers between them onto prince-place relations.

In summary, I have described the requirements to operationalise the main historical characteristics of territories. I have shown that these characteristics are interrelated and can therefore be represented as a network. Historiographical descriptions can be used to define edges among princes and places, respectively, and to quantify their weights. These edges can be aggregated to quantify prince-place relations which measure the territory of a prince. The type, number, and amount of detail of selected historical sources is subject to the focus of the analysis.

Figure 3: Providing edge weights in the 'optimal' operationalisation. 'Mapping' defines edges of power relations and spillovers in terms of historical sources. 'Aggregation' combines all power relations and spillovers to measure the extent a prince exerts power over a place. Other historical sources can moderate this power exertion

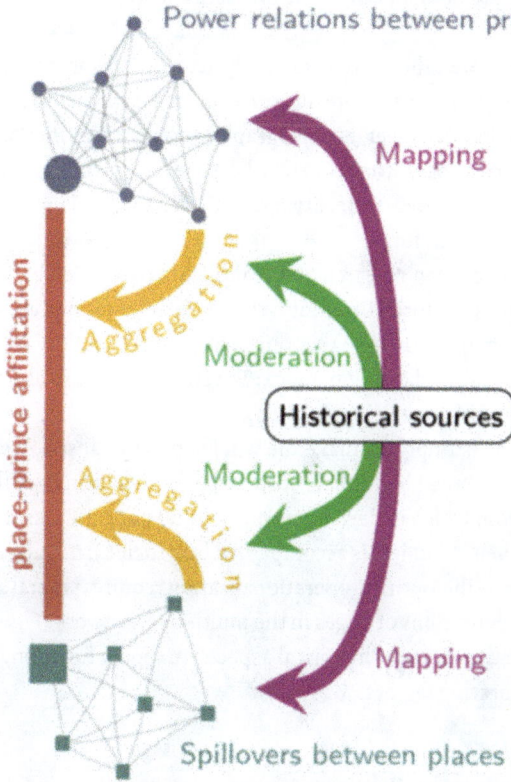

Limitations of the 'Optimal' Operationalisation

The proposed 'optimal' operationalisation faces two main problems – data availability and an inflation of assumptions – which make its practical application currently infeasible.

Data availability. To my knowledge, no structured data set currently exists that captures the main historical characteristics of territories described above. The best approximation are collections of cities and their affiliated princes which had been assembled for individual studies (Becker et al. 2020, Cantoni 2012, Kim/Pfaff 2012, Rubin 2014, Wurpts et al. 2018), mainly based on the 'Deutsches Städebuch'

(Keyser/Stoob (1939–1974). However, data on relations between places, princes, and each other are missing. Assembling the corresponding data requires detailed historiographical knowledge since individual case studies have to be interrelated. Building up this expertise and translating mainly text-based historiographical and historical sources into structured data is extremely time consuming. These extensive resources are often not available for research projects.

Inflation of assumptions. The more historically accurate the operationalisation of territories is supposed to be, the more information on the characteristics of historical territories is needed. However, historiographical research cannot provide an infinitely detailed account of historical reality because no (historiographical) reconstruction is as good as (historical) reality itself. There are too many factors and interdependencies to account for.

Hence, the gaps between research and reality have to be filled by assumptions. The larger the required historical accuracy, the more assumptions are needed. But more assumptions increase the risk that one of them is wrong, i.e., historically inaccurate. This leads to the following paradox: The strive for historical accuracy leads to historical inaccuracy in operationalisation.

Moreover, many assumptions make the whole operationalisation complicated. Assumptions about detailed historical aspects may be increasingly difficult to justify because data from which to derive assumptions do not exist. Assumptions may be entangled (if X then Y, but if X is accompanied by Z then K), making it difficult to maintain orientation. The 'optimal' operationalisation requires several assumptions with respect to the definitions of edges in the multi-layer network (Fig. 2). These assumptions concern the choice of historical aspects, mapping function, aggregation function, and moderating factors.

The Simplified Operationalisation

Since the 'optimal' operationalisation is not applicable in practice, I propose a simplified operationalisation. It is based on one incisive assumption that territories can be represented as territorial states, and can therefore be operationalised as vectorised surface geometries. Whereas territories correspond to *any* tract of land ruled by a sovereignty (e.g., prince), these tracts form a *connected* surface for territorial states.[11] The result of the simplified operationalisation is a public data set on sociodemographic attributes of territorial states that can readily be used for data-driven analyses.

---

11   Note that this distinction is not universal but specific to this study. Other studies may use the two terms synonymously.

Method: Vectorising Territorities

The idea to represent territories as territorial states is not new. Several analogue maps exist that plot the alleged geographic borders of territories in space (Hilgemann/Kinder 2020, Isphording et al. 2011, Westermann 1997). My contribution is to vectorise these maps (i.e., extract the geo-coordinates of borders) and enrich the resulting geometries with socio-economic attributes as visualised in Figure 4. Vectorisation and the Wikipedia lookup are both executed with a manual and an automatic method, whose suitability depends on available resources.

Figure 4: Approach to generate a data set of vectorised territorial states of the Holy Roman Empire during the European Reformation

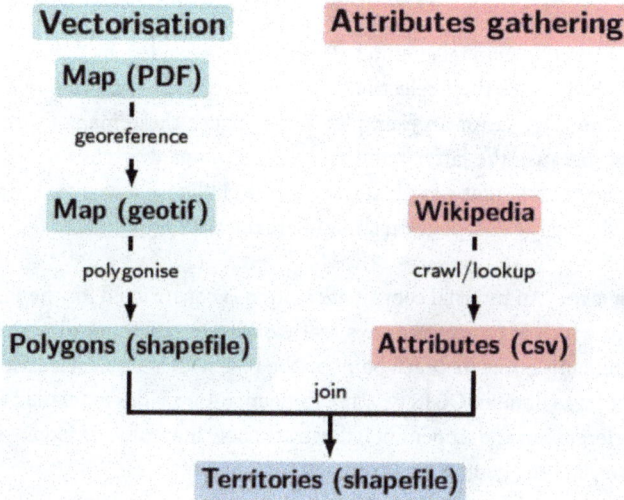

Figure 5: Maps of the Holy Roman Empire (HRE). Figure 5a: Maps of the Holy Roman Empire (HRE). Map of Ernestine Saxony from Schindling and Ziegler (1989–1995) for the manual method. Figure 5b: Maps of the Holy Roman Empire (HRE). Map of the HRE from Wikipedia (2010) for the automatic method

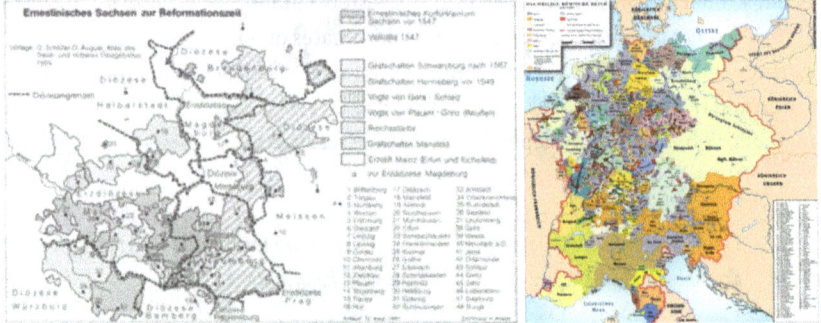

Select map.   For the manual method, I use maps provided by Schindling and Ziegler (1989–1995) since their selection captures territories that were relevant for the Reformation (Fig. 5a for an example). I cannot use these maps for the automatic method because the latter requires coloured maps whereas the Schindling and Ziegler (1989–1995) maps are black and white. I choose a coloured map from Wikipedia showing the geo-political situation in the HRE around 1400 (Fig. 5b).

Georeference map.   An internal coordinate system is constructed for the PDF of all selected maps which is projected onto a real-world geographic coordinate system. This georeferencing associates each point on the PDF with a physical location in the real world and was done in QGIS (v. 3.16). Appendix A provides a detailed description of georeferencing and Appendix B illustrates how inaccuracies in georeferencing lead to overlapping geometries in the manual method.

Polygonise.   For the manual method, I trace the border of each territorial state with the computer mouse using the polygon tracer tool of QGIS (see Appendix C for a detailed description of manual polygonisation). For the automatic method, I use the raster bands of the PDF map which store the colour of pixels as a combination of the primary colours red, green, and blue (see Appendix D for a detailed description of raster bands and the resulting geometries). I group consecutive pixels of the same raster band value into geometries with python's GDAL library (GDAL/OGR 2021). These geometries correspond to territorial states but also to noise such as labels, borders, rivers, lakes, and seas.

Post-processing. To only extract geometries that correspond to territorial states, the automatic methods requires post-processing steps, which are described in detail in Appendix E.

Filter: To discard noise geometries (e.g., lakes, rivers), I keep N geometries with the largest surface area, where N is increased incrementally until a visual inspection of a binary map (two colours for included and excluded geometries) provides evidence that included geometries capture territories. I choose N = 1000.

Buffer internally: To fill the holes inside geometries resulting from noise geometries, such as labels, I reduce the geometry to its exterior border. To fill holes in the border itself, I dilate and then erode the geometry by a small factor. This method converts sharp concave edges of the border into smooth round ones and therefore extends the border further away from the geometry's centre.

Overlay. I overlay the red, green, and blue version of each geometry from the three raster bands to match a surface geometry to its original colour on the map.

Combine Surface geometries that belong to the same territory but are separated by a river or label have to be recombined. Similar to internal buffering, I close the space caused by the separating surface geometry (label or river) (external buffering) and combine surface geometries that have the same RGB value and share a border.

Gather socio-economic attributes. I crawl Wikipedia to gather information on the territories from their Wikidata entry (fully structured crawl) or the infobox on their Wikipedia page (semi structured crawl). Exemplary attributes include 'type of rule' (e.g., duchy, bishopric, county), name of the prince (e.g., Duke Ulrich of Württemberg), and his denomination (e.g., lutheran, calvinist, catholic). I chose Wikipedia because data are open source, digitised, and cover many relevant territories from the 16th century. The socio-economic attributes were specifically selected to address questions about confessionalisation, but the data could also be enriched with other attributes. Appendix F and Appendix G describe the selected attributes and the crawls in detail, respectively. Where possible, I fill empty fields by reading Wikipedia pages or the descriptions in Schindling/Ziegler 1989–1995.

Merge vectorised and attributes data. For the manual method, I manually provide the names of territories as identifiers for geometries and for Wikipedia entries and merge the data sets on these identifiers. For the automatic method, I use a spatial join between the geo-location of the territory's capital (one of the Wikipedia attributes) and the territory's geometry. This method merges a geometry and an entry in the attributes data if the geo-location of the entry is located inside that surface geometry. Whereas the manual merge is precise, yet time consuming, the automatic merge is fast, yet imprecise, because overlapping surface geometries result in one-to-may mappings (one: Wikipedia entry, many: geometries).

Figure 6a: Manual method

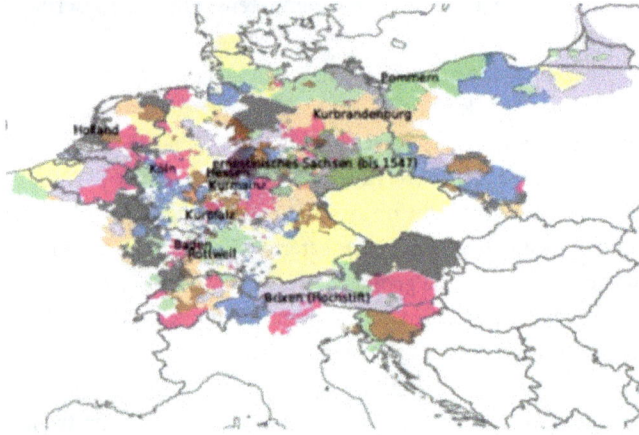

Figure 6b: Automatic fully structured method

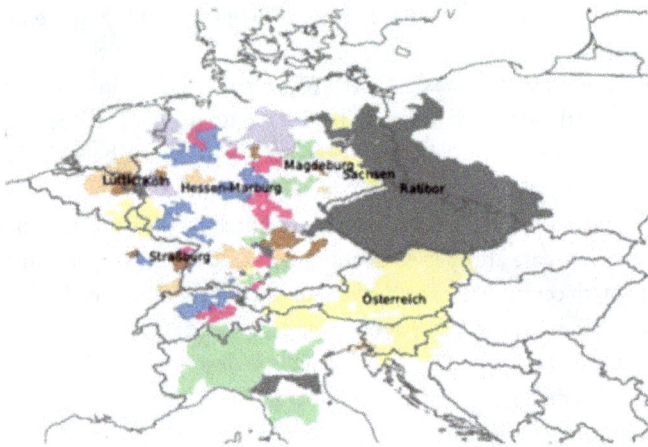

Figure 6 shows the results of the manual and automatic fully structured methods, which extracted 275, and 67 territories of the 16th century, respectively. The automatic semi structured method did not yield any territories for the 16th century but 63 territories for the full lifetime of the HRE. Appendix H provides a detailed comparison of the data sets resulting from the manual and the automatic methods in terms of missing values of Wikipedia attributes (Appendix H.1), practical usage (Appendix H.2) and descriptive statistics (Appendix H.3). The automatic method should be used if time is constrained and a high reproducibility is required. The manual method should be used if time is unconstrained and reproducibility is not a great concern.

Reflections on the Simplified Operationalisation

Uncertainty Analysis

The main advantage of the simplified operationalisation compared to the 'optimal' one is usability. Since the simplified operationalisation uses data from previous historiographical research (Schindling/Ziegler (1989–1995)) and only requires one assumption (territories are territorial states), it can be implemented and is readily usable for data-driven analyses. In contrast, the 'optimal' version remains a theoretical construct. However, that one assumption introduces uncertainty in terms of how well the vectorised territories capture relevant aspects of reality (Kaim et al. 2014). That is, how good the vectorised territories serve as a model to represent 16th century territories. To assess the uncertainty of the vectorised surface geometries, I apply the conceptual framework of Leyk et al. (2005), since it was developed for historical maps. This framework distinguishes three types of uncertainty: product-oriented, transformation-oriented, and application-oriented uncertainty.

Product-oriented uncertainty. Product-oriented uncertainty measures whether geospatial artefacts are defined correctly in the original analogue political maps. That is, is the assumption to represent territories as territorial states correct? This assumption implies that a territory is defined by a border and the power of the prince is homogeneously spread across the whole territory. However, the discussion in Section 2 has shown that territories are point-specific and power is distributed heterogeneously across localities. Hence, territorial states do not capture this historical notion. As a consequence, we lose information on heterogeneities within territories, and on relation-based influences (between princes and places, respectively) on territories, and we do not capture the perception of individuals in the 16th century that space between localities was unimportant. Modifications to the simplified operationalisation can mitigate the negative impact of the territorial state assumption on historical accuracy. For example, one could separate Europe into grid cells and compute the power of each prince per cell as a continuous variable, or one could model the location of a border as a probability distribution indicating that borders were not defined precisely.[12] These alternative modeling approaches only become feasible once more detailed data exist. By comparing our

12   The choice of the probability distribution and its parameters (e.g., variance) is a theoretical question. Robustness checks could be performed to analyse how this choice affects the results.

surface geometries to these alternative modeling approaches, we see that, as an operationalisation, surface geometries value feasibility over validity.

Transformation-oriented uncertainty.   Transformation-oriented uncertainty measures how correct the georeferencing is. In our work, this type of uncertainty is increased by three factors: (1) inaccuracies in the analogue political maps, (2) the choice of control points (cities in our case), and (3) the merge of maps with different cartographic scales. Since I used existing analogue maps, I cannot influence the first factor. The effect of the second factor, the choice of control points, can be measured by computing the root mean squared error (RMSE). It indicates how much the location of georeferenced points deviates on average from their real-world counterparts.[13] The RSMEs for the manual and automatic methods are 10.17 and 91.82 pixels, respectively. These error sizes are small relative to the size of the underlying maps. The maps used for the manual method are on average 1,730,205 square pixels large and the map used for the automatic method measures 13,699,586 square pixels. Given these sizes, the RMSEs account for 0.0053% (manual) and 0.00067% (automatic) of the respective map sizes. Both scores are tiny indicating that our choice of control points yielded accurate georeferenced maps.

The third factor concerns the merging of maps of different cartographic scales in the manual method.[14] City states are represented on a larger scale than territorial states because they are smaller and hence can be represented in greater detail. When merging the resulting surface geometries into one map, the geometries from different scales do not match because their borders provide different amounts of detail. The only way maps of different scales can be merged is to reduce all maps to the scale of the map with the smallest scale (cartographic generalisation). Several algorithms address this problem and should be applied to our vectorised territories (Douglas/Peuker 1973, Visvalingam/Whyatt 2014, Wang/Müller 1998, Zhou/Jones (2005). I leave this improvement to future research and only note at this point that the merge of different map scales is an issue of the current data.

Since I only used one map for the automatic method, different scales are not a problem there. For the manual method, the merge of different scales contributes

---

13   The root mean square error is defined as $\sqrt{1/N \sum_{(i=1)}^{N} \llbracket(x\_real-x\_georef)\rrbracket ^2}$). This is the squared distance between the georeferenced point and the corresponding real point, averaged over all control points of all analogue maps of which the square root is taken.

14   The scale of a map translates distances on the map to distances in the real world. For example, a scale of 1:50,000 means that one centimeter on the map corresponds to 50,000 centimeters in the real world. When comparing maps of different scales, the same property is shown less precise on a small scale than a large one. For example, a river on a small scale (e.g., 1:50,000) is represented as a straight line, whereas it is wiggly on a large scale (e.g., 1:50).

most to transformation-oriented uncertainty and leads to intersecting surface geometries.

Application-oriented uncertainty. Application-oriented uncertainty measures discrepancies between original and intended use of the maps. Since the analogue maps were created by historians, who like me, aimed to use them to better understand geospatial dynamics between territories, no discrepancies exist, and this source of uncertainty has minor relevance for the study at hand.

All in all, based on the uncertainty measure of Leyk et al. (2005), my vectorised surface geometries are most affected by product- and transformation-orientated uncertainty. Whereas product-oriented uncertainty is inherent to using surface geometries as our operationalisation approach, transformation-oriented uncertainty can be reduced by cartographic generalisation or by using maps of the same scale.

Comparison with other Operationalisations

How erroneous is the effect of historical inaccuracies on analyses when operationalising territories as territorial states? The short answer is: not different than for other operationalisations. When using the simplified operationalisation, I receive similar results as other studies that use different operationalisations of territories. These operationalisations are also subject to historical inaccuracies (remember, every operationalisation simplifies reality), and, like mine, simplify territories to address a specific aspect of a research question.

By using the simplified operationalisation, I found that neighbourhood and local power relations between territories are the most important factors in explaining the adoption of Protestantism (Roller et al. 2022). Weak territories wait to become protestant until their more powerful neighbours have done so. The same result was found when territories were operationalised with point geometries corresponding to the geolocation of capital cities (Cantoni 2012). This match provides evidence that the effect of local relations between territories is likely to be real.

The capital-based operationalisation appears superior to the simplified one, because it accounts for the point-specific property of territories and is therefore more historically accurate. However, its historical inaccuracies lie elsewhere and restrict the interpretation of the results. Capitals were not necessarily the representative cities of territories (François 1978), which becomes a problem when operationalising 'neighbourhood' as the inverse of the beeline distance between capitals (the closer the capitals the more 'neighbourly' they are) (Cantoni 2012). Moreover, beeline distance is an artificial measure which fails to capture spatial relations adequately (Small/Adler 2019), and a linear relation between distance and neighbourhood does not account for the heterogeneous nature of the HRE.

To address these issues, other studies have used non-capital cities (Kim/Pfaff 2012, Rubin 2014, Wurpts et al. 2018) and real-world trade routes (Becker et al. 2020) to operationalise territories and local relations, respectively. Compared to these approaches, the added value of the simplified operationalisation is that smaller localities, for which additional information cannot be retrieved, can be analysed, too. I used this advantage to study the effect of letters from protestant reformers that they sent to places within territories. When receiving locations corresponded to small villages whose princes were unknown, these letters could still be located within territorial states, and their impact on the adoption of Protestantism could be computed. This advantage enabled us to study letters of a variety of reformers, not just Luther and his students (Becker et al. 2020, Kim/Pfaff 2012), and to extend spatial relations beyond the distance to Wittenberg or Zurich, the places associated with Luther and Zwingli (Curuk/Smulders 2016, Dittmar/Seabold 2015, Kim/Pfaff 2012, Pfaff/Corcoran 2012, Rubin 2014, Wurpts et al. 2018).

This comparison of operationalisations of territories has shown that all of them are historically inaccurate and restrict the analysis to specific aspects of the research question. Hence, among the implemented operationalisations of territories none is better than the other and one's choice depends on the focus of the analysis.

Conclusion

To study the adoption of Protestantism in the Holy Roman Empire (HRE) on a large scale, we require the operationalisation of the princes' territories. To reach this aim, I identified characteristics of territories that capture their historical notion, and translated these into measures resulting in a multi-layer network of princes and places. I showed that this 'optimal' operationalisation cannot be implemented in practice because of issues regarding data availability and an inflation of assumptions.

To address these issues, I developed a simplified operationalisation where territories correspond to territorial states and are represented as surface geometries. The corresponding data set is public and can be used for empirical analyses. Despite this practicability, the simplified operationalisation introduces historical inaccuracies because territorial states are an anachronistic concept for the 16th century. However, this drawback does not seem to negatively affect the empirical analysis, as a comparison with another operationalisation of territories based on point-geometries showed. Both solutions found a strong interaction effect between neighbourhood and power relations, an indication for a robust effect.

In addition, the simplified operationalisation adds its own value to empirical analyses. Measures of neighbourhood relations are more ecologically valid than artificial ones like beeline distance. Small localities for which we lack data on rule affiliation can be incorporated in the analysis, as I showed when studying the impact of letter exchanges between reformers.

These advantages should not hide the fact that representing territories as territorial states is a poor operationalisation with respect to the historical notion of territories. Future data collection should therefore focus on capturing the main historical characteristics of territories that were identified in this contribution. To further improve operationalisations their usefulness in answering a research question should be tested early in practice, so that insights from the analysis, rather than theoretical considerations alone, can flow back into the operationalisation. Besides all strive for an 'optimal' operationalisation, one should not forget that historical accuracy is an ideal aim but one that can never be reached in practice. Every operationalisation simplifies the underlying concepts, and operationalising the same concept in different ways is important to focus on different aspects of the research question.

References

Becker, S. O., Hsiao, Y., Pfaff, S., Rubin, J. (2020). Multiplex Network Ties and the Spatial Diffusion of Radical Innovations: Martin Luther's Leadership in the Early Reformation. *American Sociological Review 85* (5), p. 857–894.

Becker, S. O., Woessmann, L. (2009). Was Weber Wrong? A Human Capital Theory of Protestant Economic History. The Quarterly Journal of Economics 124 (2), p. 531–596.

Butzbach, J. (1918). Des Johannes Butzbach Wanderbüchlein: Chronika eines fahrenden Schülers, translated by D.J. Becker. Leipzig: Insel Verlag.

Cantoni, D. (2012). Adopting a new religion: The Case of Protestantism in 16th Century Germany. *The Economic Journal 122* (560), p. 502–531.

Cantoni, D., Dittmar, J., Yuchtman, N. (2018). Religious Competition and Reallocation: the Political Economy of Secularization in the Protestant Reformation. The Quarterly Journal of Economics 133 (4), p. 2037–2096.

Curuk, M., Smulders, S. (2016). Malthus Meets Luther: The Economics Behind the German Reformation. CESifo Working Paper 6010, Munich.

Dittmar, J., Seabold S. (2015). Media Markets and Institutional Change: Evidence from the Protestant Reformation. *Tech. rep.*, Centre for Economic Performance, London school of Economics, London.

Donat, M. G., Lowry, A. L., Alexander, L.V., O'Gorman, P.A., Maher, N. (2016). More extreme precipitation in the world's dry and wet regions. *Nature Climate Change 6* (5).

Douglas, D. H.; Peuker, t. (1973). Algorithms for the reduction of the number of points required to represent a digitized line or its caricature. Cartographica: The

International Journal for Geographic Information and Geovisualization 10 (2), p. 112–122.

Dussler, H. (ed.) (1968): Reisen und Reisende in Bayrisch-Schwaben und seinen Randgebieten in Oberbayern, Franken, Württemberg, Vorarlberg und Tirol: Reiseberichte aus elf Jahrhunderten. Konrad. Weissenhorn.

Eaton, J. G., Scheller, R. M. (1996). Effects of climate warming on fish thermal habitat in streams of the United States. *Limnology and Oceanography 41* (5), p. 1109–1115.

Edel, A. (1999): Ottenheinrich. Neue Deutsche Biographie 19, p. 655–656.

Epstein, S. R. (2013). Transferring Technical Knowledge and Innovating in Europe, c.1200 – c.1800. In Prak,

M. & van Zanden, J. L. (Eds.), Technology, Skills and the Pre-Modern Economy in the East and the West, Brill, chap. 1 (p. 25–67). ISBN 9789004251571.

Faber, F. (1923). Die Reisen des Felix Faber durch Tirol in den Jahren 1483 und 1484, translated by J. Garber. Wagner. Innsbruck/München.

Flückiger, M., Hornung, E., Larch, M., Ludwig, M., Mees, A. (2021). Roman Transport Network Connectivity and Economic Integration. The Review of Economic Studies Rdab036.

François, E. (1978). Von Handelsrepubliken zu politischen Hauptstädten: Bemerkungen zur Hierarchie der Städte im frühmodernen Heiligen Römischen Reich. Revue d'Histoire Moderne et Contemporaine 25, p. 587–603.

Franco, A.P., Galiani, S., Lavado, P. (2021). Long-term effects of the Inca Road. *NBER Working Papers 28979*, National Bureau of Economic Research, Inc.

GDAL/OGR, C. (2021). GDAL/OGR Geospatial Data Abstraction software Library. ht tps://gdal.org.

Goetz, H.-W. (1981). "Dux" und "Ducatus": Begriffs- und erfassungsgeschichtliche Untersuchung zur Entstehung der sogenannten „jüngeren" Stammesherzogtums an der Wende vom 9. Zum 10. Jahrhundert. PhD dissertation, University of Bochum.

Gotthard, A. (2003): Vormoderne Lebensräume: Annäherungsversuch an die Heimaten des früh- neuzeitlichen Mitteleuropäers. *Historische Zeitschrift 276* (1), p. 37–74.

Grimm, H. (1953). Albrecht. Neue Deutsche Biographie 1, p. 166–167.

Harrington, J. F., Walser Smith, H. (1997). Confessionalization, Community, and State Building in Germany, 1555–1870. *The Journal of Modern History 69* (1), p. 77–101.

Hilgemann, W., Kinder, H. (2020). Zeitalter der Glaubensspaltung. In dtv-Atlas Weltgeschichte Band 1: Von den Anfängen bis zur Französischen Revolution. dtv. ISBN 978-3-423-03331-2.

Isphording, B., Böttcher, C., Grube, J., Clauss, M., Ackermann, M.; Kasper, R., Betker, R., Bruckmüller, E., Hartmann, P. C. (2011). Mitteleuropa im Zeitalter der

Reformation (um 1547). In: *Putzger – Historischer Weltatlas*. Cornelsen Verlag. p. 120.

Kaim, D., Kozak, J., Ostafin, K., Dobosz, M., Ostapowicz, K., Kolecka, N., Gimmi, U. (2014). Uncertainty in historical land-use reconstructions with topographic maps. *Quaestiones Geographicae 33* (3), p. 55–63.

Keyser, E., Stoob, H. (1939–1974). Deutsches Städtebuch. Verlag W. Kohlhammer. Stuttgart.

Kiechel, S. (1866). Die Reisen des Samuel Kiechel ed. by K.D. Haszler. Literarischer Verein. Stuttgart.

Kim, H., Pfaff, S. (2012). Structure and Dynamics of Religious Insurgency: Students and the Spread of the Reformation. *American Sociological Review 77* (2), p. 188–215.

Klenner, S. (1751). Der Reisende Gerbergeselle Oder Reisebeschreibung eine auf der Wanderschaft begriffenen Weisgerbergesellens. Liegnitz: Siegert.

Leyk, S., Boesch, R., Weibel, R. (2005). A conceptual framework for uncertainty investigation in map-based land cover change modelling. *Transactions in GIS 9* (3), p. 291–322.

Natural Earth (2021). Free vector and raster map data. https://www.naturalearthdata.com/.

Ninness, R. J. (2011). Protestant Imperial Knights, Multiconfessionalism, and the Counter-Reformation. In T. M. Safley (ed.), A Companion to Multiconfessionalism in the Early Modern World, Leiden: Brill, chap. 7.

Pfaff, S., Corcoran, K.E. (2012). Piety, Power and the Purse: Religious Economies Theory and Urban Reform in the Holy Roman Empire. Journal for the Scientific Study of Religion 51(4), p. 757–776.

Reinhard, W. (1999). Reformation, Counter-Reformation, and the Early Modern State a Reassessment. The Catholic Historical Review 75 (3), p. 383–404.

Richardson, L. (2007). Beautiful soup documentation. https://beautiful-soup-4.readthedocs.io/en/latest/.

Roller, R. (2021a). MapVectoriser. DOI 10.5905/ethz-1007-362.

Roller, R. (2021b). Spatio-temporal data on territories of the Holy Roman Empire: Manually extracted. DOI 10.3929/ethz-b-000472583.

Roller, R. (2021c). Static spatial data on territories of the Holy Roman Empire: Automatically extracted. DOI 10.3929/ethz-b-000472585.

Roller, R., Schweitzer, F., Christoph, S. (2022). The role of neighbourhood relations in confessionalisation. *Socarxiy*.

Rubin, J. (2014). Printing and Protestants: an Empirical Test of the Role of Printing in the Reformation. The Review of Economics and Statistics 96 (2), p. 270–286.

Schilling, H. (ed.) (1986). Die reformierte Konfessionalisierung in Deutschland – Das Problem der „Zweiten Reformation". Gütersloh: Gütersloher Verlagshaus.

Schindling, A., Ziegler, W. (eds.) (1989–1995). Die Territorien des Reichs im Zeitalter der Reformation und Konfessionalisierung: Land und Konfession 1500–1650,

Bände 1–5 (Südosten, Nordosten, Nordwesten, Mittleres Deutschland, Süd-western). Münster: Aschendorff.

Schneidmüller, B. (2000). Völker – Stämme – Herzogtümer? Mitteilungen des Instituts für Österreichische Geschichtsforschung 108 (JG), p. 31–47.

Schubert, F.H. (1961). Friedrich III. *Neue Deutsche Biographie 5*, p. 568–572. Siznax, S. (2018). wptools. https://pypi.org/project/wptools/.

Small, M. L., Adler, L. (2019). The Role of Space in the Formation of Social Ties. Annual Review of Sociology 45 (1), p. 111–132.

Tacitus, C. (1877). *vGermania*, ed. by Alfred J. Church and William Jackson Brodribb. London: Macmillan. Team, W. (2021). Wikidata API for Python. https://pypi.org/project/Wikidata/.

Vincentz, C.R. (ed.) (1918). Die Goldschmiede-Chronik. Hannover Verlag der Deutschen Bauhütte.

Visvalingam, M.; Whyatt, J.D. (2014). Line generalization by repeated elimination of the smallest area. Cartographic Information Systems Research Group, University of Hull.

Wang, Z.; Müller, J.-C. (1998). Line Generalization Based on Analysis of Shape Characteristics. Cartography and Geographic Information Systems 25(1), p. 3–15.

Watling, T. (2001). The Continuing Reformation? Dutch Crossing 25 (1), p. 3–23.

Weber, M. (1930). The Protestant Ethic and the Spirit of Capitalism. Routledge. London. ISBN 0–203-99580-5.

Westermann (ed.) (1997). Das Zeitalter der Entdeckungen und Glaubenskämpfe. In: Grosser Atlas zur Weltgeschichte. Erweiterte Ausgabe des Standardwerkes von 1956 (p. 93–105), Braunschweig: Georg Westermann Verlag. 10 edn. ISBN 3–07-509520-6.

Wikipedia (2010). Karte der Territorien im Heiligen Römischen Reich um 1400. https://de.wikipedia.org/wiki/Liste_der_Territorien_im_Heiligen_R{ö}mischen_Reich#/media/Datei:HRR_1400.png.

Wikipedia (2010). Karte der Territorien im Heiligen Römischen Reich um 1400. https://de.wikipedia.org/wiki/Liste_der_Territorien_im_Heiligen_R{ö}mischen_Reich#/media/Datei:HRR_1400.png.

Wikipedia (2021). Liste der Territorien im Heiligen Römischen Reich. https://de.wikipedia. org/wiki/Liste_der_Territorien_im_Heiligen_R{ö}mischen_Reich.

Wolgast, E. (2014). Die Einführung der Reformation und das Schicksal der Klöser im Reich und in Europa. Gütersloher Verlagshaus. Gütersloh. ISBN 978-3-579-05842-9.

Wurpts, B.; Corcoran, K. E.; Pfaff, S. (2018). The Diffusion of Protestantism in Northern Europe: Historical Embeddedness and Complex Contagions in the Adoption of the Reformation. *Social Science History* 42(2), p. 213–244.

Zachhuber, J. (2020). Religion and National Identity in Modern Western Societies: Theological Reflections on a Political Problem. In D. Ehlers; H. Glaser (eds.), *State and Religion* (p. 157–180), Nomos: Baden-Baden.

Zhou, S.; Jones, C. B. (2005). Shape-Aware Line Generalisation With Weighted Effective Area. In *Developments in Spatial Data Handling* (p. 369–380). Springer Berlin Heidelberg. ISBN 978-3-540- 26772–0.

Data Availability Statement

The data generated with the methodology of this paper are available in the ETH Research Collection (Roller 2021b, Roller 2021c). The associated source code is available in the ETH Data Archive (Roller 2021a).

Acknowledgments

The author would like to thank Peter Andorfer and his colleagues from the Austrian Centre for the Digital Humanities and Cultural Heritage for inviting her to Vienna as part of a research visit and for providing useful guidance in vectorising maps. Moreover, the author would like to thank Dominik Kremer, Finn Dammann, and the participants of the workshop 'Geography meets Digital Humanities' for providing helpful comments on an earlier draft of this paper.

Appendix A: Georeferencing

Georeferencing projects an internal coordinate system of a raster map onto a geographic coordinate system. This is achieved by locating points on the raster map for which geo-coordinates are available. If a sufficient number of these points are provided and evenly spaced across the map an internal coordinate system can be computed.

Georeferencing in QGIS is done via the Georeferencer GDAL plugin. To enable this plugin, select Plugins → Manage and Install Plugins and enable the Georeferencer GDAL plugin in the Installed tab. I upload a PDF raster map to the georeferencer and select the following transformation settings.

- Transformation type: Thin Plate Spline
- Resampling method: Nearest neighbour
- Target SRS: EPSG:4326 – WGS 84
- Output raster: file name of georeferenced map + file type (geotif =.tif)

- Save GCP points: ticked (allows to modify the internal coordinate system of geo-referenced maps)
- Load in QGIS when done: ticked (loads georeferenced map in QGIS where it can be validated)

Per map, I look up the geocoordinates of around 20 locations, mark them on the map and provide the longitudes and latitudes (Fig. 7). For most locations, I use the towns that are drawn on the map, and for some locations I use geographic landmarks like river bends or coastlines. After having marked 20 locations, I add additional locations until the residuals of the individual locations are reduced (Fig. 8). The smaller the residuals the more accurate the georeferencing. Once georeferencing is complete, I validate the result by overlaying the georeferenced map with the countries and cities maps from Natural Earth (2021) (Fig. 9). If the georeferenced cities are in the same locations as those in the validation set, georeferencing was successful and I use the georeferenced map for polygonisation.

Figure 7: Georeferencing the map of Ernestine Saxony. Geocoordinates of Dresden are added with the georeferencer tool in QGIS. The geocoordinates of Wittenberg have already been added

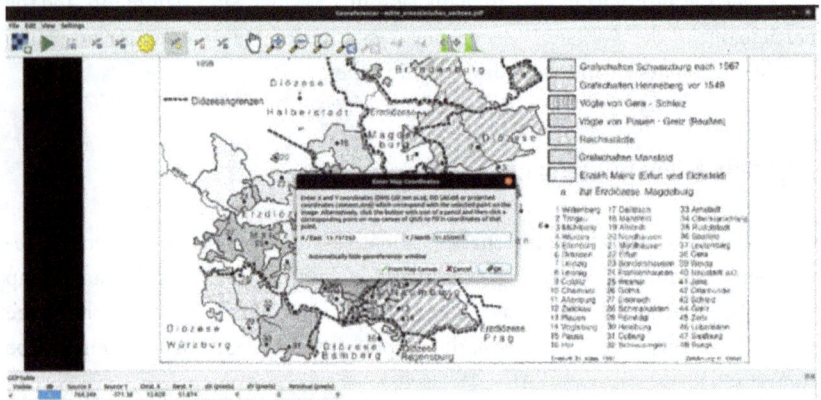

Figure 8: Residuals of two geo-coordinades provided during georeferencing

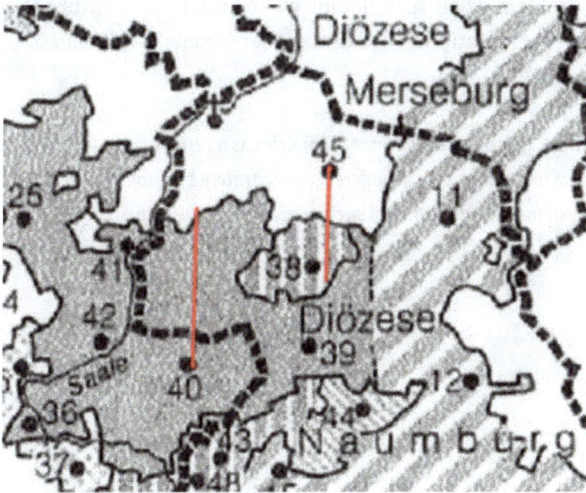

Figure 9: Validate georeferencing result with country and ciy maps from Natural Earth [31]

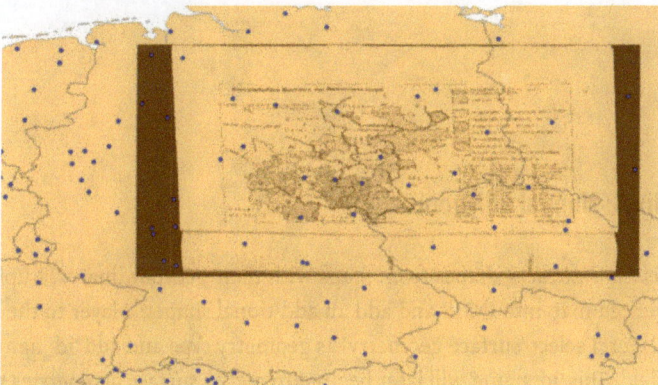

Appendix B: Manual Polygonisation Results in Overlapping Surface Geometries

Figure 10 shows the overlapping surface geometries of Ernestine and Albertine Saxony. Since these two territories were depicted on separate maps, georeferencing resulted in different projected geo-coordinate systems: one for each map. These overlaps do not cause a problem when mapping surface geometries to Wikipedia entries because this mapping is based on a manually engineered index. However, it will cause a problem when spatial joins will be used in the future to map surface geometries to other locations, such as the whereabouts of scholars.

Figure 10: Overlapping surface geometries as a result of manual polygonisation. Since maps were georeferenced separately the projected geo-coordinate systems do not align and surface geometries overlap

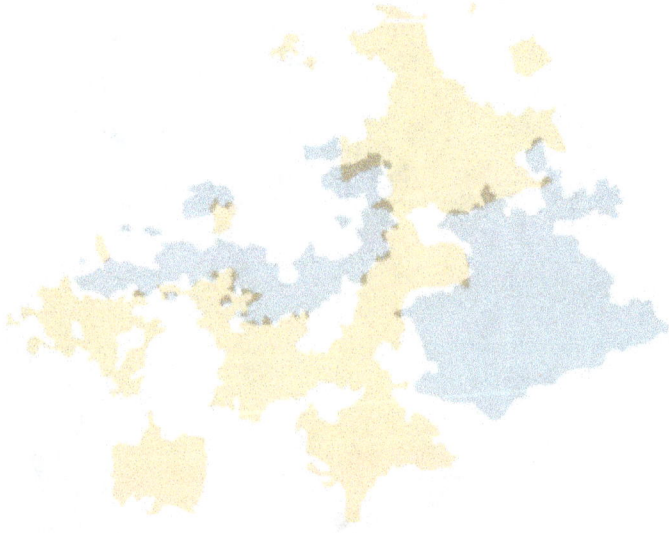

Appendix C: Manual Polygonisation

Polygonisation extracts shapes from maps with their geocoordinates. I upload the georeferenced map into QGIS and add an additional shapefile layer to the project. For this layer, I select 'surface geometry' as geometry type and add 'id_name' as attribute field. This 'id_name' will later be used to merge surface geometries with the Wikipedia entries into territories. I activate the new shapefile layer, enable editing, and add a surface geometry feature by tracing the border of the territorial state on the map with the mouse cursor (Fig. 11a). Once the surface geometry is saved, I provide an 'id_name' (Fig. 11b). To avoid intersections and small gaps between surface geometries, I tune the snapping options by selecting Project → Snapping Options → Advanced Layer configuration → Avoid intersection + enable items on previous layer (Enable snapping on intersection) + 10 pixels. I screen the generated surface geometries for invalid shapes with QGIS' validation function: Processing → Tools → Vector geometry → click validate. I export the resulting surface geometries as a shapefile.

Figure 11a: QGIS polygon tracer. Polygon tracer in progress

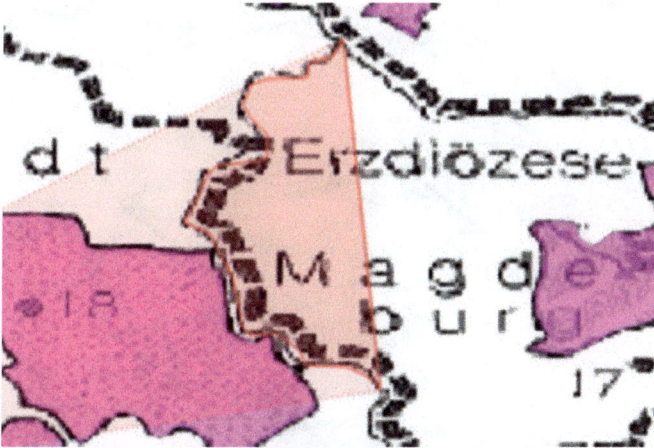

Figure 11b: QGIS polygon tracer. Final surface geometry after tracing

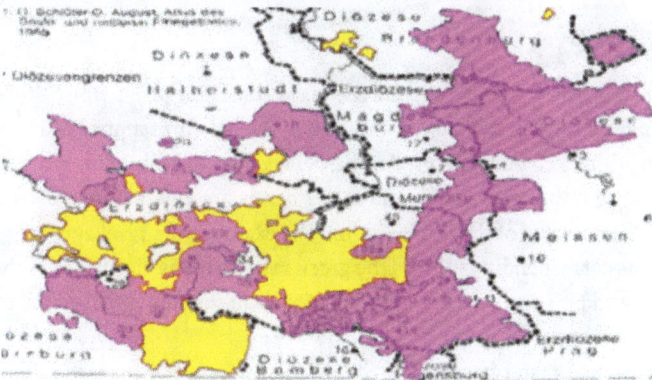

Appendix D: Raster Bands

Figure 12: Raster bands layed ontop of each other define an image

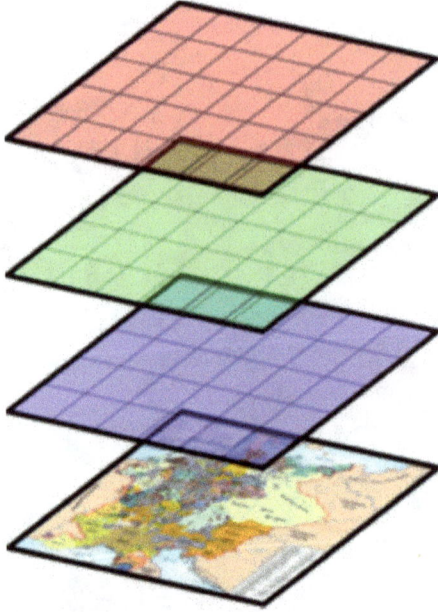

The original and georeferenced PDF-maps consist of pixels which store colour values and are arranged in a grid, the raster. The colour of a pixel is a mixture of the three primary colours red, green, and blue. Values of each primary are stored in a separate grid, the raster band, and raster bands are laid on top of each other to yield the colour value of the pixel (Fig. 12). For example, if a pixel appears green on the map, its corresponding value in the green raster band is high whereas the values in the red and blue raster bands are small. Pixels of the same colour have the same raster band values.

For the three raster bands I extract 611, 854 (red), 604, 621 (green), and 585, 356 (blue) surface geometries, respectively. These numbers differ because not all surface geometries have all raster band values. For example, the blue colour of water has no red whereas borders and imperial cities, coloured in red, have no blue. However, the majority of surface geometries has three raster band values and surface geometries across the three raster bands are therefore duplicated. It is important to keep these duplicates to later merge surface geometries of the same territory by colour.

Appendix E: Post Processing

The following figures show the results of the individual post-processing steps, required in the automatic method. Figure 13 shows the kept (blue) and discarded (orange) surface geometries on a map after the *Filter* step. The surface geometry corresponding to the North Sea was removed manually. Figure 14 compares an extracted surface geometry before and after internal buffering. Holes caused by labels are closed. Figure 15 shows the surface geometries that are kept and discarded during the *Overlay* step, where surface geometries of the three raster bands are matched. Since surface geometries corresponding to most seas and lakes do not have red raster band values they are not matched and filtered out. Figure 16 shows some examples of combined surface geometries that belong to the same territory but were separated by a river or label.

Figure 13: Result after filtering surface geometries

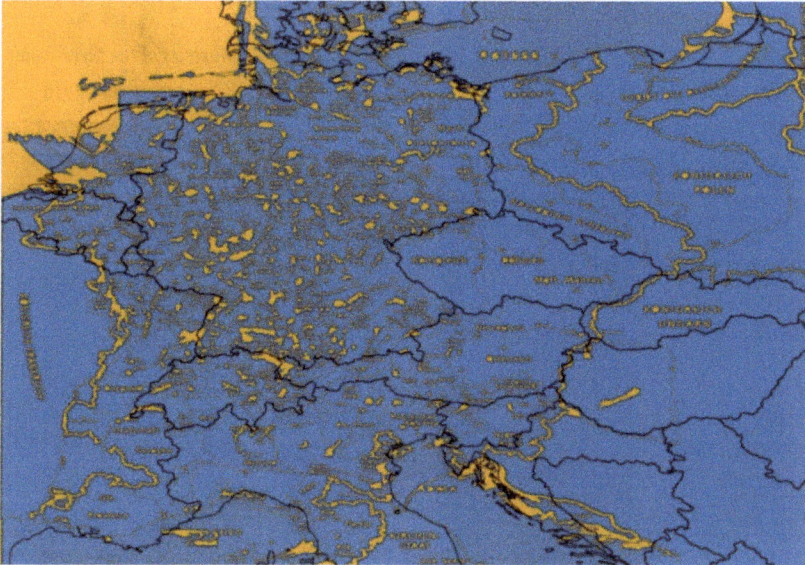

Surface geometries identified as territories (blue). Surface geometries identified as noise (yellow)

Figure 14: *Extracted surface geometry corresponding to parts of the Electorate of Saxony. 14a: After polygonisation, labels leave holes in the surface geometry. 14b: After internal buering, the holes are closed*

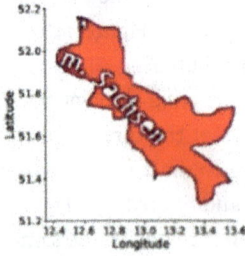

(a) *After polygonisation*

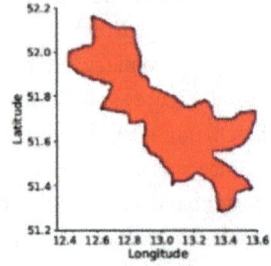

(b) *After internal buffering*

Figure 15: *Extracted surface geometries after overlaying surface geometries of the three raster bands. 15a shows the surface geometries that could be mapped to all three raster bands in colour and those that could not in white. 15b shows that the unmapped surface geometries are mainly seas and lakes. These surface geometries are blue and therefore do not have values in the red raster band and hence no corresponding red surface geometries. The arrangement of sea surface geometries into concentric ellipses captures the colour style of the seas on the map where areas of dark blue fade out into lighter ones (banding)*

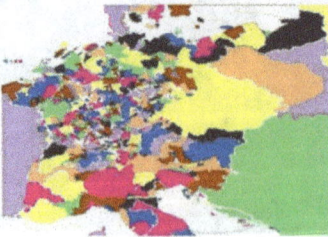

(a) *Kept surface geometries*

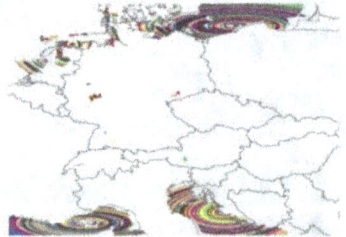

(b) *Discarded surface geometries*

Figure 16: Selection of territories with their merged constituent surface geometries. On the original map, Austria is split into separate territories such as County of Tirol and Duchy of Krain. Since these territories all have the same face colour on the original map the algorithm interprets them as constituent surface geometries of one territory

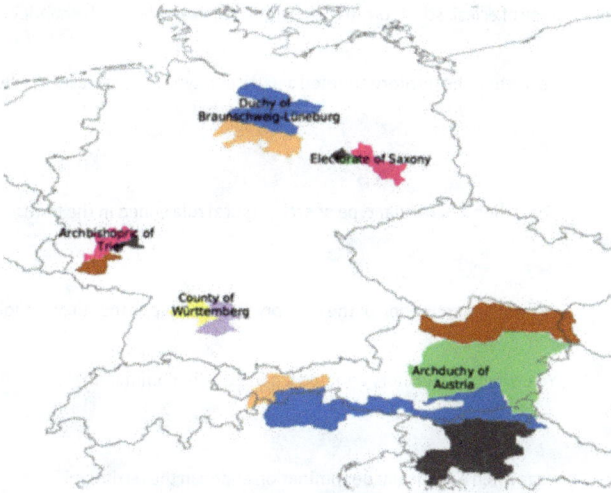

Appendix F Attributes from Wikipedia

Appendix F.1 Manual

id_name	Unique name of the territory during a particular historical period. Used to map Wikipedia entries to surface geometries. For example, Ernestine Saxony (after 1547).
territory_name	Name of territory independent of historical period. For example, although Ernestine Saxony changed its territory and type of rule over time, all its instances are called Ernestine Saxony.
territory_start	Founding year of the territory. This is equivalent to the earlier of the start dates of secular and ecclesiastical rule.
territory_end	Year when the territory ceased to exist. This is equivalent to the later of the end dates of secular and ecclesiastical rule.
territory_secu-lar_rule	Type of secular rule in the territory. For example, margraviate or duchy.

territory_start_secular_rule	Year when the territory adopted a particular type of secular rule.
territory_end_secular_rule	Year when a particular type of secular rule ended in the territory
territory_ecclesiastical_rule	Type of eclesiastical rule in the territory. For example, archbishopric or abbey.
territory_start_ecclesiastical_rule	Year when the territory adopted a particular type of ecclesiastical rule.
territory_end_ecclesiastical_rule	Year when a particular type of ecclesiastical rule ended in the territory.
territory_religion	Official denomination of the territory. For example, lutheran or catholic.
territory_start_religion	Year when the territory adopted a particular denomination.
territory_end_religion	Year when a particular denomination ended in the territory.
alliances	Whether the territory was part of the Schmalkaldic League (SL), an alliances of protestant princes, or part of the Catholic League (CL), and alliances of princes who were loyal to the Emperor.
start_alliance	Year in which territory joined alliance.
capital_name	Name of the territory's capital. For example, Dresden for Ernestine Saxony after 1647.
capital_lat_long	Latitude and longitude of the capital in decimal degrees.
book	Volume of Schindling and Ziegler (1989–1995) where the map of this territory was taken from. The book series covers five regions of the Holy Roman Empire, one per book: **SW**: Südwesten (southwest), **SO**: Südosten (southeast),

MD: Mittleres Deutschland (central Germany), **NO**: Nordosten (northeast), and **NW**: Nordwestern (northwest).	If book is given but id_name is empty, the territory is covered by Schindling and Ziegler (1989–1995) but not included because its geometry is too complicated. This is the case for the Imperial knights in the siuthwest of the HRE. If book is empty but territory_name is given, the territory is covered on Wikiedpia but not by Schindling and Ziegler (1989–1995). For example, the margraviate of Baden-Hachberg or the county of Reuss. These territories were discovered during the research and considered to be important. It can be used for other analyses that do not require a geometry.
region	Bookchapter in Schindling and Ziegler (1989–1995) where the map of this territory was taken from. For example, Kurpfalz (Electoral Palatinate) and ernestinisches sachsen (Ernestine Saxony).
Source	URL to the website where information on the territory was found. Mostly Wikipedia.
table_on_wikipedia	Whether or not the Wikipedia page of this territory has an infobox.

Appendix F.2 Automatic

Appendix F.2.1 fully structured crawl

old_name	Name of territory together with its type of rule or an indication to a specific Wikipedia page. For example, "Überlingen#Freie Reichsstadt" or "Wissembourg#Geschichte".
modern_name	Name of territory.
type_of_rule	Type of secular or ecclesiastical rule in the territory. For example, margraviate or bishopric.
modern_country	Country the territory is part of today. For example, "Germany" for Ernestine Saxony.
wikipage	Identifier of the territory's Wikipedia page used by wptools (Siznax 2018).
wikibase	Unique key to access the Wikidata page of the territory.
description	Short summary of the territory's history.
instance_of	Higher-order category on Wikidata the territory belongs to. Often this attribute refers to the modern state of the territory. For example, the previous imperial city Buchau is today called Bad Buchau, because of its thermal springs and rehabilitation facilities. Buchau is an instance of a "spa town".
inception	Founding year of the territory.
dissolved	Year when the territory ceased to exist.

religion	Official denomination of the territory. For example, lutheran or catholic.
geoLoc	Longitude and latitude of one point inside the territory in decimal degrees.
capital	Name of the territory's capital. For example, Dresden for Ernestine Saxony after 1647.

Appendix F.2.2 Semi Structured Crawl

The meaning of the following attributes is equivalent to the ones in the fully structured crawl: old_name, modern_name, type_of_rule, modern_country, instance_of, inception, dissolved, religion, capital.

| infobox | Whether or not the Wikipedia page of the territory has an infobox. |
| infobox_keys | List of territory attributes covered in the infobox. |

Appendix G Wikipedia Crawl

Appendix G.1 Gathering Socio-Economic Attributes of Territories

Appendix G.1.1 Manual: Wikipedia Lookup

I select all territories that are covered in Schindling and Ziegler (1989–1995) and look up information on attributes on their Wikipedia pages (Appendix F.1). If Wikipedia did not provide data on these attributes, I checked the territory-specific texts in Schindling and Ziegler (1989–1995). If information was still not available after this step, I marked it as missing value.

Since territories changed over time the unit of analysis is the state of a territory in a specific year. For example, if a territory became lutheran in 1540 and all other attributes remained unchanged, two version of the territory are included in the data one before and one after 1540. The manual Wikipedia lookup resulted in 558 unique temporal states of 303 territories.

Appendix G.1.2 Automated: Wikipedia Crawl

Select territories. Wikipedia provides a list of 806 territories that have existed in the HRE at some point during its 1,000 years reign [56]. I use this list as a starting point and later filter out territories that have existed in the 16th century. I use the German version of Wikipedia pages because they are more detailed than the English version. I use the python package wptools to access the Wikipedia page as html (Siznax 2018), and the package Beatifulsoup to parse its content (Richardson 2007). From the list I can extract the name of the territory, the type of rule, and the country the territory is part of today. Since Wikipedia does not provided temporal information in a structured way, I gather static attributes of territories. My unit of analysis therefore is a territory rather than the state of a territory in a specific year, as was the case in the manual method. I use this crawled list of territories to access the Wikipedia pages of the individual territories and crawl information from them in a fully structured and a semi structured way.

Access attributes (fully structured). The fully structured method accesses the Wikidata page of the Wikipedia page. Wikidata is the official database behind Wikipedia and is fully structured because it uses the same structural format for all its data. I use the wikidata-API to crawl attributes of each territory (Team 2021). See Appendix F.2 for a detailed description of all attributes. For example, the dates of inception and dissolution are used to select territories that have existed during the 16th century, and the geo-location are used to merge territories in the vectorised and attributes data. The fully structured crawl resulted in 127 territories for the 16th century.

Access attributes (semi structured). Since Wikidata is not a rich data source for territories yet, I turn to another source of attributes and crawl the infoboxes of the Wikipedia pages (see Figure 17 for an example of an infobox). These infoboxes seem promising because they provide structured information about the page's topic and in the case of territories in the HRE, are subject to a standardised format. However, editors are not forced to follow this standard, as is the case on Wikidata, and can therefore add, remove, or change keys. Thus, infoboxes are semi structured. For example, the possible keys to access the dates of inception are "Periode" (period), "Vorläufer" (predecessor), "Entstanden aus" (arisen from), and "Entstehungszeit" (period of formation). I checked the infoboxes of several Wikipedia pages of territories to get relevant keys for our attributes of interest, which are the same as for the fully structured method. The semi structured crawl resulted in 806 territories for the complete lifetime of the HRE. Filtering for the 16th century discraded all territories.

Figure 17: Wikipedia infobox of the Margraviate of Baden

Territorium im Heiligen Römischen Reich	
Markgrafschaft Baden	
Wappen	
Alternativnamen	Markgrafschaft Baden
Herrschaftsform	Grafschaft
Herrscher/ Regierung	Markgraf
Heutige Region/en	DE-BW
Reichstag	3 Virilstimmen auf der weltlichen Bank im Reichsfürstenrat[1]
Reichskreis	Schwäbischer Reichskreis
Hauptstädte/ Residenzen	bis 1535: Baden ab 1771: Karlsruhe
Dynastien	Haus Baden
Konfession/ Religionen	bis 1535: römisch-katholisch ab 1771: gemischt römisch-katholisch/lutherisch
Sprache/n	Deutsch
Aufgegangen in	Kurfürstentum Baden 1803

Appendix H Camparison between Manual and Automatic Method

Appendix H.1 Comparison in Terms of Missing Wikipedia Attributes

Table 1 shows the number of missing values for selected attributes for the manual method and the fully- and semi structured crawls. I see that the automatic methods yielded almost three times as many territories as the manual one (806 vs 303). This is because the automatic crawl was not restricted to the 16th century and therefore returned entries on all territories that have ever existed in the HRE. Filtering for 16th century territories discards most of the entries as the large number of missing values for the dates of inception and dissolution show. In the manual data many missing values occur for the type of ecclesiastical rule. This is not of great concern because many territories did not have an ecclesiastical prince so their type of rule is only secular. In contrast, the large number of missing values for alliances is not balanced by another attribute and therefore has to be used with caution in future analyses.

	Manual		Automatic	
	Temporal* (558) UoA: temporal state of territory	Aggregated* (303) UoA: territory	Fully[†] (806) UoA: territory	Semi[†] (806) UoA: territory
Name	0	0	0	0
ID maps to surface geometry	35	20	-	-
Date of inception	58	35	413	679
Date of dissolution	49	27	472	600
Type of secular rule	19	14	17	17
Type of ecclesiastical rule	492	260	-	-
Religion	21	13	732	615
Start date of denomination	37	19	-	-
End date of denomination	29	16	-	-
Alliance	456	250	-	-
Capital	9	5	594	598
Geo-coordinates of the capital or of another location within the territory	9	5	451	0

( ): Total number of entries
UoA: Unit of analysis
* Historical period is restricted to the 16th century
[†] Historical period includes the complete HRE period (800-1806). Restricting the historical period to the 16th century discarded all entries.

Appendix H.2 Comparison in Terms of Practicability

Table 2 compares the manual and the automatic methods for vectorisation along seven practice-oriented criteria. This comparison is intended to help researchers to choose a suitable method based on their resources and research problem.

First, transformation-oriented uncertainty summarises the accuracy of the vectorisation process. We see that the manual method fares worse than the automatic one because of the merge of different cartographic scales.

Second, coverage measures the extent to which extracted territories cover a large are of the Holy Roman Empire. Figure 18 shows the extracted 16th century territories from the manual and automatic fully structured method. We see that coverage is larger in the manual method indicating that many Wikidata entries lack information on geolocation. We also see that the methods yield different territories for the same geographic area [15] which is caused by a mismatch in historical periods of the original maps.[16]

Table 2: *Comparison between manual and automatic vectorisation method.*

	Manual	Automatic
1. Transformation-oriented uncertainty	medium	low
2. Coverage	high	low
3. Mapping ambiguity	low	high
4. Relevance	high	low
5. Temporality	medium	low
6. Speed	low	high
7. Reproducibility	low	medium

---

15   For example, the Duchy of Silesia is united in the automatic method but divided in the manual one.

16   Whereas original maps for the manual method show the geo-political situation in the 16th century, the original map for the automatic method shows the situation around 1400.

Figure 18: Coverage for manual and automatic fully structured method

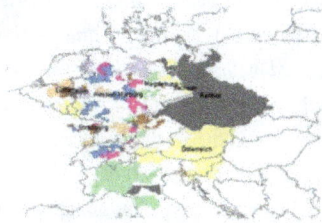

(a) Manual method   (b) Automatic fully structured method

Third, mapping ambiguity assesses to what extent surface geometries are mapped ambiguously to Wikipedia entries. A perfect mapping is one-to-one because one surface geometry is uniquely mapped to one Wikipedia entry and vice versa. The manual method results in a one-to-one mapping because I used manually engineered identifiers.[17]

---

17   However, in future applications, the manual method is prone to mapping ambiguity since surface geometries overlap due to the vectorisation at dierent scales. For example, if we would like to assign locations of individuals on their travel routes to territories the manual data will result in many-to-one mappings (one individual is placed into many territories).

*Figure 19: Mapping ambiguities and their dissolution in the fully structured and semi struc-
tured versions of the automatic method. Coloured points correspond to Wikipedia entries
mapping to the extracted surface geometries (one-to-one and one-to-many mappings). Black
diamonds correspond to Wikipedia entries that map to several surface geometries (many-
to-one mapping). Figures 19a and 19c show the ambiguous mappings for the fully and semi
structured methods, respectively. One-to-many mappings occur more often than many-to-one
mappings indicating that mismatches in historical periods between the selected entries on
Wikipedia and the original map cause more ambiguities than overlapping surface geometries
resulting from external buering (filling holes between surface geometries). Figures 19b and
19d show the result of the mapping corrections. Unique pairs of Wikipedia entries and surface
geometries were chosen uniformly at random leading to dierent mappings in 19b and 19d, as
the dierent point locations in the same surface geometry show*

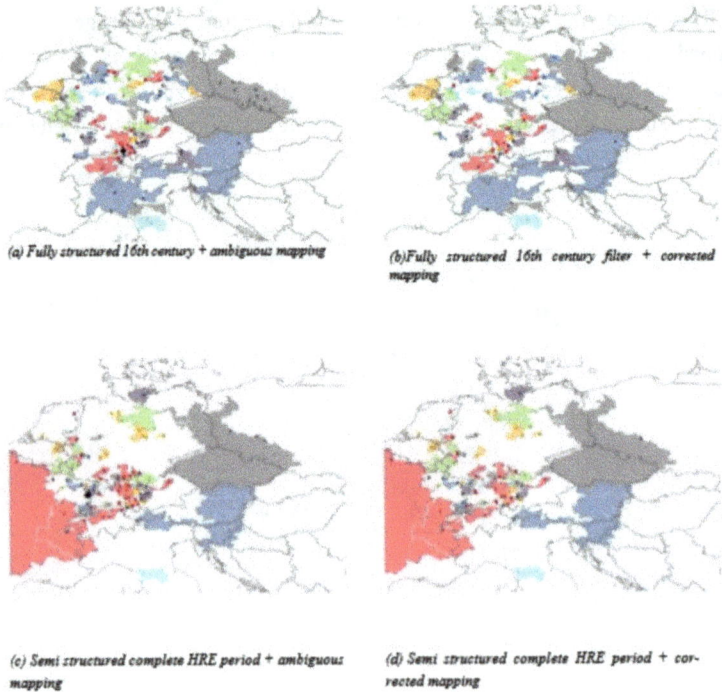

(a) *Fully structured 16th century + ambiguous mapping*

(b) *Fully structured 16th century filter + corrected
mapping*

(c) *Semi structured complete HRE period + ambiguous
mapping*

(d) *Semi structured complete HRE period + corrected mapping*

Fourth, relevance indicates whether the analogue maps provide territories that
are relevant for the subject under study. In our case, relevant territories are those,
that played an important role during the European Reformation in the 16th century.
The maps used in the manual method were specifically chosen to analyse the Reformation based on an informed decision whereas the map for the automatic method
was constructed to display the 15th century, i.e., the time before the Reformation. So

the maps used for the manual method have a higher relevance than the one for the automatic method. This result is not generically valid for all manual and automatic methods but only applies to the specific maps that were chosen in this study.

Fifth, temporality indicates whether the analogue maps account for temporal changes of territorial borders. This is an important criterion because territories in the HRE were volatile structures often changing their realms due to territorial gains and losses. Only the maps used for the manual method account for temporal changes. However, only the most important changes of famous territories such as Ernestine and Albertine Saxony are recorded. Most of these maps are static. Similar to the relevance criterion, this result specifically applies to the maps used in this study and is not generally valid for all manual and automatic methods.

Sixth, speed indicates how time-consuming the two methods are. For both methods, maps have to be georeferenced manually which takes a lot of time. After this step, the automatic method is very fast since it relies on source code. The only manual part is the tuning of parameters when filtering non-territory surface geometries. In contrast, the manual method is very time consuming because territorial borders have to be traced by a human. Since polygonisation can be done in parallel, several individuals could in principle perform this task, which speeds up the process, but requires more resources. Speed-wise, the automatic method beats the manual one.

Seventh, reproducibility indicates how easy others can generate the presented results. Neither method will yield 100% reproducibility because both methods rely on manual georeferencing. Beyond this step, the automatic method is highly reproducible since code and maps are publicly available. In contrast, the manual method is not reproducible because the scanning of the analogue maps and the polygonisation are manual tasks whose results differ between individuals.

In summary, this comparison shows that both methods have their strengths and weaknesses. The automatic method should be used if time is constrained and a high reproducibility is required. The manual method should be used if time is unconstrained and reproducibility is not a great concern. In our analysis for the Reformation, the maps used for the manual method provided more relevant territories than the maps used for the automatic method. Moreover, the manual maps accounted for temporality of territorial borders whereas the maps in the automatic method did not. This comparison shows that the methods and accompanying maps have to be assessed with respect to a specific research problem. In our case, the manual method yielded better results which is why I prefer it to study geopolitics during the Reformation. However, once more appropriate coloured maps become available, the automatic method may become the more suitable candidate.

Table 3: Descriptive statistics of manual and automatic data

	Manual[*]	Automatic	
		Fully structured[*]	Semi structured[†]
# Wikipedia entries[*]	303	127	117
# surface geometries	272	487	487
# Territories after mapping, restrict to one-to-one mappings	275	67	63
Period of existence lifetime of territory in years	mean: 433.34 SD: 236.85 median: 441	mean: 609.76 SD: 221.10 median: 623	-
Confessional stability Number of years for which territory retains a denomination after 1517	mean: 146.43 SD: 107.54 median: 129	-	-
Timing of confessional switch Year in which territory became Protestant	mean: 1549 SD: 26 median: 1541	-	-
Power status Types of rule are ranked 1: large power, 15: small power	mode: 2 range: 1-151	mode: 2 range:1-11	mode: 2 range: 1-11
Surface area in km^2 crs: ESRI:54012	mean: 3316.94 SD: 6575.05 median: 911.83	mean: 7136.65 SD: 22754.47 median: 2025.12	mean: 8518.53 SD: 27017.29 median: 1189.08
# Territories in alliances S: Schmalkaldic League C: Catholic League N: no alliance	S: 40 C: 8 N: 228	-	-

The unit of analysis is a territory for all methods.
[*] One-to-one mapping and 16th century.
[†] One-to-one mappings and complete HRE period (800-1806).
#: Number of
SD: standard deviation

Appendix H.3 Comparison in Terms of Descriptive Statistics

Table 3 shows descriptive statistics for the manual and automatic methods. Within methods, we see that the standard deviations for all measures are large showing that territories vary a lot, and a typical territory does not exist. Between methods, we see that only the power status yields similar results. The most common type of rule is an imperial territory (rank 2), such as an imperial county or an imperial city (see Appendix I) for a complete ranking of types of rule), and all data sets include the most and the least powerful territories. Since the manual data are temporal whereas the automatic data are static, temporal statistics can be computed only for the manual data. Of interest is that territories tended to become Protestant in 1541, a rather long time before the Peace of Augsburg in 1555, where princes were officially entitled to choose the denomination for their subjects.

Figure 20: Frequency of territories along selected attributes

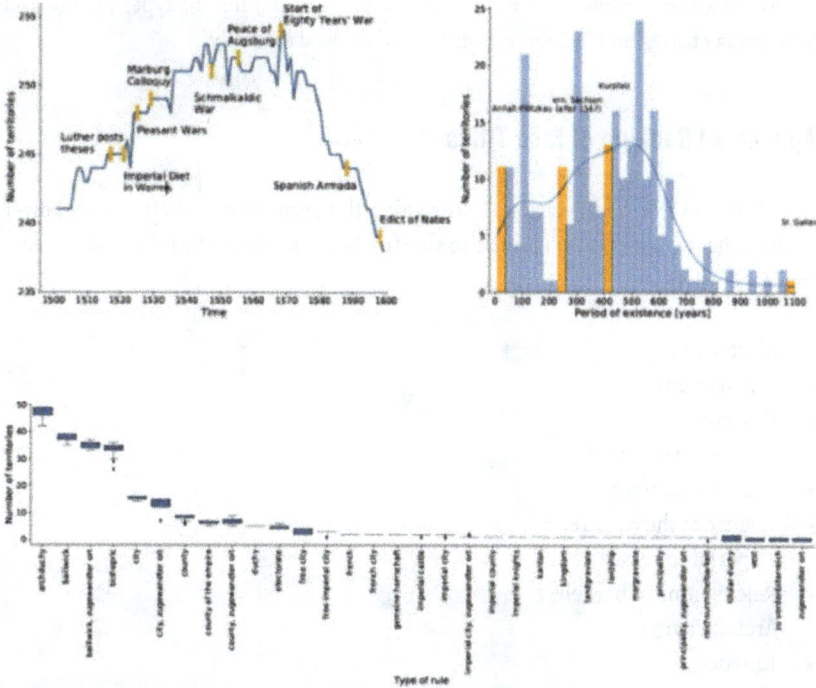

To explore the manually assembled territories, I discuss visualisations and descriptive statistics on selected attributes of the data. Figure 20a shows the number of extracted territories that existed at different points in time in the 16th century. We see that the number ranges between 228 and 246 and that most territories existed in the middle of the 16th century. This is because Schindling and Ziegler (1989–1995) concentrated on territories that drove the confessionalisation in the HRE which gained momentum around 1555 when princes were allowed to choose the denomination of their subjects (Peace of Augsburg).

Figure 20b shows the number of extracted territories that had existed for a certain number of years. We see that most territories have a lifetime of 400 to 600 years. Given that the political system had been stable for such long periods, the importance of the Reformation as transformative movement gains additional weight.

Figure 20c shows the average number of territories per type of rule over a 10 year sliding window. We see that the distributions for all types of rule are narrow indicating that the territories in the data stuck to one type of rule in the 16th century. Note that the types of rule were no standardised titles but fuzzy categories with ambiguous modern interpretations. For example, many Wikipedia entries mix up imperial and free cities. Whereas the imperial city was only subordinate to the Emperor the

free city was subordinate to a territorial prince but had extensive rights and priv-
ileges. As a consequence, the crisp categorisation into different types of rule and
Wikipedia entries on HRE territories have to be used carefully.

Appendix I Ranking of Rule Titles

Based on an informed decision, I rank rule titles according to their power. Lower
ranks indicate more power (similar to sports where the winner has the lowest place-
ment, i.e., 1).

- Electorate: 1
- Imperial city: 2
- Free city: 2
- Free imperial city: 2
- Imperial castle: 2
- County of the empire: 2
- Imperial county: 2
- Reichsunmittelbarkeit: 2
- Archduchy: 3
- Kingdom: 3
- Duchy: 4
- Titular duchy: 4
- Principality: 5
- Bishopric: 5
- Imperial knights: 5
- Margraviate: 6
- Landgraviate: 6
- County: 7
- City: 7
- Lordship: 8
- Vest: 8
- Gemeine Herrschaft: 8
- Zugewandter Ort: 9
- Kanton: 9
- Bailiwick: 10
- French: 11

Authors

Finn Dammann is a research assistant at the Institute of Geography at Friedrich-Alexander-Universität Erlangen-Nürnberg. His research interests lie in digital geography, GIScience and interdisciplinary infrastructure research. He works on questions of contested spatialities of digital sovereignty in Germany, on new methods at the intersection of GIScience and Critical Cartography as well as on Political Geographies of digital infrastructures.

Marie Flüh, M.Ed., is a research assistant at the Institute for German Studies at the University of Hamburg. Currently, she is involved in the DFG-Project CompAnno (Comparative Annotation to Explore and Explain Text Similarities). Her interests in research and teaching revolve around Computational Literary Studies, emotions in literary texts, Didactic and literature of the 18th, 19th and 20th century.

Georg Glasze is Chair of Cultural & Political Geography at FAU Erlangen-Nürnberg. His interests include the construction of geographical knowledges and the changes in socio-spatial relations within the digital transformation as well as the geopoliticisation of the digital transformation.

Guenther Goerz is Professor em. of Computer Science (AI) at FAU, head of the Digital Humanities group and member of the school of Humanities. He has been a visiting scholar at project LILOG (IBM), at several universities in Europe and the US, at the MPIWG Berlin and MPI Bibliotheca Hertziana, Rome. He was the principal investigator of project WissKI (DFG).

Dominik Kremer works at the Department of Digital Humanities and Social Studies at Friedrich-Alexander-Universität Erlangen-Nürnberg. After a doctorate in Applied Computer Science at Otto-Friedrich-Universität Bamberg and experiences as an IT consultant in the industry, he joined the working group for Digital Health Geographies at FAU in 2020. His research addresses climate change and climate resilience, place-based GIScience and geo-content management in education.

Johannes Liem is a PostDoc at the Department for Art and Cultural Studies, University for Continuing Education Krems, Austria. His research focuses on visual and narrative communication of spatio-temporal data. He received his Ph.D. in computer science from City, University of London, UK.

Eva Mayr is a senior researcher at the Department for Arts and Cultural Studies at the University for Continuing Education Krems, Austria. Her research focuses on the cognitive processes involved in interacting with visualisations, especially in "casual", informal learning settings. She received her PhD in applied cognitive and media psychology from the University of Tübingen, Germany.

Boris Michel is professor for digital geography at the Martin-Luther-University Halle-Wittenberg. His research focusses on urban studies ,critical cartography and the uneven geographies of the digital transformation.

Julia Nantke, Prof. Dr. is assistant professor for German language and literature with a focus on Digital Humanities at the University of Hamburg. She is leading several projects in the domain of Computational Literary Studies. Her main research areas are CLS, the materiality and mediality of literature, digital scholarly editing and literary theory.

Saminu Salisu is a PhD student at the Vienna University of Technology and was a research assistant at the University for Continuing Education Krems, Austria. His research interests are visual analytics, visualisation of uncertainty, and spatio-temporal visualisation.

Mareike Schumacher, Prof. Dr., is assistant professor for Digital Humanities at the University of Regensburg. In 2022 she published her first book on the topic of place and space in novels. Her research interests include Computational Literary Studies, Digital Gender Studies, Narratology, Ecocriticsim and Public Humanities.

Blake Walker is Professor of Digital Geography at FAU Erlangen-Nuremberg and leads the Digital Health Geography Working Group.

Florian Windhager is a senior researcher at the Department for Arts and Cultural Studies at the University for Continuing Education Krems, Austria. He holds a PhD in Digital Humanities from the University of Vienna which focuses in line with his current research on visualisation methods in the field of digital humanities and cultural heritage fields.

GPSR Authorized Representative: Easy Access System Europe, Mustamäe tee
50, 10621 Tallinn, Estonia, gpsr.requests@easproject.com

www.ingramcontent.com/pod-product-compliance
Lightning Source LLC
Chambersburg PA
CBHW070110030426
42335CB00016B/2087